Moritz Busch

**Bismarck in the Franco-German War, 1870-1871**

Vol. 2

Moritz Busch

**Bismarck in the Franco-German War, 1870-1871**
*Vol. 2*

ISBN/EAN: 9783337383824

Printed in Europe, USA, Canada, Australia, Japan

Cover: Foto ©ninafisch / pixelio.de

More available books at **www.hansebooks.com**

# BISMARCK

IN THE

# FRANCO-GERMAN WAR

## 1870-1871.

*AUTHORISED TRANSLATION FROM THE GERMAN OF*

## DR. MORITZ BUSCH.

IN TWO VOLUMES.

Vol. II.

NEW YORK:
CHARLES SCRIBNER'S SONS,
743 AND 745 BROADWAY.

# CONTENTS OF VOL. II.

| CHAP. | | PAGE |
|---|---|---|
| XII. | Increasing Anxiety for Decisive Action in several directions. | 1 |
| XIII. | The Difficulty in the Reichstag about the Convention with Bavaria removed—The Bombardment put off. | 32 |
| XIV. | Prospects before Paris improve | 80 |
| XV. | Chaudordy and Facts — Officers breaking their Parole—French Misconstructions—The Crown Prince entertained by the Chief | 118 |
| XVI. | First Weeks of the Bombardment | 169 |
| XVII. | The Last Weeks before the Capitulation of Paris | 210 |
| XVIII. | Negotiations for the Capitulation of Paris | 245 |
| XIX. | From Gambetta's Retirement to the Conclusion of the Peace Preliminaries. | 332 |

# BISMARCK

IN THE

# FRANCO-GERMAN WAR.

### CHAPTER XII.

INCREASING ANXIETY FOR DECISIVE ACTION IN SEVERAL DIRECTIONS.

ABOUT the middle of November I wrote home: "It is still possible that we may get back before Christmas. From expressions attributed to the King in the last few days many think it likely. For my own part I don't put much faith in it, although everything is going well, and Paris will probably be reduced to meal and horse-flesh in three or four weeks, and must accordingly 'sing small,' especially when Hindersin's big guns begin to assist to rapid decisions a government made reasonable by starvation. I can understand how our good friend S. finds the thing slow. Certainly the war makes no account of his comfort or that of those who feel with him. Let him possess himself in patience a while longer, like our soldiers, who have to wait for the end in hunger and dirt, while he and other fine people in Berlin lie on comfortable sofas and have their cups and platters full. These omniscient critics of the bar and the tap-room, with their eternal grumbling and fault-finding, are a queer sort, ridiculous and very unsatisfactory."

In all this there was certainly some truth. But when it became clear that the Parisians had been provisioned for longer than we believed, when the big guns of General Hindersin kept silence for weeks after, and the German question would not get solved in the way we wanted, the discontent, even in the house in the Rue de Provence, increased daily, while rumours that people who had no business to interfere were preventing the beginning of the bombardment gained greater and greater force week after week.

Whether these rumours were well-grounded I must leave an open question. It is certain, however, that there were other causes also at work to prevent the bombardment beginning as soon as people wished, and that the effectual blockade of Paris itself was something unprecedented. Let me quote, for instance, what Major Blume said of it in 1871 :—

"Foreign military critics had declared the blockade of Paris absolutely impossible till it actually took place, and they had very good grounds for their opinions. When the inhabitants were first shut in, there were nearly 400,000 armed men in the city, some 60,000 of whom were line troops, and nearly 100,000 Gardes Mobiles of the city and the neighbouring departments. The line and the Mobiles were armed with the chassepot, and whatever the defects of their military training, they were certainly capable of defending themselves behind walls and ditches, and, if properly led, of making dangerous sorties. The fortified *enceinte* of Paris was 18 miles, the line connecting the forts, 34 miles; the line through the most advanced outposts of the besieging army, 50 miles long; the direct telegraph line, which joined up with each other the headquarters of the several army corps, extended for not less than 90 miles. The German army, which completed the investment on Sept. 19, consisted of no more than 122,000 infantry, 24,000 cavalry, and 622 guns. The effective strength of the different divisions had been greatly reduced by the battles they had fought and their march as far as Paris. The Guards, for instance, numbered only 14,200, and the Fifth Army Corps only 16,000 infantry. Thus the investment of Paris was a bold undertaking, far more so than even the French used then to represent it, and a very little self-examination would convince them now how little right they have to comfort themselves with fine-sounding phrases about the glorious defence of their capital. For four long weeks there was only a single German foot-soldier per yard over the enormously long line of investment. Gradually the Eleventh North German, the First Bavarian Army Corps, and the relief troops melted in to fill up the gaps. The fall of Strassburg freed the Guards' division of the Landwehr, and at the close of October our two armies round Paris numbered 202,000 infantry, 33,800 cavalry, and 898 guns. Besides the strain of outpost duty, and the perpetual necessity of strengthening the line of investment, these troops had every now and then to spare strong detachments to sweep clear the immediate neighbourhood of the besieging army. Taking all things into account, the number of the German troops directly engaged in the investment of Paris hardly ever exceeded 200,000 men."

Blume proceeds to explain what he believes to have been the reasons why no attempt was made in September to take the city by assault, and why a regular siege was not opened against it afterwards. The forts and the *enceinte* which protected the city could not have been carried by storm. As to a regular siege, or even an artillery attack on single forts, the chief obstacle, apart from the numerical weakness of the troops who would have had to undertake it, was our great poverty in suitable siege guns. These could not be brought up till after Toul fell and the railway was opened to Nanteuil, which was not till the last week of September. Nanteuil was still fifty miles from Paris, and after the railway up to it had been cleared for traffic, the first thing was to provide suitably for the health and comfort of the troops. Round Paris itself there were no stores or warehouses, little indeed but wine-shops. The army had to live from hand to mouth. Reserve magazines had to be organised and filled; and till that was done the siege guns had to wait. Even after the guns had got to Nanteuil there was plenty of trouble. Nearly 300 cannon of the heaviest calibre, with five hundred rounds of shot and ammunition for each of them, "necessary as a first supply," had to be dragged fifty miles on waggons " over execrable roads." The necessary four-wheeled carts could not be collected in France, and long columns of ammunition waggons had at last to be brought from Germany. Through these causes and others Major Blume asserts that in December, when the preparations began for the artillery attack on Mount Avron and the forts on the south of Paris, the park of artillery was of very moderate strength. Besides the forty rifled six-pounders, there were only 235 guns, nearly half of which were rifled twelve-pounders. They were hardly fit, as Blume says, to do more than make a sort of moral impression on the city. But that, he adds, "was all that was wanted, and in the circumstances it was no use arranging for a regular siege, or for parallels of investment for the reduction of the forts."

"About the middle of January 123 guns were playing on the southern front of Paris. They threw into the city from two to three hundred grenades daily, sufficient to make every place on the left bank of the river 'lively,' and to drive most of the inhabitants from their houses. The actual material damage was certainly trifling. After the fall of Mézières, however, a good many more heavy guns were placed in position, and the successes of our batteries in the north enabled us to prepare an attack of decisive moment against Saint-Denis, and to bring the northern half of Paris also under fire. The powers of resistance had, however, by that time been completely exhausted. Shortly after the last unsuccessful sortie on January 19, the city laid down its arms, and the armistice and peace followed in due course."

I return to the middle of November, and I shall leave my journal to speak for itself as much as I can.

*Wednesday, November* 16.—The Chief is still out of sorts. People attribute it partly to worry over our negotiations with several of the South German States, which seem once more to be hanging fire, and to his annoyance with the military authorities, who are supposed not even to have asked his opinion on several points which involved more than merely military questions.

After three o'clock I spent some time again with the officers of the 46th, who have been run from the outposts into this haven of rest for a few days, and are making themselves comfortable in the Château of Chesnay. H., who will now probably soon get his iron cross, tells us a pretty little anecdote of the last few weeks. In the struggle near Malmaison they had to get over a breach in the wall of a park, which, however, was still too high for him to climb without laying aside his drawn sword. He was in some perplexity, when he noticed on the other side a handsome, strapping French lad, who had been taken prisoner and disarmed. Calling him up he asked him to hold the sword. The lad laughingly did as he was told, returned him his weapon afterwards with a smile and a bow, and did the same good turn for the sergeant-major who was clambering up behind H. Naturally the soldiers would have shot the man down on the slightest sign of an inclination to keep the sword. These Gauls let themselves be taken prisoner now, H. thinks, without making any difficulty. The reason of this is no want of food in the Paris army so far. The deserter Zouave sergeant caught at the outposts at La Celle looked an extremely well-nourished person. Everybody here is eager and impatient for the beginning of the bombardment, and everybody maintains for certain that it has been so far prevented by some ladies of high station interceding that the city should be spared. To-day people expected—from what signs or on what grounds I omitted to inquire—a great sortie of the Parisians. I tell them that such an attempt would have far fewer chances of success now than some weeks ago, as Prince Frederick Charles and his troops are already at Rambouillet.

Count Waldersee dines with us. The Chief again complains that the military authorities don't inform him of everything of importance that goes on. It was after repeated entreaties that he got them to agree to send him, at all events, what they were telegraphing to the German papers. In 1866 it was a different story. He was then summoned to every consultation. "And so I ought to be," he says; "my business requires it; I need to know all that goes on in military matters, so that I may be able to make peace at the right time."

*Thursday, November* 17.—After breakfasting with us, Delbrück, who lived two or three doors away, towards the Avenue de Saint-Cloud, set out to-day for Berlin, where the Reichstag is to open its sessions. At breakfast we learned that Keudell had been elected, but that he would soon come back to us. Before breakfast I had looked through several French balloon letters, also a heap of Paris newspapers, and among them *La Patrie* of the 10th, with an interesting attack on the provisional government by About—saying pretty much the same thing as *Figaro* has been saying recently—the *Gazette de France* of the 12th, and the *Liberté* of the 10th. Afterwards I sent to Berlin a translation of the letter which the president of the Roman Junta has directed to the *Allgemeine Zeitung*. In the afternoon we heard that Prince Frederick Charles had arrived at Orleans.

Alten and Prince Radziwill were the Chief's guests at dinner. Somebody said that there was a rumour that Garibaldi, with his 13,000 "free companions," had been taken prisoner. The Minister said, "That would be very serious: 13,000 Francs-tireurs, who are not even Frenchmen, made prisoners—why on earth were they not shot?" He complained once more that the military authorities so seldom ask his opinion. "There, for instance, is this capitulation at Verdun, which I should certainly not have advised. They have promised to give back the arms after peace is made, and the French magistrates are to order and settle everything meanwhile as they think proper. The first is a trifle, for in making peace we may stipulate that the arms are not to be given back. But 'as they think proper!' Our hands are tied fast, and meantime they can go against us in everything and act just as if no war were going on. They might openly encourage a rising for the Republic, and according to the agreement we could not protect ourselves."

Somebody then spoke of the article of the Diplomatist in the *Indépendance Belge*, which prophesies the return of Napoleon. "No doubt," said the Chancellor, "if he has read the article, he is picturing something of the kind to himself. After all, it is not quite impossible. If he made peace with us he might return with the troops he has in Germany. It is something like our Hungarian legion on a large scale. He is really the regular government. After the restoration of order he would not need more than 200,000 men to maintain it. It would not be necessary to overawe the large towns with troops, except Paris. Perhaps Lyons and Marseilles should be made safe; but he could trust all the rest to the National Guard, and if the Republicans rose he could shoot them down."

A telegram stating what Granville had said about the Russian declaration respecting the Treaty of Paris was brought in, and the Prince began upon it at once. "It means pretty much this, that Russia claims the right to set herself free from a part of the Treaty of 1856, and on her own initiative takes what can only be given her by the collective powers. England cannot allow a pretension like this, which would make any and every treaty worthless. Future complications are much to be feared." The Minister laughs, saying: "Future complications! Parliamentary speeches! Risk nothing! The accent is on the word 'Future.' That is the sort of talk when people mean to do nothing at all. No, nothing is to be feared, as four months since nothing was to be hoped from these people. If at the beginning of the war the English had said to Napoleon, 'Don't fight,' this would never have happened." After a while he went on: "People have always said that the Russian policy is diabolically artful—full of shuffles, and quirks and dodges. It is nothing of the kind. Dishonest people would have made no such declaration; they would have gone on quietly building war ships in the Black Sea and waited till somebody asked them about it. Then they would have said they knew nothing about it, they had 'sent to inquire,' and they would have wriggled out. They might have kept that sort of thing up a long time in Russia, till at last everybody had got used to things as they were." Bucher said,

"They have already three war ships in the Black Sea built in Sebastopol; and if they were told, You can't have any here, they might answer that they really couldn't get them away, as the passage of the Dardanelles was closed against them in 1856."

Another telegram announces the election of the Duke of Aosta as King of Spain. The Chief says, "I am sorry for him and for Spain. He is elected by a narrow majority—not by two-thirds as was originally intended. There are about 190 votes for and 115 not for him." Alten is happy over the monarchical sentiment of the Spaniards, which even now has been victorious. "Ah, these Spaniards," says the Minister. "Did a single man of these Castilians, with their elevated feelings, even whisper his indignation when this war was set afoot by their former election, by Napoleon's interference with their freedom of choice and by his treating them as his vassals?" Somebody said it was all over now with the candidature of the Prince of Hohenzollern. "Yes," replied the Chief, "because he chose that it should be. Only a fortnight since I said to him, 'There is still time.' But he had ceased to care for it." In the evening at tea-time somebody said that Borck was quite delighted to learn that we should pass our Christmas at home. He had said to the King, "People must be beginning to think about the Christmas gifts for the Queen." "Ah," said Her Majesty, "and how long is it now till Christmas?" "Five weeks, your Majesty." "Well, we shall be home by that time." A story or a misunderstanding, I believe. Let me make a note of it, however.

*Friday, November* 18. — Thick mist in the morning, which cleared up about eleven, and gathered again a little in the afternoon. At breakfast we learn that General von Treskow has driven 7,000 moblots out of Dreux and occupied the town. I asked whether I might telegraph the fact, and was told, "Yes," so that I did so. Afterwards I went out with Wollmann to Ville d'Avray for another look at Paris. When we got back the Bavarian Minister of War, von Pranky, was with the Chief, in the salon. In the office we talked about Keudell as likely to come back to-morrow or on Sunday, and about a small sortie made against the position of the Bavarians, no details of which, however, had come in. The evening edition of the *National Zeitung* of the 15th, under the head of Great Britain, has notices of Regnier and his visits to us in Metz and to Eugénie. He is a well-to-do proprietor, married to an Englishwoman, and a friend of Madame Lebreton, one of the Empress's ladies, who escaped from France before the war. He seems a volunteer diplomatist, and as we had previously guessed among ourselves, he appears to have undertaken his *rôle* of mediator on his own prompting. At dinner the guests were Count Bray, the Minister von Lutz, and von Mancler, a Würtemberg officer. Bray is a tall, lanky man with long, smooth-hanging hair plastered down the side of his head and behind his ears, clean-shaven all but a short poverty-stricken whisker, with thin lips, very thin hands and uncommonly long fingers. He says little, radiates a chill all round him, and certainly does not feel himself at home where he is. He might easily be taken for an Englishman. The usual Jesuit of our comic papers is very much his sort of figure. Lutz is the exact opposite, middle-aged, round, ruddy, with a black moustache, dark hair brushed high back from his forehead, with spectacles, brisk and talkative. Mancler is an uncommonly handsome young fellow. The Chief is very good-humoured and sympathetic, but the conversation this time has no particular significance, turning mostly on beer questions, in discussing which Lutz was much interested, and gave us a great deal of information.

*Saturday, November* 19.—Nothing to do in the morning but to read through the papers. The Chief is occupied, I suppose, with the Bavarian affair. Bray and Lutz have been with him again in consultation from one o'clock. In the evening the Minister dined with the King, and Counts Maltzahn and Lehndorf, and a certain Herr von Zawadski with us. He is a green hussar, wearing a white patch with the red cross, the badge of the Knights of St. John, and the iron cross on a white ribbon. He has a full red face and wears a moustache. There is nothing to note about the conversation. Bets are made that there will be a great sortie to-morrow. Somebody has been told that the Versailles people are to give us a new St. Bartholomew's night this evening, but nobody turns white at the news.

*Sunday, November* 20.—The band of a Thuringian regiment woke the Chief up with a morning serenade. He sent them down something to drink. Afterwards he came out to the door, and took a glass in his hand, saying: "*Prosit!* (good luck!) We shall drink to our speedy return to our mothers." The conductor asked him whether it would be long till that time. The Minister answered: "Well, we shan't spend our Christmas at home, though the Reserves may. The rest of us will have to stay here among the French. We have a great deal of money to get out of them. But we are sure to get it pretty soon," he added, laughing.

In the afternoon I made an excursion through Ville d'Avray to Sèvres. Between the two, up on the hill by the railway bridge, there is a magnificent view over one quarter of Paris which lay before me in the bright afternoon sunshine. I returned through Chaville and Viroflay. In the former village I came across a piece of soldiers' wit. They had converted the figures on the pillars at the two sides of a doorway into caricatures. A fisherman, or porter, with his trousers turned up to the knee had been made into a sort of *sans-culotte*, by giving him a muff and a pocket-handkerchief, covering his shoulders with red epaulettes, strapping a knapsack on his back, sticking a military cap behind his ears, and arming him with a rusty musket. I had no time to make out what the abbé on the other side represented. They had stuck a three-cornered hat with a tricolour cockade on his head, made him hold a huntsman's horn at his mouth, hung a wine-bottle round his neck by a string, and fastened a lantern in front of him.

At dinner our guest was General von Werder, a long man with a dark moustache, who is Prussian Military Plenipotentiary at St. Petersburg. Soon after he came in, the Chief said, with a look of gratification on his face, "It is possible that we may yet come to terms with Bavaria." "Yes," cried Bohlen, "something of the sort is already mentioned in the telegrams of one of the Berlin papers, the *Volkszeitung*, the *Staatsbürger-Zeitung*, or one of that kind." The Minister said, "I don't like that. It is too soon. After all, with the lot of respectable people who have nothing to do and who find things dull, there is little wonder that nothing can be kept quiet." Afterwards, I can't now recall in what connection, he happened to mention this anecdote of his youth: "When I was quite small, there was a ball or something of the sort given at our house, and when the company sat down to table, I looked out for a place for myself and found one somewhere in a corner where several gentlemen were seated. They puzzled over the little guest, and talked to each other about me in French: 'Who can the child be?' '*C'est peut-être un fils de la maison, ou une fi*' ('Perhaps it is a boy or the family, or a girl'). '*C'est un fils, monsieur*' ('It is a boy, sir'), said I, quite unabashed, and they were not a little astonished."

The conversation then turned on Vienna and Count Beust, and the Chief said that Beust was apologising for the uncivil note which had just appeared, declaring that Biegeleben, and not he, was the author. The conversation passed from him to the Gagerns, and, finally, to Heinrich Gagern, of whom people once thought so much. Talking about him, the Chief said, " He lets his daughter be brought up as a Catholic. If he thinks Catholicism the right thing there is nothing to be said ; but then he ought to become a Catholic himself. What he is doing is mere inconsistency and cowardice." "I remember that, in 1850 or 1851, Manteuffel had been ordered to try to arrange an understanding between Gagern's people and the Conservatives of the Prussian party—for as far, at least, as the king was willing to go on the German question." "He tried it with me and Gagern, and one day we were invited to his house to supper for three. Politics at first were hardly mentioned. Then Manteuffel made some excuse and left us together. As soon as he had gone, I tackled Gagern about politics, and explained my whole position in a very sober and business-like way. You should have heard Gagern. He put on his Jupiter face, lifted his eyebrows, bristled up his hair, rolled his eyes about, fixed them on the ceiling till they all but cracked, and talked at me with his big phrases as if I had been a public meeting. Of course that got nothing out of me. I answered him quite coolly, and we remained as far apart as ever. When Manteuffel came back to us, and Jupiter had had time to disappear, Manteuffel asked me. ' Well, what have you made up with each other?' 'Indeed, said I, 'nothing is made up. He is frightfully stupid—and takes me for a public meeting, the mere phrase-watering-pot of a fellow! Nothing is to be done with him.'"

We spoke of the bombardment, and the Chief said, "I said to the King once more, so late as yesterday, that it was now full time for it, and he had nothing to say against me. He told me that he had ordered it, but the generals said they were not ready." The conversation then turned on General von Möllendorff, who had just died, and who was said to have been a thoroughly fine old gentleman. Count Bismarck Bohlen told a story of him. "In the affair at Schleswig, when shots were being fired in the distance, Wrangel rode up to Möllendorff in a state of great excitement to ask where the firing was going on. Möllendorff could not say. Wrangel abused him, saying that it was his duty to know, and burst away from us in a very theatrical style. After a little, Möllendorff said, 'This Wrangel is really half a brute and half a play actor. I sit here quietly master of the situation.'" The Minister capped the story with this other. "After the days of March, I remember that the troops were in Potsdam and the King in Berlin. When I went out to Potsdam a great discussion was going on what was to be done. Möllendorff, who was there, sat on a stool not far from me, looking very sour. They had peppered him so that he could only sit half on. One was advising this and another that, but nobody very well knew what to do. I sat near the piano, saying nothing, but I struck a couple of notes, 'Dideldum Dittera' (here he hummed the beginning of the infantry double-quick step). The old fellow got up from his stool at once, his face beaming with delight, embraced me, and said, 'That's the right thing!—I know what you mean—march on Berlin.' As things fell out, however, nothing came of it."

After a little the Chancellor asked his guest, "What may

every visit to the Emperor cost you now?" I don't remember what Werder replied; but the Chief went on: "In my time it was always a pretty dear thing, especially in Zarskoje. I had always at that time to pay fifteen or twenty, sometimes five-and-twenty roubles, according as I went at the request of the Emperor or on my own account. In the former case it was dearer. The coachman and footman who had fetched me, the house-steward who received me—and when I had been invited he had his sword at his side—the runner who preceded me through the whole length of the castle to the Emperor's room, and that must have been a thousand yards, all had to get something. You know him, of course, the fellow with the high round feathers on his head, like an Indian. He certainly earned his five roubles. And I never got the same coachman to take me back again. I could not stand these drains. We Prussians had very poor pay—25,000 thalers (£3750) salary, and 8000 thalers (£1200) for rent. No doubt I had a house for that as big and fine as any palace in Berlin. But the furniture was all old, faded, and shabby, and if I count in repairs and other expenses, it came to quite 9000 thalers (£1350) a year. I found out, however, that I was not expected to spend more than my salary, so I eked it out by keeping no company. The French ambassador had £12,000 a year, and was allowed to charge his government with the expense of all company which he could at all consider official." "But of course you had free firing, which comes to a good deal a year in St. Petersburg," said Werder. "I beg your pardon," answered the Chief, "I had to pay for that myself. But the wood would not have been so dear if the officials had not made it dear. I remember once seeing a fine load of wood on a Finland boat; I asked the people their price, and what they named was very moderate,

I was about to buy it, when they asked me (he said this in Russian) whether it was for the Treasury. I was imprudent enough to say not for the Imperial treasury, but (he again used the Russian words) for the Embassy of the King of Prussia. When I came back to settle and get the wood taken home, they had all run away. If I had given them the address of a merchant with whom I could have come to a private understanding, I should have had it for the third of what I should otherwise have paid. The ——" (he used again the Russian word for the Prussian ambassador) "was in their eyes another officer of the Czar's, and they thought, 'No, when he has to settle with us he will say that we have stolen the wood, and throw us into prison till we let him have it for nothing.'" He went on to tell other stories of the way in which the Tchinovniks torment and plunder the peasants, and came round again to the wretched pay of the Prussian ambassador compared with the others. "It is the same thing," he added, "in Berlin: a Prussian Minister gets 10,000 thalers (£1500), while the English ambassador gets 63,000 (£9450), and the Russian, 44,000 (£6600); then he charges his government with the expense of all official entertainments, and when the Emperor stays with him he usually gets a full year's extra salary. No wonder we cannot keep pace with them."

*Monday, November* 21.—The negotiations with Bavaria don't yet seem to be quite concluded, but he hopes he has brought them to a good end on essential points. The way in which it has been managed is not to be made out from what one hears. It seems clear to me that the result is a compromise in which we have maintained what is essential and given way to the wishes and demands of others in everything else. No sort of pressure certainly has been put upon them. It is conceivable that the question whether

Elsass-Lothringen is to be retained or given back, has constrained them to settle. Elsass-Lothringen can only be asked from France in the name of and for all Germany. The north has no immediate need of it, but to the south, as history can tell the Particularists, it is as necessary as daily bread. Bavaria is a sharer in the benefit. It is only through her complete union with the north, which will show every consideration for all her wishes, that Bavaria can secure this wall of defence for herself in the west. It would not look well that the more and more emphatic hope and wish of the whole of Germany to recover that stolen property should be disappointed through the struggles of the Munich politicians against a closer union with the rest of the country. Some people in the north may possibly have contributed to make the Bavarians less obstinate. I don't know how much there may be in what I was told to-day at breakfast: "We might have had them earlier. But the ———— sent some good friend of his to Munich who knew his feelings, who has dealt with them and shown them how satisfactory the minor concessions really were, so that Bray has already, probably, in his conference with the Minister, taken a paper out of his pocket saying, Look here; such and such men who are reasonably national, ask only so much. After which very little would remain to be said."

Keudell is back and looking very well. About one o'clock the Chief has a conference with Odo Russell, who was previously accredited from the Court of St. James's to Rome. He has probably to discuss with the Minister the pretensions of Russia in respect to the Black Sea. After three, when the Chief goes to the King, I start with H. for the Hôtel de Chasse, where we drink middling French beer among a crowd of officers and army doctors, and chat with the conversable landlady who dresses in black silks and manages her business from her pulpit-like throne. The Minister distributes among us a good many out of a parcel of three thousand cigars which he received, I believe, as a present from Bremen. I get my share. They are Prensados and excellent. The Chief is not with us; we have Knobelsdorff as our guest.

In the evening L. has a story that Garibaldi has inflicted a heavy defeat on us, in which six hundred of our cavalry were killed. Stupid chatter! Why not say six thousand at once? It costs no more breath. L. supposes that something must be decided near Orleans to-morrow, as our men have surrounded the French. In the evening, a little before nine, Russell is again with the Chancellor, and remains till close on eleven.

*Tuesday, November* 22.—Detestable rainy weather in the morning. While we are sitting at late breakfast Lutz has a talk with the Chief in the salon. The latter opens the door once and asks, " Can any of you gentlemen tell me how many members Bavaria has in the Customs parliament?" I go to look it up in old *Weber's Illustrated Calendar*, but found no information in what is usually a good authority on such points. There must, however, have been forty-seven or forty-eight. After three the Russian General Annenkoff spends nearly an hour and a quarter with the Minister. At dinner we have Prince Pless and a Count Stolberg. The talk runs on a great discovery of fine wines which were hidden in some hill or cellar in Bougival. It has been duly confiscated according to the rules of war, as it falls under the head of sustenance. B., who is our high steward, complains that none of it has come our way. And, indeed, on every occasion the foreign office is served as shabbily as can be. They seem to try to palm off the most inconvenient lodgings on the Chief, and to succeed pretty generally in finding them. "Yes," says he, laughing. "They certainly don't behave nicely to me. It is most ungrateful of these military people whose interests I have always defended in the Reichstag! They will find me a changed man soon. When I started for the war I was all for them, when I get back I shall be a complete parliamentarian." Prince Pless praises the Würtemberg troops, who make an admirable impression, and who come next our own men in soldierly bearing. The Chancellor agrees with him, but must put a word in for the Bavarians. It seems to gratify him particularly that they make such short work in shooting down the Franc-tireur robbers. "Our North Germans go too much by the letter. When a bushranger of that sort shoots at a Holstein dragoon, the soldier flings himself from his horse, runs after the man with his heavy sabre, catches him and brings him to his lieutenant, who either lets him off or hands him over to his superior officer, who is sure to do so. The Bavarian knows better, and makes war in the good old way, not waiting till he has been shot at from behind, but shooting first." We have caviare and pheasant pasty on the table, the one provided by the Baroness von Keudell and the other by the Countess Hatzfeld; and Swedish punch is handed round.

In the evening there is Bernstorff's note on the subject of the French frigate *Desaix*, which captured a German vessel in English waters, a letter to Lundy is prepared for our newspapers on the English supplying munitions of war to the French; we advise them that they are no longer to defend Bazaine from the charge of treason, as "injurious to his feelings," and a telegram is despatched to say that for some days back the French Government has been refusing to let any foreigners out from Paris, including even diplomatists, to whom our lines are still open as usual.

L. tells us that the prefect, von Brauchitsch, has ordered the French magistracy at Versailles, under penalty of 50,000 francs (£2000), to provide before December 5 a magazine of articles necessary for us, the stock of which is beginning to run low. Garibaldi has had a small success over our troops, after all; our loss in killed, wounded, and missing not, however, exceeding 120 men.

At tea-time we heard that H., who was with us in Meaux, had come back and been received by the Chief. According to Bohlen, he is a somewhat mysterious personage, an agent of Napoleon's, though he is engaged on— perhaps, indeed, joint proprietor of—a very radical, democratic newspaper in the Rhine Province, and though he gives himself out and, in Prussia, is considered to be a high-toned patriotic republican. It is in that capacity that the Governmental President von —— introduces him to us. What there may be in the object of his present visit to bring the two halves of this double nature together is far from clear. We talked afterwards of a gentleman who, in despair at the goings on of certain personages in the Hôtel des Réservoirs, meant soon to enrol himself among the democrats, if he had not already done so.

*Wednesday, November* 23.—Early this morning I said to one of the councillors, "Do you know how matters are now getting on with the Bavarian negotiations? Will the affair be settled, do you suppose, this evening?"— "Yes," he said, "unless something new turn up; but any trifle might break them off." —"Do you know what was the point on which the negotiations nearly came to grief a short time ago?"— "You would never guess; it was the question of collars or epaulettes." As I was called away at the moment, I could not solve this riddle; but I learned afterwards that the question had been whether the Bavarian officers were in future to wear the mark of their rank, as hitherto, on their collars or on their shoulders, like the North Germans. . . . At dinner we had a hussar with the Geneva sash, and an infantry soldier with shoulder straps; the former the Silesian Count Frankenberg, a big, tall, dignified-looking man, with a large ruddy beard; the latter, Prince Putbus. They were both decorated with the Iron Cross. They talked over the excitement in Berlin over the delay of the bombardment, and about the grumbling there on that account. The report that one of the reasons of the delay was the interference of ladies in a high position appears now to circulate everywhere. . . . The conversation turned on the attitude of the French peasantry, and Putbus said that a Bavarian officer had burned down the whole of a fine village and ordered the wine in the cellars to be run into the streets, because the peasants there had behaved treacherously. Somebody else remarked that the soldiers, somewhere or other, had frightfully beaten a curate, who had been apprehended for some alleged treachery. The Minister again praised the energy of the Bavarians, but as to the second case, he added, " We must either treat the country people with as much consideration as possible or altogether deprive them of the power to harm us, one thing or the other." And, after musing a little, he added, " Politeness as far as the last step of the gallows, but hanging for all that. One can afford to be gruff only to one's friends, being convinced that they won't take it ill; how much sharper one is, for instance, with one's own wife than with other ladies."

There was some talk about the Duke of Coburg, and afterwards about the aqueduct at Marly, which had not been touched by the guns of the forts; and then Prince Putbus spoke of a certain Marchioness Della Torre, who had, he said, had a somewhat stormy past, who liked campaigning, who had been with Garibaldi before Naples, had been staying here with us for some time, and was going about with the Geneva Cross. Somebody spoke of the picture which had been ordered from Bleibtreu, and another of the guests spoke of the rough sketch of a picture representing General Reille bringing Napoleon's letter to the King on the hill before Sedan. They said that the General was taking off his hat as if he was about to shout Hurrah! or Vivat! The Chief remarked: "He behaved himself throughout with propriety and dignity. I had a talk with him alone while the King was writing the answer. He represented to me that we ought not to impose hard conditions on so large an army which had fought so well. I shrugged my shoulders. Then he said that before they would give in to such conditions, they would blow themselves up sky-high with the fortress. I said, 'Do it if you like.' '*Faites sauter.*' Then I asked him whether the Emperor was quite sure of his army and his officers. He said, 'Certainly!' And whether his orders would still be obeyed in Metz. Reille said they would, and we have since seen that at that time he was right. If he had made peace then, I believe he would now have been a reigning sovereign; but he is—as I said sixteen years since, when nobody would believe me—stupid and sentimental."

In the evening L. told us that a misfortune had happened to one of the newspaper correspondents here. Dr. Kreissler, who furnishes news to the Berlin papers, is said to have disappeared some eight days ago, during a journey he made to Orleans, and it is feared that he may have been killed by the Francs-tireurs, or at least taken prisoner.\* We should not have been so sorry if the same fate had overtaken a correspondent of some Vienna and

\* It was subsequently discovered that Dr. Kreissler had been made prisoner.

Frankfort papers, which are hostile to Prussia, viz. a certain Voget, who, it appears, imagines himself privileged to circulate all sorts of lies all over the world under shelter of the German authorities. At the very beginning of the war, at Saarbrücken, he got into a quarrel with our officers; and he has now been impudent enough to say that the Prussians left the Bavarians in the lurch at Orleans, by not coming up to their assistance at the right time, thus making them the real cause of the defeat. To banish him from the army would be a much more sensible thing than what we did about poor Hoff.

About ten o'clock I went in to tea, and found Bismarck-Bohlen and Hatzfeld still there. The Chief was engaged with the three Bavarian plenipotentiaries in the salon. After a quarter of an hour or so, he threw open the folding-doors, put his head in, looked round kindly, and, when he saw that there were several of us, came up to us and sat down at the table with a glass in his hand. "Now," said he excitedly, "the Bavarian business is settled, and everything signed. *We have got our German unity, and our Emperor.*" There was silence for a moment. Then I begged to be allowed to take the pen, with which he had signed the document. "In God's name," said he, "take all three of them, if you like; but the gold pen is not there." I went and took possession of the three pens which were lying beside the document, two of them still wet. (W. afterwards told me that the one the Chancellor had used was that with feathers on both sides.) Two empty champagne bottles stood on the table. "Bring us another," said the Chief to a servant, "it is a great occasion." After musing a little, he remarked, "The newspapers won't be satisfied, and a historian writing in the ordinary spirit may very likely condemn our convention. He may say [I am giving his exact words, as I always do where I use quotation marks], 'The stupid fellow might easily have asked for more; he would have got it; they would have had to give in to him; his might was his right.' I was more anxious that these people should go away heartily satisfied. What are treaties worth which people are forced to sign? I know that they went away satisfied. I don't want to press them, or to take full advantage of the situation. The convention has its defects, but it is the stronger on account of them. I count it the most important thing which we have accomplished during recent years." . . . "As for the Emperor, I reconciled them to that during the negotiations by representing that it would be much pleasanter and easier to concede certain points to the German Emperor than to the neighbouring King of Prussia." . . . Afterwards, over a second bottle which he drank with us and Abeken, who had come in, in the meantime, he began to talk about his death, and mentioned the exact age at which it would happen. . . . "I know it," he said, when somebody remonstrated, "it is a mystic number."

*Thursday, November* 24.—Hard work in the morning. Wrote several articles in the sense of yesterday evening's conversation with the Chief on the convention with Bavaria. In the afternoon, we went together for a walk in the park of the château, and W. told me how a Colonel K. had put an advocate somewhere in the Ardennes in prison for treasonable relations with a band of Francs-tireurs. The courtmartial had condemned him to death, and he had begged for remission of the sentence. The Chief, however, had heard of it, and had made them write to-day to the War Minister to use his influence with the King to let justice take its course.

At dinner, Count Tilly, of the General Staff, and Major Hill were the principal guests. He again complained that the military authorities talked too little to him, and asked his opinion too seldom. "It was so, for instance, with the appointment of Vogel von Falkenstein, who has just raised the Jacoby trouble. If I have to speak about that business in the Reichstag, I shall wash my hands of it all. They could have done nothing more disagreeable to me." "When the war began," he went on to say, "I was a keen partisan of the military people. I shall side with the parliamentarians for the future, and if they worry me further, I shall take my seat somewhere on the extreme left." The convention with Bavaria was mentioned, and the difficulties in connection with it were set down to the account of the National Party, on which the Minister said, "It is quite extraordinary how many very intelligent people understand nothing whatever about politics." Then changing the subject suddenly, he said: "The English are beside themselves. Their journals are shouting for war, on account of a letter in which there is nothing but a statement of a particular view of what is right. For that is all there is in Gortchakoff's note," which he went on further to discuss. Afterwards he began to speak once more of the delay in the bombardment; which was making him anxious for political reasons. "We have collected there an immense siege park," he said; "all the world is expecting us to begin, and up to this moment the guns are standing idle. It has certainly damaged us with the neutral powers. The effect of the success of Sedan has been lessened quite enormously in consequence, and for what object, after all?"

*Friday, November* 25.—Before breakfast, I telegraphed the capitulation of Thionville, which happened during the night. I prepared, for the King's reading, an article in the *Neue Freie Presse*, describing Granville's note as feeble and colourless, and I took care that all our newspapers should reproduce the telegrams of July last, assuring Napoleon of the concurrence of the French people in the declaration of war he then sent us.

In the afternoon I spent an hour with W. in the gallery of historical portraits in the château, which of its kind is of the greatest value, and which includes a very interesting half-length of Luther. Afterwards we had a walk through the principal streets of the town to the two chief churches, and to Hoche's monument. We met, as usual, crowds of priests, nuns, and monks, and marvelled at the number of wine-shops and coffee-houses which supply Versailles. One of these establishments is called the "Smoking Dog" (*Au Chien qui fume*), a dog with a tobacco pipe in his mouth being painted on the signboard. The people at the door-steps, and especially the women, were everywhere polite. The newspapers say that mothers and nurses turn their backs when a German pats a child on the cheek. I have never seen anything of the kind; on the contrary, they were always quite pleased, and said, "*Faites minette à monsieur!*" ("Curtsey to the gentleman"). No doubt, the upper classes are seldom seen in the streets, and when they do appear, the ladies are in mourning—for the misfortunes of their country, of course—and because black is becoming.

During his usual evening visit, L. told us that Samwer had been away again for some time, and had not, as the newspapers told us, been appointed prefect anywhere, but that the town has had the privilege of harbouring another interesting personage, the American spiritualist Home, who has come over here, I believe, from London with introductions to the Crown Prince.

*Saturday, November* 26.—Wrote several articles; one on the extraordinary list of honourable mentions by Trochu in the *Figaro* of the 22nd. The Chief read out to me portions of passages which he had marked in pencil, saying, "Many of the heroic deeds of these defenders of Paris are such commonplace affairs that Prussian generals would never think them worth mentioning. Some of them are mere brag; others manifest impossibilities. Trochu's heroes have made more prisoners, if you count them up, than the French have done altogether during the whole siege of Paris. Captain Montbrisson distinguished himself by marching at the head of an assaulting column, and getting himself lifted over a park-wall to make a reconnaissance—as it was his bounden duty to do. Then you have the farce of a soldier called Gletty, who made three Prussians prisoners —*par la fermeté de son attitude.* It was the firmness of his attitude which brought our Pomeranians to their knees! It might be all well enough in a Paris theatre on the Boulevards, or in a circus, but fancy it in real life! Then there was Hoff, who killed neither more nor fewer than seven-and-twenty Prussians in different single combats. This three-times-nine man must certainly be a Jew, perhaps the cousin of Malzhoff in one of the Wilhelmstrasses. At all events he is a *miles gloriosus.* Lastly, we have Terreaux, who captured a *fanion* (colour) along with the staff to which it was fastened. Properly speaking, that is the colour of a company, which we do not have in Germany. Such is the stuff a commander-in-chief publishes officially. This list of honourable mentions reminds me of the battle-pieces of "Toutes les Gloires de la France" (in Versailles), where every drummer-boy from Sebastopol and Magenta has had his portrait taken for beating his drum."

Count Schimmelmann (a light blue hussar, with a face of a somewhat Oriental type, apparently in his last twenties) and Hatzfeld's brother-in-law (a brisk and self-confident American) were the Chancellor's guests to-night. He said to us: "I was yesterday the victim of a whole swarm of mishaps, one after the other. First, I was to have had a conversation with Odo Russell, who had important business. I sent him a message to wait a couple of minutes for me, as I was occupied with another pressing matter. After a quarter of an hour I came out, and found him gone, and the peace of Europe may perhaps have depended upon it. Then about twelve I go off to wait on the King, and fall by the way into the hands of ——, who compels me to listen to a letter, and holds me prisoner a long while. In that way I lose a whole hour, during which telegrams of great importance ought to have been despatched. The people concerned may perhaps not have got them to-day at all, and decisions may have been come to and relationships established in the meantime which may have very serious consequences for the whole of Europe, and may completely alter the political situation. All this happened," he said, "because it was a Friday."

Afterwards he asked, "Have any of you gentlemen told the Mayor to provide properly in the Trianon for the King of Bavaria?" Hatzfeld replied that he had himself seen the Mayor about the matter. The Chief replied, "Excellent; I hope he will come. I never imagined that I should have to play the part of house-steward of the Trianon. What would Napoleon I. and Louis XIV. have said to that?" Somebody remarked that the American spiritualist Home had been here several days, and had been invited to dine with the Crown Prince. Bucher described him as a dangerous man, and added that he had been condemned in England for some underhand business about a legacy. After dinner he told me that, according to the newspapers, Home had some time ago swindled a legacy in his own favour out of a rich widow, that the lawful heir had prosecuted him, and that he had ultimately been condemned by the court to pay a large sum in damages. It was to be feared that he had been sent here now by somebody to influence important personages to our injury, and Bucher said he would try to induce the Chief to get the fellow turned away.

In the evening I extracted several articles from the *Moniteur* for the King's reading, and read Treitschke's paper upon Luxemburg and the German Empire in the *Preussische Jahrbücher*. From half-past eleven till after half-past twelve at night, there was another violent cannonade into space from the forts or the gunboats. The Chief remarked, " It is a long time since they heard themselves speak. Don't let us grudge them the pleasure."

*Sunday, November* 27.—In the morning we received the speech made at the opening of the Reichstag. I sent it immediately to L., so that he might translate it and get it printed in the newspapers. After twelve, Russell appeared again. The Chief asked him to wait for ten minutes, and spent that time walking up and down with Bucher in the garden. As there was nothing to do, I made a call alone with H. in La Celle, and on the road back was stopped three times by the sentinels, a thing which never happened to me before. After spending an hour in a pleasant chat with H. and the other officers, in the stately château over the market-place, I started for home. An official who was going back to the town in a handsome carriage gave me a place beside him. He had found the horse and carriage shut up in a stable at Bougival, and had taken them quietly away. He appears also to be the discoverer and distributor of the great find of wine which was made there, but which is now pretty nearly finished.

Count Lehndorf and a Bavarian officer (Count Holnstein), a handsome, straight-built man, with a full red face and a pleasant open manner, apparently, we thought, about thirty years of age, were at dinner. I hear that he is the Master of the Horse to King Ludwig, and one of his confidants. The Chief spoke first about the Russian affair, and said: "Vienna, Florence, and Constantinople have kept quiet about it so far; but Petersburg and London, which have spoken, are the important places. It will all come right in the end." Then he told several anecdotes of his sportsman's life—of chamois-hunting, "for which he has not breath enough now"; of the heaviest wild boar he had killed, "the head alone weighed between 99 and 101 lbs."; and of the biggest bear he had shot. Our relations with Munich came up later in the evening, and Holnstein remarked that before the war broke out, the French embassy had been completely mistaken about the attitude of Bavaria. It had got its information from two or three red-hot Catholic and anti-Prussian drawing-rooms. It considered the victory of the patriots certain, and had even believed that the King would have to go. The Chief replied, "I never doubted that Bavaria would side with us, but I certainly could not have hoped that she would have decided so soon." Afterwards we talked about the shooting of the treacherous Africans; and Holnstein said that a shoemaker in Munich, from whose windows the procession of the Turco prisoners who had been marched in there could be very well seen, had made a good deal of money by charging for the view, and had handed over 79 guldens (£8) to the fund for our wounded. Numerous spectators came even from Vienna to see the spectacle. The Chief said, "It was against my inclination that these black fellows got taken prisoners at all." Holnstein answered, "I believe, too, that you don't do so now." The Chief replied, "If I had my will, I should put every soldier under arrest who takes such a fellow prisoner and hands him over to the authorities. They are a robber gang who ought to be shot down. The fox may plead that it is its nature, but for these fellows, it is most horrible and monstrous. They tortured our soldiers to death in the shamefullest way."

After dinner, at which we always smoke, the Minister gives us each a big, full-flavoured, first-rate cigar, saying, "Pass the bottle." His grateful countrymen have recently been particularly mindful to supply him with cigars, and on his sideboard stands box upon box of weeds, so that, God be praised, he has enough of what he likes in that way.

L. told us that Home left yesterday, if I understood him rightly. He has ordered the *Moniteur* to be sent after him to London, having subscribed to the paper for a month. Perhaps this and the whole affair of his journey to our head-quarters may have been only a ghostly spiritualist hocus-pocus; but it looks suspicious that this Cagliostro from Yankee-land should have asked whether he might speak to the son of Worth, the great London tailor, who "lets duchesses wait in his salon," and who was caught in one of the balloons. It is said that Home will come back again. L. tells us, further, that our Versailles friends have been made happy these last few days by a supply of pleasant news. Thiers and Favre, some say Trochu too, have been in the town to negotiate with King William. Garibaldi, whom our generals have driven away from Dôle, has recaptured Dijon, according to the myths of our Versailles friends, and in so doing made prisoners no fewer than 20,000 German soldiers. A German prince or Highness has fallen into the hands of the French in the neighbourhood of Paris. The King offered Marshals Bazaine and Canrobert in exchange for him, but the offer was not accepted. Prince Frederick Charles, finally, has been defeated at Rambouillet, Dreux, and Châteaudun, the very opposite being the fact; and so on. "Hope springs eternal in the human breast."

## CHAPTER XIII.

THE DIFFICULTY IN THE REICHSTAG ABOUT THE CONVENTION WITH BAVARIA REMOVED—THE BOMBARDMENT PUT OFF.

MONDAY, *November* 28.—Early in the morning I telegraph the capitulation of La Fère, with 2000 men, and the victory of Manteuffel on the Somme at Ladon and Maizières. Afterwards I prepared an article on the Convention with Bavaria. The Chief asks about Home, and I tell him that he is gone, but is expected back. He orders me to write at once to the military authorities that if Home returns without a permit, he is to be immediately put in prison, and word brought to the Chief. If he appears with a permit, he is to be watched as a treacherous spy and swindler, and his arrival reported at once to the Minister.

In the afternoon Bucher and I made a carriage excursion to St. Cyr; Prince Pless and Count Maltzahn were with us at dinner. The Minister spoke, first of all, of the American spiritualist, and told us what he thought of him, and what he had arranged to have done about him. Bohlen said: "And you know, too, that Garibaldi also has taken himself off." Somebody said: "If we could catch him he ought to be shot, for he had no business to shove himself into this war." "He should first be put in a cage and exhibited publicly," said Bohlen. "No," said the Minister, "I would try another plan. I would send the prisoners to Berlin, with bits of pasteboard round their necks, and the word 'Gratitude' printed on them. After which they should be shown through the town." Bohlen said: "And then to Spandau." The Chief answered, "Or you might write on the card 'From Venice to Spandau.'"

Afterwards we talked about Bavaria, and the situation in Munich. Somebody, in what connection I don't recollect, once more referred to the circumstances of Reille's appearance at Sedan, and it seemed as if the King then expected more from the letter of the Emperor Napoleon, as, indeed, according to what the Minister said once before, he had been justified in doing. The Emperor ought not to have surrendered himself a prisoner there with no object; he should have concluded peace with us. The generals would have stood by him. Then we talked about the bombardment, and, in connection with it, of Bishop Dupanloup and his present intrigues, and afterwards of the part he had played in the opposition at the Council. "I remember," said the Chancellor, "that the Pope wrote a very clear letter to the French Bishops, or to several of them, ordering them not to mix themselves up with the Garibaldians." Somebody said that something lay very much at his heart. The Chief answered, "What is nearest my heart just now is what may be going on at the Villa Coublay. If they would give me the command-in-chief for four-and-twenty hours, and I were to take the responsibility on myself, I should give just one order—'Fire!'" The Villa Coublay is a place not very far from here, where the siege artillery is collected in a park, instead of being brought into the forts and batteries, and the Chancellor has made the most urgent representations to hasten the bombardment. "You have 300 guns, all told," he went on; "and fifty or sixty mortars, and for every piece you have five hundred rounds—surely that is enough. I have spoken to artillerists who say that at Strassburg they did not use half of what is already piled up here, and, compared with Paris, Strassburg was a Gibraltar." "Perhaps you might have to fire some barracks in Mont Valérien, and overwhelm Forts Issy and Vanvres with your grenades, so as to clear them out. The *enceinte* is very weak, and the ditch no bigger than the length of this room." "I am convinced that if we could throw grenades for four or five days into the town itself, and they once saw that we can fire further than they can, namely, 9000 yards, they would sing small in Paris. No doubt the fine quarters lie on this side of the town, and the people in Belleville would not care a straw though they were all wrecked. Indeed, they would rub their hands over the destruction of the houses of the rich." "We might certainly have left Paris alone, and gone further, but now that we have begun it we must put it through. The plan of starving them out may take a long while yet, perhaps till the beginning of the year. They have certainly meal up till January. If we had only begun the bombardment four weeks ago, we should in all probability have been by this time in Paris, which is the vital point. As it is, the Parisians fancy that London, St. Petersburg, and Vienna are keeping us from firing, and the neutral Powers believe, in their turn, that we can't do it. Some day, however, the real reasons will be revealed."

In the evening I telegraphed to London that the Reichstag had again voted a hundred million thalers (£15,000,000) towards the prosecution of the war with France, and that eight social democrats only voted against it, also that Manteuffel had occupied Amiens. Afterwards several articles were prepared, one to defend the Chancellor and explain how satisfactory his position had been in the negotiations with Bavaria, and how much had been due both to his moderation and his sagacity. The vital point, as I said, was not that any particular concession should be got out of the Munich people, but that the South German States should feel at home in the organisation of the new German state. Any pressure or constraint to extract further concessions from them would be ingratitude, especially as they have fully discharged their patriotic obligations. It would, besides, be bad policy to press any more urgent claims on our allies. The discontent which would be the inevitable consequence would do us far more harm than half-a-dozen slightly improved paragraphs in a treaty could ever do us good. It would at once reveal to the neutral powers, Austria and the rest of them, the place where a wedge might be driven home, which might loosen and in the end split to pieces the unity just realised.

L. told us that somebody had been stealing from the Gallery of Historical Portraits in the château—two portraits, of a Princess Mary of Lothringen and of the La Vallière, having been carried off. An investigation was set on foot immediately, and it was shown that the thief had used a double key, and must have been familiar with the ways of the custodians, so that the theft can hardly be set down to any foreigner. It is perfectly certain, however, that the French will say that we carried the pictures off with us.

From half-past nine till after one in the morning the sound of a brisk renewed cannonade from the north side could be made out.

*Tuesday, November* 29.—In the morning the mouths of the French cannon growl out to us a savager salute than ever, while I have the gratification to telegraph new triumphs of the German arms. Yesterday, for instance, Garibaldi had severe losses at Dijon, and Prince Frederick Charles's troops defeated the more numerous French army opposed to them at Beaune la Rolande. When I laid the second of these telegrams before the Chief, he said, "To say many hundred prisoners is to say nothing; many hundreds means at least a thousand. To put our loss at a thousand men, and say nothing more of the enemy than that he sustained severe losses, would be a piece of clumsiness of which we ought to have too much sense to be guilty. I beg you in future to make up your telegrams more carefully."

At breakfast we learn that the thunder of the cannon was to support a sortie of the Parisians in the direction of Villeneuve, where the Bavarians are, which was repulsed. A few shots were still to be heard from the forts as late as one o'clock. Something more seems to have been expected, for several batteries are standing ready to start, on the Avenue de Saint-Cloud.

In the afternoon I sent off another article on the convention with Bavaria, which is to be reproduced in various forms in Berlin. A grudging dissatisfaction seems to be the prevailing mood there. Afterwards I ran off to the little place at Chesnay, where my lieutenants are having all sorts of fun. I found them, for instance, singing the song of the eleven thousand virgins of Cologne.

We had Lieutenant-Colonel von Hartrott at dinner. The conversation turned on the distribution of the Iron Cross, and the Chief observed, "The doctors ought to have it on their black and white sashes; they are under fire, and it takes much more courage and sense to let yourself be shot at without doing anything than to go with a storming party." Blumenthal said to me that he at any rate could not earn one, for it is his duty to keep himself out of danger of being shot. Accordingly he always looks out for a place from which he can have a good view of everything, with very little chance of being hit; and he is quite right; a general who exposes himself needlessly ought to be put under arrest. We talked next of the handling of the army, and he said, "Modesty and moderation are the only things to ensure victory; conceit and insolence being certain defeat." Then he asked Hartrott whether he was a Brunswicker. "No," he said, "I am from the district of Aschersleben." "I made out from your accent," said the Minister, "that you came from the Harz, but not from which side." Aschersleben suggested Magdeburg, which reminded him of his friend Dietze, of whom he said, "He is the most estimable man I know, his house is the pleasantest and most comfortable for a visitor I have ever been in. There is good hunting and capital keep, and his wife is perfectly charming. Then he is full of that genuine native heartiness—the *politesse de cœur*—nothing made up. What a difference between a hunting party given by a man who goes out without a gun, and whose delight it is to see his friends shoot well, and one where it is perfectly understood that the master is to have most of the shooting, and that bad temper and swearing at the servants are a matter of course, if he does not get it." Abeken wondered whether *politesse de cœur* was native French or imported. "Not a doubt," said the Chief, "that the phrase was borrowed from us. The thing itself exists only among the Germans. I should call it the courteousness of good-will and of kindly feeling in the best sense of the word—the courteousness of a man inclined to be helpful to one. You come across it among our common soldiers, often certainly in the clumsiest forms. But the French have none of it; their courteousness is begotten only of hatred and envy." He went on to say that the English had something of the sort, and praised Odo Russell, whose natural and straightforward ways were thoroughly to his liking. "One thing only made me at first a little suspicious of him. I had always heard, and my own experience had confirmed it, that an Englishman who could speak good French was a doubtful character, and Odo Russell speaks French quite admirably. But then he speaks German just as well."

At dessert he said, "I see that I eat too much, or perhaps too much at a time. I can't get out of the stupid habit of eating only once a day. Some time ago it was even worse. I used to drink my cup of tea early in the morning, and tasted no food at all till five o'clock at night. I smoked 'even on,' and it did me a great deal of harm. Now my doctors make me take at least a couple of eggs in the morning, and I don't smoke much. But I ought to eat oftener, only if I take anything late I am kept awake all night digesting it."

In the evening I had again to telegraph the news of our victory at Beaune, the French attempt to break through in the direction of Fontainebleau, with the bulk of the Loire army, having been utterly baffled. Afterwards I was directed to send off a telegram to the War Ministry in Berlin, requesting them to issue letters of caption, and to send them to us for publication in the French papers, after all the French officers who have broken their parole and made their escape from captivity, a practice which is becoming alarmingly frequent among these gentlemen. Afterwards he showed me a report from an adjutant of Kératry, the commander of the Breton army, on the absurd and theatrical pardoning of a soldier, which I was told to reproduce, with a little commentary, in our *Moniteur*, and which I give here as a specimen of the way in which these new-fangled dilettanti officers show off, and how they get themselves noticed and praised in the newspapers. A few days ago, Count Kératry authorised the following publication :—

"CAMP DE CONLIE, *November* 18, midnight.

"The General commanding (Kératry) authorises me to send you the following despatch: 'This was a day never to be forgotten in the army of Brittany. A soldier who had been condemned to be shot at two o'clock was pardoned. He had been guilty of great insubordination to the Commandant of the Camp, General Bonedec. Since his condemnation, the army chaplain and officers of the general staff had interceded on his behalf. General Kératry's answer was that it was out of his power to pass the thing over. Accordingly all the troops in camp were gathered about one o'clock to-day, to be present at the execution of the sentence. About two, everything was in readiness. The condemned man stood between two field chaplains, expecting every moment would be his last. He had shown considerable fortitude the whole day, as he knew that there was no longer the faintest hope of pardon. At the appointed hour, the sentence was read before all the troops. Then came the first rattle of the drum: at the second all would be over. The coffin was ready, and the grave dug. It was a frightful moment. Just when the last signal was to have been given, Monsieur de Kératry stepped forward, cried 'Halt!' and in a clear ringing voice said (really just as in a genuine melodrama), 'Officers and men of the army of Brittany! One of our soldiers, guilty of an act of insubordination, has been sentenced to death by court-martial; I grant him a free pardon; but in future every offence against discipline will be punished without mercy. I hope that this lesson may be sufficient to prevent any offence against the Articles of War or disobedience to the orders of your officers, and that I shall be rewarded for my leniency by a discipline beyond reproach. That justice may be impartial, I remit all the other sentences at present in force.' This speech was received with tremendous acclamations, and shouts of 'Vive Kératry' (just as in the theatre). The officers of the general staff, who had asked for the man's pardon, were deeply touched. All the troops then marched past the General commanding; and although ordered to march in silence, they kept shouting 'Long live Kératry!' In the evening the officers of the general staff expressed their gratitude to the Count. His gracious act has made a deep impression on the soldiers. The result will, I hope, be that they will give him a confidence never to be shaken."

The ludicrously theatrical nature of the people at present in authority in France could not be better illustrated than by the publication of such a document. The brave French soldiers who have to fight for the maintenance in power of such stage-heroes, are much to be pitied.

A single example, to show the line our servants take about the delay of the bombardment, and the sort of myths which circulate in their circles. As I was, for the last time to-day, going up the staircase leading to my room from the story in which the Chief lives, Engel, in great delight, called after me: " Doctor, things are right now; all will soon be over with Paris." " How is that? I don't think it can last long. But you are not going to begin the bombardment?" " No, Doctor, I know, but I mustn't say a word." " Oh, speak quite freely." Then he whispered something to this effect in my ear, on the stair-landing: " The King told our Excellency to-day, at the War Minister's, 'The bombardment comes off on the 2nd!'"

After ten o'clock the French began another furious cannonade from their forts, with what object, nobody can make out. At tea, when the Chief was with us, fuller favourable accounts came in of yesterday's battle. We then spoke of the delay of the bombardment—a subject coming every day more prominently into the foreground—and of the Geneva Convention, of which the Chief remarked that we must tolerate the thing, but that it was nonsense, and that war could not be carried on that way. It appears that Delbrück has not telegraphed quite distinctly what are the prospects of the arrangements with Bavaria being carried in the Reichstag. It seems as if the Reichstag could not make up its mind to decisive action, and the convention concluded at Versailles were to be attacked both by the Progress party and the National Liberals. The Chief said: "As for the Progress fellows, they are quite consistent. They would like us back in 1849. But these National Liberals! If they will not take what, at the beginning of the year they were struggling for with all their might, and what they may now have by putting out their hand, we must dissolve their Reichstag. The Progress party would be weakened by a new election, and several of the National Liberals would not come back either. But the convention would for the present be torn to pieces. Bavaria would reconsider her position; Beust would stick his finger in the pie, and nobody knows what might happen. I can't well go off to Berlin. It is very inconvenient, and takes up a good deal of time when I am really wanted here." In this connection he spoke also of the state of matters in 1848: "At that time things looked well for a while for a union of Germany under Prussia. The little princes were mostly powerless and in despair. If only they could have had a good deal of property secured to themselves—domains, appanages, &c.—most of them would have willingly consented to everything else. The Austrians had their hands full with

Hungary and Italy. The Emperor Nicholas would, at that time, have made no protest. If before May, 1849, we had put our backs into it, been decided, and settled up with the minor princes, we might have had the south, for the armies of Bavaria and Würtemberg were inclined to side with the revolution in Baden, which at that time was not an impossibility. But time was lost through delays and half measures, and the opportunity was gone."

About eleven a telegram came in from Verdy about the sortie this morning. It was directed against La Haye, and about five hundred red-breeches were taken prisoners. The Chief complained bitterly that they would go on taking prisoners, instead of shooting them down at once.

"We had more than enough prisoners," he said, "already, and the Parisians were relieved of so many 'consumers,' whom we should have to feed and for whom we had no room."

*Wednesday, November* 30.—In the morning T. was written to at length, and the reasons explained to him why we did not urge the demands which he and those who feel with him think absolutely essential in Bavaria. At the same time we communicated similar observations to S. During the latter half of the night and towards morning there was heavy firing from great guns beyond the thicket between this and Paris. Wollmann thinks he also heard the growl of the mitrailleuses and the rattle of musketry. Other people knew nothing of that. . . . . The Chief appears to have seriously entertained the idea of asking the King to relieve him of his office, and according to ―― he put the notion aside just before the decisive moment.

In the afternoon Wollmann and I took a carriage excursion to Marly. The Chancellor, Abeken, and Hatzfeld also rode out in that direction a little after us, so that we met them up at the aqueduct. We saw there that heavy firing was going on north of Paris in the direction of Gonesse. White clouds of powder smoke rose into the sky, and flashes of fire from the guns lightened through it.

Prince Putbus and Odo Russell dined with us, and the Prince told us of the only time he had made an attempt to speculate in stocks on the strength of his knowledge of state secrets and of the bad luck he had had of it. "I had been charged," he said, " to talk over the Neuenburg (Neufchatel) business with Napoleon, in the spring of 1857, I believe. I was to ascertain his attitude, and I knew that he would express himself favourably, and that that would point to a war with Switzerland. On my way through Frankfort, where I then resided, I went accordingly to see Rothschild, whom I knew personally, and told him to sell out a certain stock which he held for me, as it would certainly not rise. 'I should not advise you to do it,' said Rothschild, 'the stock has good prospects, and you will see that soon.' 'Well,' said I, 'if you knew what I know, you would think differently.' However that might be he said, he should not like to advise selling out. Of course I knew better, so I sold my stock and went off. In Paris, Napoleon was quite clear and very amiable. He could not accede to the King's wish to be allowed to march through Elsass and Lothringen, as that would have roused too much feeling in France. Otherwise he entirely approved of the enterprise, and it would give him nothing but gratification to see that Democrats' nest routed out. So far I had succeeded perfectly. But I had not calculated on our own policy in Berlin, which had meanwhile shifted in another direction—probably in view of Austria—so that the thing was given up; there was no war, the stock kept steadily rising in the market, and I could only regret that it was no longer my property."

Then we spoke of the bombardment, of the Villa Coublay, and of what seemed the impossibility of getting the necessary ammunition forward quickly. The Chief said, "I have told the gentlemen twice over that we have lots of horses, which have every day to be exercised to keep them in health, and which might surely be employed for once in another way. . . ."

Somebody told us that the Villa Caffarelli had been purchased for our embassy in Rome, and Russell and Abeken said it was a very handsome one. The Chancellor said "Yes indeed, and we have some fine houses in other places, as, for instance, in Paris and London. But according to our continental ideas, the latter is too small. Bernstorff has so little space that when he receives or is at work, or has any grand affair on, he has to get his room cleared out for it. His Secretary of Legation has a better room in the house than Bernstorff himself." "The residence of the Embassy in Paris is a fine house very comfortably arranged. It is certainly the best house any of the Embassies have in Paris, and it is worth so much that I once asked myself the question whether I ought not to dispose of it and give the Ambassador the interest of the capital to pay his rent with. The interest on 2½ million francs (£80,000) would be a nice addition to his income, which is only 100,000 francs (£4000). But the more I turned it over, the less I liked it. It is not seemly or worthy of a great power, that its ambassadors should have to rent a house which they might get notice to quit, when all the state papers would have to be trundled through the streets in wheel-barrows during the flitting. We must have houses of our own, and we ought to have them in every embassy town. The house in London is in a very peculiar position. It belongs to the King, and everything turns on the energy with which the ambassador of the day looks after his own interests. It may happen—occasionally it does happen—that the King gets no rent at all. . . . " The Chief praised Napier, who was formerly English ambassador in Berlin. "It was very easy to get on with him," he said; "Buchanan, too, was a good, dry man, but trustworthy. Now we have Loftus. The position of an English ambassador in Berlin raises curious questions and involves special difficulties on account of the relationship between the two Royal Houses. It needs great tact and discretion (a quiet hint probably that Loftus does not answer these demands and requirements)." The Minister (perhaps to mark still more clearly his opinion of the character of the then representative of Her Britannic Majesty) then turned the conversation to Gramont, saying "He and Ollivier always seem to me the real people. If such a thing had happened in my hands, after doing mischief like that, I should at least have enlisted or become a Franc-tireur on my own account, though I might have been hanged for it. That big strong fellow Gramont is very well made for soldiering." Russell said he had once seen him in Rome in blue velveteens at a hunting party. "Yes," said the Chief, "he is a good sportsman. He has the right build of muscles for it. He would have been a capital head gamekeeper. But—Minister of Foreign Affairs—one can hardly conceive how Napoleon could have appointed him to such a position."

In the evening L. told us that he had seen two heavy siege guns, with eight horses each harnessed to them, passing through Versailles to-day, probably for a battery at Sèvres or Meudon.

Bohlen told us at tea that Hatzfeld had yesterday been invited to the Royal table. Abeken sorrowfully remarked, "I have never had the good fortune to be commanded to dine and have never got any farther than tea." About ten o'clock the Minister came in. He spoke once more of the bombardment. "If what the General Staff asserted at Ferrières, that in three days they could reduce a couple of forts to ruins, and then push forward against the feeble *enceinte*, were correct, it would be a good thing for us. But now—it has been too long put off—only one month till Sedan, and already three months here, for to-morrow is the 1st of December. The danger of an intervention of the neutral Powers grows greater daily. That would begin in a friendly sort of way and might end in all sorts of mischief. . . . Had I known three months ago how things would be I should have been very anxious." Later in the evening, Abeken came back from the King, to whom he has for some time been reporting matters for the Chancellor. He had heard that there had been three sorties to-day, one directed against the Würtembergers, one against the Saxons, and the third against the Sixth Army Corps. The King thought that it might have been an attempt to break through our lines and escape. "Where could they go?" said the Minister; "they would put their heads in a sack. Such an attempt would be the best thing that could happen for us. Where they came on with eight battalions we should meet them with ten: and better troops too. Of course they may have received dark hints about the Army of the Loire, they don't know that it has already been defeated. By the way," turning to me, "you might put into a telegram what Putbus told me to-day, that some of the wounded to whom we gave permission to return to Paris, declined to do so."

There was no more firing to-night

I have already remarked somewhere that there are only a few reasonable men in France. To-day I have come across one. A leading article of the Lyons *Décentralisation*, headed

'A Voice from the Provinces,' and signed L. Duvarennes, runs as follows:—

"On the day after the Empire fell, the Paris Deputies thought themselves obliged to form a Government. Impartial history will take note of this quite as much as of the attitude of a Chamber elected, at least in part, rather in the interests of a dynasty than of the nation. Out of their action issued the Provisional Government and the premature proclamation of the Republic, which has not yet received the necessary legal sanction of the representatives of the country.

"Although we may not excuse, we can readily understand the excitement of those first days; and how the French people, unaccustomed to administer its own affairs, surprised by what then revealed itself to it as a sort of eternal justice asserting its indefeasible rights and appearing to be a success—we can understand how arbitrary action seemed in many parts of the country to assume the shape of freedom.

"But we have several times already pointed out to whom, in our opinion, we owe this false idea of the situation, and as one naturally suspects the man who is to profit by a crime, of being its real author, the adherents of the dethroned government have an interest so clear and unmistakable in the maintenance of disturbance in France, that we are entitled distinctly to charge them with striving to secure it by every means in their power" (the writer is in error here).

"What ought to be the attitude of the Government, if it really wishes to defend the country in its hour of danger? What has it done in that way? It was bound first of all to make an appeal to the nation and by every possible means to bring itself into that harmony with its representatives which the situation required for the public well-being. It ought by its example to have inculcated the union of all Frenchmen. But it must be admitted that unity, which implies a disciplined obedience, was everywhere absent, and that we have too many actual governments to be able to tell which of them is the lawful government of the country.

"Tours orders elections and Paris will not hear of them. Paris proceeds to elections which France, acting from Tours, has refused. Lyons is under one flag, France under another. Marseilles holds itself aloof. Blood flows in the streets of Perpignan, and Esquiros leaves his place in Ghent and is received with shots from revolvers. Duportal stays at his post at Toulouse, preaching up a peasants' war, in defiance of the government at Tours. Is this unity? Can one call it Government? In presence of such facts is it possible to question the necessity of a regularly established authority?

"There is another class of citizens resisting the elections —the people at present at the helm. Probably they are afraid that the country would send them back to their old occupations. Certainly the obstinacy with which they cling to their dictatorship justifies every kind of distrust. They see that the power they have laid hold of is slipping out of their hands, they struggle to confirm themselves in it, and people hereabouts are beginning to talk of a plebiscite, to establish a sort of bastard representation of the people for the duration of the war. We shall not exchange our liberties for such a mere phantasm of freedom; we shall go on demanding a free, equal, and universal expression of the popular will. It is not the time to ask people to cast into the ballot-boxes a simple Yes or No for a particular set of candidates. After the Plebiscite, which has been hissed off the stage, they ought to let the curtain stay down on the comedy, and we say distinctly, for the honour of the country, that a proposal for that sort of election can scarcely be seriously meant. But there is no reason why we should not immediately elect municipalities, restoring to the communes of our towns and villages their most sacred rights, of which they have been shamefully robbed by the pretensions of the Parisians to be the mouthpiece of France. Let us name our municipalities, and elect our mayors. In one word, let us be free, and from these communes will issue a real representation of the country.

"Under the reign of yesterday's Cæsar, we had plenty of fine speeches stigmatising the official precautions taken about the freedom of elections. Was all this patriotism (of MM. Gambetta and Favre) nothing but a wretched farce? We might have believed it sincere, if the Cæsar of to-day had not been equally ready to give his own declaration of the popular will. We want free elections; we want the Commune; we want people really charged with the decision of our destinies; we shudder to think of the hydra of anarchy, which is already rearing its hideous head. That is why we shall never cease to demand communal elections, and the creation of those elected into a *Parliament of national defence*, if we are to defend ourselves any longer, and, at any rate, into a Parliament representing France."

*Thursday, December* 1.—This morning only a couple of shots were fired from the forts. I telegraphed that yesterday's sortie had led to a desperate struggle with the Würtemberg Division, the larger half of the 12th, and portions of the 6th and 2nd Army Corps, and that the result had been that the enemy had been repulsed along the whole line. The wounded had declined to avail themselves of the permission to return to Paris. Afterwards there was the usual study of the journals with pencil marking and extracts.

At breakfast Abeken appeared with his hair cut. He asked Bismarck-Bohlen how he looked. The answer was, "Admirably, Privy Councillor, but the lock on the one side is longer than on the other." "No matter for that, I always wear it so. But have you really nothing else to say against it?" "It is quite perfect, Privy Councillor." The old gentleman went away whistling, greatly pleased with himself, and Hatzfeld watched him as he went out with a wondering smile.

At dinner we had a First Lieutenant von Saldern who was present as Adjutant at the last engagements of the 10th Army Corps with the Army of the Loire. According to him this Corps was for a long time surrounded by a superior body of French, who were trying to break through one wing of our troops towards Fontainebleau. They defended themselves for seven hours against the enemy's assaults with magnificent courage and firmness. The troops under Wedel, and above all those of the 16th Regiment, specially distinguished themselves. "We made over 1600 prisoners, and the total loss of the French is estimated at from 4000 to 5000 men," said Saldern. "Yes," said the Chief, "but prisoners are now a serious trouble to us, an extra burden" . . . When Saldern told us, in the course of his narrative, that one of the French soldiers was shot only ten paces in front of our needle-guns, the Chief said, "But he *was* shot." Afterwards he gave Abeken his instructions for the report he was to make for him to the King, "and say to his Majesty," said he finally, "that if we permit a Frenchman to appear in London (in the Conference then being held for the revision of the peace of 1856), we are not bound to do so, as the Government has never been recognised by the Powers, and cannot be long in existence. We may allow it, to gratify Russia, on this question only, but if anything else is brought forward, he must leave the room."

The Chief then told us the following incident: "After being with Roon to-day, I took a walk which may have done some good. I went to see Marie Antoinette's rooms in the château, after which I thought to myself, You should take note how the wounded are getting on. I asked one of the sentinels, 'What do the people get to eat?' 'Well,' he said, 'not very much, a little soup, meant for broth, with some bits of bread and pickles of rice in it, not boiled very soft, and very little fat.' 'And about the wine,' I said, 'and do you get beer? They got about half a glass of wine a day. I asked another, afterwards, who had got none at all. A third told me he had had some three days ago, but none since. I questioned about a dozen, including some Poles, who did not understand me, and could only express their delight to have anybody asking for them, by smiling. Also the poor wounded soldiers did not get what they ought, and the rooms were cold, because they were not allowed to be heated for fear of spoiling the pictures on the walls. As if the life of a single soldier were not worth more than all the lumber of pictures in the château. Then the servants told me that the oil lamps were only allowed till eleven, and that after that the men had to lie in the dark till the morning. I had previously talked with an officer severely wounded in the foot. He said he ought to be satisfied, though things might be managed better. People took pretty good care of him, but for the rest ——. A Bavarian companion of St. John plucked up heart and told me that beer and wine were given out, but probably half or more went a-missing somehow, as well as warm things and other gifts from friends at home. Then I went off to the head doctor. 'What about

the provision for the sick,' I said; 'do they get proper things to eat?' 'Here is the official list of returns.' 'Don't show me that,' I said, 'people can't eat paper—do they get their wine?' 'Half a litre daily.' 'Pardon me, the people say that is not so. I have asked them, and it is hardly to be supposed they are lying when they say they have got none.' 'Here, sir, is my proof that everything is done properly, and according to my orders. Come with me, and I shall ask them about it before you.' 'I must excuse myself,' I said, 'but they shall be asked by the auditor whether they get what goes to the inspector for them.' 'That would be a great reflection on me,' said he. 'Yes,' said I, of course, 'but I shall take care that the matter is inquired into, and at once.'"*
He went on to say, "Frauds happen mostly among two classes, the meal-worms, who have to do with the provisions, and the building people, especially the hydraulic engineers. Unfortunately, too, there are some among the doctors. Not long ago, perhaps a year and a half since, I remember that there was a great investigation into frauds in the supply of the soldiers, and to my astonishment I found that about thirty doctors were involved." Then he asked suddenly, "Does any of you know who is Niethammer? He must come of a very learned family." Somebody thought he was a philologian, another said there was a friend of Hegel's of that name, Keudell remembered that there was a diplomatist so-called, who had no good-will to us. The Chief said he must have been in relation with Harless, a Bavarian theologian, who was an enemy of ours.

* We shall see afterwards that little more came of this suspicion, which appearances abundantly justified, than that some small defects were discovered in the provision for looking after the sick throughout. I have told the story as an evidence of the Minister's sense of justice and kindly feeling for people.

In the evening Dunker's interpellation on the imprisonment of Jacoby, as it appeared in the *National Zeitung*, was prepared for the King's reading.

The Chancellor came in later, after half-past ten, when we were at tea. After a while, he said, "The papers are not pleased with the Bavarian Convention; I expected as much. They are out of humour because certain officials, who will have to conduct themselves entirely according to our laws, are to be called Bavarian. It is the same thing, essentially, with the military people. The beer tax is not to their mind, as if we had not had the same thing for years in the Customs Union. They would cavil in this way over every detail in the treaty, though everything essential has been obtained and properly secured. They are behaving as if we had been at war previously with Bavaria, as we were with the Saxons in 1866, instead of the Bavarians being our allies, and fighting at our side. Rather than see any good in the Convention, they would prefer to wait till they could have their unity in a form agreeable to themselves. They would have to wait a long while. Their course leads to nothing but distraction, while the matter must be settled at once. If we put off, Time, the old enemy, will come in, and sow tares among our wheat. The Convention secures us a great deal, and those who want everything will make it possible that we may get nothing whatever. They are not content with what is in their hand—they want more uniformity—if they would only think of five years back, and what they would then have been satisfied with. . . . A Constituent Assembly! But the King of Bavaria might decline to allow one to be elected. The Bavarian people would never force his hand, and neither should we. Yes, criticism is easy when people don't in the least realise the real circumstances."

He then turned to a different subject: "I have seen the

account," he said, "of the surprise of the Unna Battalion. Inhabitants of Châtillon took part in it, and others undoubtedly added to the difficulties of our troops. If they had only burnt down the place in their first rage! Afterwards, in cold blood, it is not so easy to do."

A little after, he took up some gold pieces, and played with them in his hands for awhile. "It is startling," he said, "how many well-dressed people go about begging here. It was the same in Rheims, only it is much worse here. How seldom one sees gold pieces now of Louis Philippe's, or Charles the Tenth's! I remember when I was young, in my twenties, one still saw pieces of Louis the Sixteenth and Eighteenth, the thick ones. Even the name, Louis d'or, has almost gone out, though with us it is still the correct thing to talk of Friedrichs d'or." He balanced a gold Napoleon on the tip of his middle finger, as if he were weighing it, and went on: "A hundred million double Napoleons would be about the amount of the war indemnity so far, in gold—it will come to more after a bit—4000 million francs. Forty thousand gold thalers make a hundredweight, thirty hundredweights are the load for a good two-horse cart—I know that I once had to take 14,000 gold thalers home, and how heavy they were! That would take about eight hundred carts." "We should get those faster than the carts for the ammunition for the bombardment," said somebody, whose patience, like that of most of us, was about worn out over the putting off of the bombardment. "Yes," said the Chief, "but Roon told us a few days ago, that he has several hundred lorries at Nanteuil, meant for the transport of the ammunition. We might use four horses for awhile, for carriages which have now six, and spare the extra two for the transport of ammunition. We have already 318 cannon, but we want forty more, and he might get them also, said Roon. But others won't hear of it." Afterwards, Hatzfeld said: "They have been refusing to hear of it for six or seven weeks now. Bronsard and Verdy said, so long ago as at Ferrières, that we could lay Forts Issy and Vanvres in ruins in six-and-thirty hours, and then advance on Paris itself. Yet, after all that, nothing is done." I asked what Moltke thought about the matter. "Oh, he does not trouble himself," said Hatzfeld; but Bucher said, "Moltke wants the bombardment."

Before going to bed, I cast my eye over our *Moniteur*, with a whole column full of the names of French officers who had been taken prisoners, broken their parole, and got off from the places where they had been interned. There were captains and lieutenants, infantry and cavalry, northern Frenchmen and southern Frenchmen. Two had got away from Dresden, and no fewer than ten from Hirschberg. If we can trust the reports in the English and Belgian newspapers, there is little enough already in Paris, of what holds body and soul together; but things are still bearable, at all events, for well-to-do people. They have plenty of bread, dried vegetables and preserved meats. There is very little fresh beef, and it is very dear. Horse and donkey-flesh, "both better than they are called," says a letter, have to serve for it with most of the Parisians. The rat is beginning to be much in request. Dogs and cats are articles of luxury, and can no longer put out their noses with impunity on the Boulevards at night.

The stock of oil is about done, there is no more wood for firing, and the supplies of coal are running low. About the middle of November a pound of butter cost twenty-five to twenty-six francs, a goose thirty-five, a pound of horse-flesh three to four francs, and fresh vegetables and milk were no longer within the reach of people of moderate means.

*Friday, December* 2.—In the morning I again explained the Chief's attitude about the convention with Bavaria in letters and an article. At breakfast we were told that another sortie was going on against the Würtemberg troops and the Saxons, and that this time the French had developed great masses of infantry. We had several degrees of cold, a very serious affair for the wounded on the battlefield. In the afternoon the long article in the *Times* on Gortchakoff's answer to Granville's despatch was translated for the King.

Alten, Lehndorff, and an officer in dragoon uniform were the Chief's guests at dinner. The officer was a Herr von Thadden, a son of Thadden-Treglaff. The Chief said that after coming back from a carriage round he had just been looking to the better quartering of our soldiers on guard. "Up to this time the fellows have been billeted," he said, "in Madame Jessé's coach-yard, where they can get no fire. I could not allow that any longer, and ordered the gardener to clear out the half of the hothouse for them. 'But madame's plants will be frozen,' said the gardener's wife. 'It is a pity,' I said, 'but it is better than that the soldiers should be.'" He then spoke of the danger that the Reichstag might disallow, or at least modify, the convention with Bavaria. "I am most anxious about it," said he. "These people have no idea of the real situation. We are standing on the point of a lightning conductor; if we lose our balance, after I have had the greatest difficulty in getting it, we tumble to the bottom. They want more than what was got without using any pressure, and what they would have been delighted with, or with the half of it, in 1866. They want amendments, they want to put in more unity and uniformity. If they alter a single comma, we shall have the negotiations all over again. Where are they to be held?

Here in Versailles? And if we are not finished by the 1st of January, which would be delightful to many in Munich, the unity of Germany is done for, perhaps for years, and the Austrians can do what they like in Munich."

The first dish after the soup was mushrooms, served up in two different ways. "You must eat these with much feeling," he said; "they are a love-gift from the soldiers, who found them in some quarry or cellar, where a crop of mushrooms is being raised. The cook has fitted with them a capital sauce, first-rate! Even a better love-gift, certainly a more unusual one, was sent me by the soldiers: what regiment was it that sent me the roses?" "The 47th," said Bohlen. "Yes, that bouquet of roses was gathered under fire, probably in a garden of the outpost circle. By the bye, that reminds me that in the hospital I came across a Polish soldier, who could read no German. A Polish prayerbook would be a comfort to him; has anybody such a thing?" Alten said no, but he could supply him with some Polish newspapers. The Chief replied: "No good; he would not understand them, and they would put him up against us. Perhaps Radziwill has something. A Polish novel, 'Pan Twardowski,' or something of that sort, might do." Alten said he would make a note of it.

The conversation then turned on to-day's sortie, as twice over we heard the thunder from the Seine. Somebody said, "The poor Würtemberg fellows have no doubt lost a great many men this time, too." "Most likely the poor Saxons also," said the Chief. Somebody mentioned Ducrot, who was probably in command of the sortie, and said he ought to take care not to get taken prisoner. "Certainly," said the Minister, "he should either get killed in battle, or if he has no mind for that he should take himself off in a balloon." . . . The Chief looked round: "Where is

Krausnik? He has surely not forgotten to bring the apple-poultice for the soldier which I promised him. He was wounded only in the arm, but he looked a miserable object, and had fever—suppuration, I am afraid."

We began to talk of speculation in stocks, and the Minister again repeated that very little could be made out of it, through the possession of which must always give one a very restricted forecast of political events. Such things only produce their effects on the Exchange a little later, and nobody can guess on what day the effect will begin. "Yes," he went on, "and if one could procure a fall of stocks by intrigues of that sort, it would be a disgraceful affair. The French Minister G. did so, as R. recently told us. He doubled his capital by it—it might almost be said that the war was promoted with that object. M., too, as they say tried the same business—not on his own account, but with the money of his mistress—and when it was likely to turn out well, he died under suspicious circumstances. A man who wants to make use of his position will arrange to have the Bourse telegrams for all the Exchanges sent on along with the political despatches to suitable officials at the various legations. Political telegrams have precedence, and twenty or thirty minutes might be gained that way. Then you must have a Jew who can run fast, to take proper advantage of the extra time. There are people, doubtless, who have done it. In this way one might earn his 500 or 5000 thalers daily, which in a couple of years would come to a good deal of money. My son shall never say that his father made him a rich man in any such fashion. He may get rich some other way, if he wants. I was better off before I was Chancellor of the Confederation than I am now. I was ruined by the Dotation. Since that time I have been a man in difficulties. I considered myself before as a simple country squire, but after I came to belong in a sort of way to the peerage, the demands on me have increased, and my estates don't bring it in. The time when I always had something to the good was when I was ambassador at Frankfort, and in St. Petersburg, when I needed to keep no company and kept none." Then he told us of his ground-fir and wood pulp concerns in Varzin, out of which he seemed to expect to make a good deal. His tenant paid him interest on the capital which he had sunk in the mills and other plant. "How much might it be?" said somebody. "Forty to fifty thousand thalers. He pays me 2000 thalers," he added, "for a water-power, which was of no use before; he buys my pine logs which I could hardly sell previously, and after thirty years he is to hand me back the whole of the mills in the condition in which he received them. At present there is only one, but there will soon be another where the water falls with greater force, and afterwards a third." "And what may your tenant make of it?" "Pasteboard for book-covers, paper for packing and for making boxes and so on, especially for Berlin, and cakes of ground-pine flour which are sent to England, dissolved there, mixed up with other stuffs, and turned into paper." All this he explained to us in detail, as knowing all about the processes.

*Saturday, December* 3.—During the night there was heavy firing again in the north, but, in the course of the day, only single shots came from the big guns. Yesterday there must have been severe fighting on the east and north-east of Paris, with heavy losses on our side too. Apparently the French had established their footing at night in the villages of Brie, Villiers, and Champigny, which were included within our lines. I forward by telegraph to Germany a communication from the General Staff about these events, which leaves the continued occupation of these positions by our troops ambiguous, speaks only of the repulse of the French, who burst out in heavy masses, by the Saxons (who seem to have lost a whole battalion), the Würtemberg troops, and the 2nd Army Corps, and goes on to describe a victory at Longwy and at Artenay. At half-past one the Chief goes to visit the Grand Duke of Baden, whose wife's birthday it is, and afterwards dines with the King. We have Count Holnstein with us, who went off last Saturday night to see the King of Baden at Hohenschwangau and got back here at mid-day to-day. "A journey that can never be forgotten," said Bohlen to him. I asked Bucher about it. "The Count was absent while the Emperor question was going on, and he brings back good news," he answered. We were struck to-day by the French firing four cannon-shots some six times in the course of the day, two at intervals of about four seconds, and two almost simultaneously.

The *Gaulois*, which has emigrated from Paris to Brussels, seems an accurate sort of print. Its editors, one of whom was that amiable person, Angelo de Miranda, go on as if they were still writing in Paris, shut off from all the world. For example, these children of the father of lies tell us, that about the middle of October Prussia paid 450,000 thalers (£67,500), through a London house, to certain people living in France, on which account these people are supposed to be Prussian spies. They say that Moltke died and was buried three weeks since, but that any German soldier who mentions the fact is at once shot. To get out of the way of the serious business which there is likely soon to be about Paris, King William has, it seems, taken himself off to Germany, probably to open the Reichstag. Lastly, thirty-six heads of families at Mutzig, near Strassburg, whose sons are with the French army, have been put to death, their ears and noses cut off, and their corpses fastened on the church walls, where they have been for a month past. In other respects the chief editor, Tarbé, is not at all bad. He attacks Gambetta, whom he calls a tyrant, and whom he charges particularly with acting in the interest only of the republic, not of France, the republic meaning nothing but his own dictatorship and absolute sovereignty; and with sacrificing his country to secure his own power. In Paris Tarbé appears not to have been in a position to express these views with sufficient distinctness. So he left Paris, and tried to slip through the German lines with three of his sub-editors. He succeeded, but he could not start his paper again in any of the French provincial towns, as he might not have been allowed to attack Gambetta even there. So he is going to fight and lie from Belgium. Notes about this mendacious print were communicated to the *Moniteur* and the German papers.

Afterwards I wrote an article on the neutrality of Luxemburg, and the perfidious way in which the people there have taken advantage of it to assist the French in their struggle with us in various particulars. The line of argument was as follows. At the beginning of the war we declared that we should on our part respect the neutrality of Luxemburg. The reciprocal neutrality of the grand duchy and people of Luxemburg was presumed without any express declaration. This presumption has turned out unfortunately. While we kept our promise honestly, inconvenient as it was, interfering especially with the forwarding of our wounded, neutrality was frequently violated by Luxemburg in the most flagrant fashion. We had previously had reason to complain that the fortress of Thionville had been revictualled by supplies brought in during the night through the connivance of the officers of the grand-ducal railway

and of the police authorities. After the capitulation of
Metz numerous French soldiers passed through the Grand
Duchy on their way back to France and the French army
operating against us in the north. The French consul
established an official "bureau" at the railway station at
Luxemburg, where such soldiers were supplied with money
and legitimation papers for their journey. The grand-
ducal government allowed all this to go on without making
an attempt to interfere with this assistance to the enemies
of Germany. It can have no reason to complain if we pay
no further respect to its neutrality in our military operations,
and if we require it to make up the loss which we have
had to undergo through its permitting these violations of
neutrality.

*Sunday, December* 4.—Lovely weather. Scarcely a shot
fired in the north. I am telegraphing that the French have
made no new attempts to break through our lines either
yesterday or to-day, and that Prince Frederick Charles has
been again pressing forward and capturing some more guns.

The Bavarian ex-minister Von Roggenbach, first lieutenant Von Sarwadsky, and the Bavarian companion of St.
John, von Niethammer, a man with an uncommonly noble
countenance, whose acquaintance the Prince made recently
in the hospital, were at dinner. The Minister first mentioned that he had again been visiting the wounded in the
château. Then he said, "Frankfort and Petersburg excepted, I have never been as long in any strange place as
I have been here. We shall certainly spend our Christmas
here, and a little ago we did not expect that. At Easter
we may be still in Versailles seeing the trees once more
growing green, and keeping our ears always open for news
of the army of the Loire. If we had known, we should have
had asparagus beds in the garden out there." Afterwards,

turning to Roggenbach, he said, "I have seen the extracts from the newspapers. How they are wrestling over the Convention! They don't leave one good hair on its head. The *National Zeitung*, the *Kölnische*, the *Weser Zeitung*, which is as it always is, the most rational of all. Well, criticism must please itself. But I am responsible if nothing comes of it all, and the critics are not. It is all one what they say against me if the thing can only be put through in the Reichstag; history may say, if it pleases, that that poor creature of a Chancellor ought to have made something much better out of it, but then I was responsible. If the Reichstag amends it, every South German country diet may do the same, and a peace such as we want, and need, is done for. Elsass cannot be claimed from France, unless a political personality has been meanwhile created, and there is a Germany to recover it for."

We spoke of the peace negotiations which would likely spring out of the soon-expected capitulation of Paris, and of the difficulties that might ensue. "Favre and Trochu," the Chief began, "may say, 'We are no longer the Government; we once were, but we have resigned and are merely private individuals—I am only Citizen Trochu.' I should soon bring the Parisians to their senses. I should say, You two millions of people are answerable to me with your lives. I shall leave you to starve for four-and-twenty hours till we get what we want out of you. And twenty-four hours on the top of that, for what happens is all one to me. The delay will do *me* no harm, but . . . I could manage well enough with myself, but there is something standing behind me, behind my back, or rather lying on my chest, so that I cannot breathe. . . . Ah! if I were squire, I could answer for my own hardheartedness; but I am not squire. Within the last few days something very foolish has come up through sentimental feeling for the people inside. Great magazines of provisions are to be prepared for the Parisians. They are to be brought over from London and Belgium, the magazines are to be between our lines, and our soldiers are only to look on, and not to help themselves out of them when they are in want. It is to save the Parisians from starving after the capitulation." "We have certainly enough in the house here, but the troops outside are often hard put to it, and they are suffering that the Parisians may be able, when they know they are looked after outside, to put the capitulation off till they have really swallowed their last loaf and slaughtered their last horse. I am not asked about it, else I should be hanged rather than give my consent." "But I have myself to blame; I was imprudent enough to invite people's attention, only the diplomatic world's to be sure, to famine as inevitable." (I had also had to do the same in the newspapers.)

Swiss cheese was handed round, and somebody asked whether cheese went well with wine. "Some kinds of cheese with some sorts of wine," said the Minister; "high-flavoured cheeses like Gorgonzola or Dutch, don't suit. Others suit well. When people used to drink hard in Pomerania, some two centuries or so since, the Rammin folk were the hardest drinkers. One Stettin man had once got wine which did not taste right to him, and he wrote to the wine merchant about it. The answer he got back was, 'Eet Kees to Wien, Herr von Rammin, denn smekt de Wien wie in Stettin ook to Rammin.' ('Take cheese to your wine, like a Rammin man, for the wine tastes the same in Stettin as in Rammin.')"

L. told us when he came in, about eight o'clock, to fetch his notes, that the Ambassador von der Goltz had told him in 1866 that he had despatched a courier to the

German head-quarters to say that the Emperor Napoleon would offer no objection to the annexation of Saxony, but the messenger arrived a couple of hours too late (the facts, as is well known, were different). I then told L. to explain at length, in an article in the great newspaper for which he corresponds, what is the feeling here about the convention with Bavaria. He could say something like this: In the first place, we cannot dictate to Bavaria the conditions of her entrance into the Confederation with the rest of Germany, as we did to Saxony in 1866. She is our victorious ally, not our defeated enemy. We could not have put pressure on her in time of peace, much less now, after she has been fighting by our side, with whatever motives—and probably a wish to maintain her own independence, to a certain reasonable extent, may have been one of them. And finally, if the Reichstag alters anything in the convention the diets of Southern Germany may correct anything they think convenient, and the negotiations will be endless; while it is of the utmost moment that the convention should soon be complete, in view of the annexation of Elsass-Lothringen.

After ten o'clock, some six shots came from one of the forts, one sharp after the other, and some more shortly after. The Würtemberg troops fought, it appears, wonderfully well in Ducrot's first sortie towards the Marne, and the Saxons also, who lost several hundreds in prisoners. We have taken eight hundred French prisoners.

I went down to tea after half-past ten. Bismarck-Bohlen and Hatzfeld were sitting there with three sharp-shooters, who were waiting for the orders of the Chief. It was half an hour later before he came back from the Grand Duke of Baden's. He wrote rapidly a letter in pencil to the general commanding the Fourth Army Corps, which one of the sharpshooters took away with him. Then he told us how the Grand Duke had just had the news from the King that our people were now in possession of the Forest of Orleans and close up to the town. After the others and the sharp-shooters had left, I asked, "Your Excellency, should I telegraph the good news straight off to London?" "Yes," he said, smiling, "if the general staff will allow us to say anything about the movements of the army." He then read Reuter's telegram with accounts from the French side. He stopped at the word "tardé," which was probably a mistake in writing out, saying, "A Saxon must have telegraphed this." Then, with a look at me, "I beg your pardon."

The gentlemen came in with Abeken who had had the honour to drink tea with the King We spoke of Gortchakoff's note, of England, of Count Holnstein's journey and its happy results, of his audience by King William. Bohlen said, "They are quite beside themselves in Germany. It will be a splendid spectacle to-morrow with their Emperor. They will illuminate; they are already making preparations for a feast of dazzling magnificence." "Well," said the Chief, "it may have, I fancy, a good effect on the Reichstag. It was very good of Roggenbach to be ready to go off to Berlin at once" (to preach reason to those of the members of parliament who were dissatisfied).

*Monday, December* 5.—Charming weather, but this morning very cold. While he was still in bed the Chief had a written report from Bonsart, that the Third and Ninth Army Corps under Prince Frederick Charles had had a great victory, that the railway station and one of the suburbs of Orleans had been taken by Mannstein; that the Grand Duke of Mecklenburg had appeared in the west of the town; that over thirty cannon and several thousand prisoners had fallen into our hands. All sorts of war material, including nine cannon, had also been captured by our troops at Amiens, after a victory there. Finally, here, before Paris, the French had been driven back behind the Marne. I telegraph this in our usual fashion, and this time the Minister has no fault to find with my long despatch.

Soon after he called me back, and I wrote out a polemical article on the Bavarian affair, in which the ideas I had put forward hitherto were somewhat differently given, and which I dropped into the cigar-box which hangs below on the wall of my bureau, for letters requiring rapid dispatch. It was something in this style: "The rumour that the Chancellor of the Confederation accepted the convention with Bavaria as it now stands, only because he believed that the Reichstag would throw it out, or, at all events modify it, is altogether groundless. In the course of December these conventions will have to be finally accepted and concluded in every particular, if they are to come into force, as they are meant to do, on the first day of the new year. Otherwise, everything remains in uncertainty. If the representatives of North Germany alter the Convention, the South German diets become entitled to alter it back again, and nobody can say whether they may not decide to exercise their right. In that case the nation would have a long while to wait for political unity." ("Ten years, perhaps," the Chief had said, "and *interim aliquid fit*—something happens in the meantime.") "Nor can the peace that is coming be what we want without them. The conventions may be defective, but all that can be put right afterwards by the Reichstag acting along with the Federal Council, and through the pressure of public opinion, and of national feeling among the people. Hurry had nothing to do with it. If this pressure fails, the present situation of German affairs is still manifestly according to the wish of the majority of the nation. The Nationalists in Versailles are very much concerned and disturbed about the tone Berlin takes in the matter; but there is some comfort in noticing that the *Volkszeitung* has been fighting against the convention with Bavaria; for people are accustoming themselves to recognise by degrees that everybody with political insight regularly goes against everything which that paper praises or recommends, and inclines to the side which it criticises and warns them away from."

About three I went for a walk with Bucher to the wooded hills south of the city, from which we can see its whole extent. Shortly before dinner I telegraphed, according to news which the Chief had just received, that Orleans was last night taken possession of by the Germans. About the same time L. came to let me know that Bamberg had told him that he, L., was to resign the editorship of the *Moniteur officiel*, by order of the Federal Chancellor, to him, Bamberg. .... I am glad that he is still permitted to get information for his correspondence from us. He has several times done us really good service in that way.

The Royal messenger Bamberger sat at dinner on the Chief's left. He was thinking of starting for Berlin to persuade people to accept the conventions with South Germany without alteration. Besides him, the Minister had as his guests a dragoon officer with a yellow collar, Colonel von Schenk, and a lieutenant or captain of the light-blue hussars. The latter, a grey-headed gentleman with moustaches, was the von Rochow who killed Hinkeldey in a duel. The conversation first turned on doctors, and their knowledge of things, and the Chief thought very little of them. Then we talked of the conventions, and somebody said that the attitude of the princes in the matter had been right. " Yes, but the attitude of the Reichstag," interrupted the Chancellor, " I can think of nothing but, gentlemen, gentlemen, you are spoiling the whole of our fowling. You remember Kaiser Heinrich. But it turned out well there in the end. Well, if this fails, man after man of them might offer himself to be shot dead on the altar of his country, but it would be of no use to anybody." Then he thought a moment, and went on with a half smile, " People should make members of Parliament as responsible as ministers, no more and no less, on a footing of perfect equality. There might be a law that they could be put on trial for high treason, for obstructing important State agreements, or, as they have done in Paris here, for approving a war made without just cause, and in lightness of heart (they were all for it, except Jules Favre). Some day, perhaps, I shall introduce such a law."

We then spoke of the last fights before Paris, and somebody said that the Pomeranians had been under fire. " Probably also my good fellows from Varzin," said the Chief; " forty and nine—seven times seven. How are they getting on, I wonder?" Rochow then told some stories about several peculiar habits of General von Alvensleben, in whose quarters he had passed the night.

We spoke again of the delay in the capitulation of Paris, which was to have taken place in four weeks at latest. "Yes," sighed the Chancellor, " if it would only come to that, all my troubles would be over." Bamberger suggested, "I suppose we shall not allow them merely to capitulate; we shall require them to make peace with us?" " Quite so," said the Chief, " that is my view, too, and we must force them to it by starving them. But there are people here who want to be praised for their humanity above everything, and who spoil everything with it; besides which, our first duty of humanity is to think of our own soldiers, and see that they don't suffer needless misery, and are not killed for nothing." "——'s view of the bombardment is just the same. Then they spare the potato-grubbers, who ought to be shot, of course, if we want to force the city to submit by starvation."

After eight o'clock I was repeatedly called for by the Chief, and wrote two longish articles. The second was founded on a note in the *Indépendance Belge*, and pointed out that there was nothing in the circumstance that the House of Orleans was connected with that of Habsburg Lothringen through the Duc d'Alençon, to make us Germans inclined to give it any preference, or to regard it at all more favourably. It came pretty much to this.

"It will be remembered that when the princes of the House of Orleans offered their services for the war against us, they were refused by Trochu. The *Indépendance Belge* now tells us that the Duc d'Alençon, the second son of the Duc de Nemours, who was not at the time able to follow in his father's and uncle's footsteps, on account of ill-health, is now ready to try his luck in the same direction, and it significantly adds :—" It will be remembered that the Duc d'Alençon is married to a sister of the Empress of Austria." We understand the hint, and believe that we meet it in the spirit of the true policy of Germany as follows.

"The Orleans princes are well known to have been quite as hostile to us as the other dynasties which have angled for the French crown. Their press teems with lies and insults against us. We have not forgotten the pretty song to the glory of the murderous Francs-tireurs, which the Duc de Joinville started after the battle of Wörth. In France the Government which is most agreeable to us is that which has least power to hurt us, having too much to do at home in strengthening itself against its rivals. For us, except in that way, Orleanists, Legitimists, Imperialists, and Republicans, are equally worth and equally little worth. As for the hint of the Austrian relationship, we can see what that would come to. . . . There is one party in the Austro-Hungarian Empire which sides with, and another which sides against Germany. The latter would like to see the Empire repeat the old policy of Kaunitz in the Seven Years' War, of a perpetual conspiracy with France against German, and above all, against Prussian interests. It is the policy which has recently been associated with the name of Metternich, which was pursued from 1815 to 1866, and which people have since been attempting to carry out more or less energetically. This is the party of which Metternich junior, the latter-day resurrection of old Prince Metternich, has for years been the most emphatic spokesman. It wants a Franco-Austrian alliance against Germany, and it was one of the chief instigators of the war now raging. The House of Orleans may fancy that its connection with Austria improves its prospects, but it is the very reason why it has nothing to hope for, at all events from us."

While we were drinking tea, and after Bucher and Keudell and I had been sitting awhile together, the Chief came in, and Hatzfeld afterwards. The latter had been with the King, and told us that he had learned that in the battle near Orleans, and during the pursuit which followed, Prince Frederick Charles had captured seventy-seven guns, several mitrailleuses, and four gun-boats. Some 10,000 unwounded prisoners fell into our hands. The enemy's troops dispersed in different directions. All the important points were taken by storm, and we suffered considerable losses in consequence, the 36th, for instance, having lost a great many, it is believed as many as 600 men. In the last battle before Paris, also, we lost heavily, in consequence of the overwhelming numbers of the enemy. You may imagine, Hatzfeld went on to say, that we did not have a very lively time at the King's. "The Russian state councillor, Grimm, told us all sorts of feebly interesting things about Louis XIV. and Louis XV. The Weimar man proposed a riddle to which nobody could give the correct answer." "Radowitz was a great man in finding out these things," said the Minister. "He used to give his solution of every possible thing with the utmost confidence, and that was the way in which he won most of his successes at Court. He could tell us exactly what la Maintenon or la Pompadour wore on such and such a day. She had this or that round her throat, her head-dress was ornamented with humming-birds, or bunches of grapes; she wore a pearl-green or a parrot-green dress with such or such flounces and laces—all quite as well as if he had been there himself. The ladies were all ears for this toilette lecture, which came trippingly from his tongue."

The conversation turned afterwards on Alexander von Humboldt, who, if we can trust to what was said about him, must have been a courtier not at all of the entertaining kind. "In the time of his late Majesty," the Chief told us, "I was the only victim when Humboldt used of an evening to entertain the company in his own fashion. He used to read aloud to us—often for an hour at a time—a biographical account of some French scholar or architect in whom nobody but himself took any interest. There he stood, holding his paper close up to the lamp. Occasionally he let his hands drop, to interpose some learned expansion of what he had been saying. Nobody listened to him, but he kept on without a pause. The Queen worked steadily at some tapestry work, and certainly did not hear a word of his discourse. The King looked over pictures—

copper-plates and wood-cuts—making a good deal of rustling in turning them over, with the quiet purpose apparently of preventing himself having to listen to anything that was being said.  The young folks kept at the side and in the background, talking quite unrestrainedly, tittering, and occasionally overpowering the voice of the lecturer, who went rippling on all the same for ever like the brook.  Gerlach, who was usually present, sat on a little round stool, over the edge of which his portly person overflowed on all sides, and he slept and snored so loud that the King once wakened him up, saying, 'Gerlach, don't snore so any longer.'  I was his only patient audience, for I kept quiet, as if I were listening to the discourse, while I was thinking of other things.  At last, we had in the cold meat and the white wine."  "It vexed the old gentlemen very much when he could not get speaking.  I remember once that somebody present took up all the conversation, quite naturally, as he was telling us in a charming way about things that interested us all.  Humboldt was beside himself.  He moodily heaped on his plate—so high" (showing us with his hand) "pâté de foie gras, fat eels, lobster claws, and other indigestibles—a regular mountain of them—it was marvellous what that old man could eat.  When he was able for no more, he began to be restless again, and made one more attempt to run away with the conversation.  'On the peak of Popocatepetl,' he began, but it was no use, the story-teller was not to be put down.  'On the summit of Popocatepetl, 14,000 yards above the level of the sea,' he repeated, in a loud, excited voice.  It was still no use; the story-teller went on just the same, and the company gave their attention to him alone.  It was unheard of—an outrage!  Humboldt sat down storming, and fell a-musing sadly on the ingratitude of mankind, even at Court."

"The Liberals made a great deal of him, and counted him one of themselves. But the breath of his nostrils was the favour of princes, and he never felt himself comfortable except in the sunshine of royalty. That did not prevent him from gossiping about the Court afterwards with Varnhagen, and telling all sorts of evil stories about it. Varnhagen made books of them, which I bought like other people. They are frightfully dear when one thinks of the dozen lines in big type that sprawl over a page." Keudell said he supposed, however, that for history they were indispensable. "Yes," said the Chief, "in a certain sense they are. There are points on which they are not worth much, but as a whole they express the acrid tone of Berlin society at a time when there was no good in it. Everybody about that time used to talk with the same malicious impotence." "Without such books, it would be quite impossible for one nowadays to have the least conception of the kind of world it was unless one had seen it. Plenty of apparent, but no real good-breeding. I can remember, though I was then but a little fellow (it must have been in the year 1821 or 1822), the Ministers of the day were frightful creatures, much stared at, and full of a mysterious importance. There happened to be a great gathering at Schuckmann's, what was called at that time an 'Assembly.' What a frightful creature of a minister that man was! My mother went to it. I can remember her as if it were yesterday. She had long gloves on, up to here" (pointing up past his elbow), "a short-waisted gown, her curls done up in pads at both sides, and a big ostrich feather on her head." Whether or not he had meant to tell us some story, he broke off here, and went back to Humboldt. "Humboldt," he said, "had really much to tell one that was worth listening to, when one was alone with him—about the time of Frederick William III.—and especially about his own first residence in Paris. He had a kindness for me as I was always so respectful a listener, and I got a great many good anecdotes from him. It was just the same with old Metternich. I spent a couple of days with him once on the Johannisberg. Thun said to me, some time after, 'I don't know what glamour you have been casting over the old prince, who has been looking down into you as if you were a golden goblet, and who told me, that he had no insight at all, if you and I did not get on well together.' 'Well,' said I, 'I will tell you; I listened peaceably to all his stories, only pushing the clock several times till it rang again. That pleases these talkative old men.'" Hatzfeld remarked, that Moltke had written to Trochu, to tell him the real state of things at Orleans. "He gave him liberty to send out an officer to convince himself of the truth, offering him a safe-conduct to Orleans." The Chief said, "I know. I should have liked better that they had let the proposal originate with him. Our lines are at present thin in several places; and, besides, they have their carrier-pigeon post. When we invite them to come out and see for themselves, it looks as if we were in a great hurry for the capitulation."

*Tuesday, December* 6.—Before breakfast, I telegraphed particulars of the battle at Orleans to Berlin and London. Afterwards I drew up articles for the *Moniteur*, and for several German papers, on the breach of their parole by several captive French officers, some of whom are again to be pursued with letters of caption. Even General Barral, now in command of the army of the Loire, made his escape in this disgraceful fashion. He gave a written promise on his word of honour, after the surrender of Strassburg, not once but twice over, that he would not in this war bear arms again against the Prussians and their allies, and that he would do nothing whatever to the injury of the German armies. He then went off to Colmar, and from thence to the Loire, when he re-entered the French service —an unprecedented infamy. The gentlemen of the Tours government made no objection to him. These gentlemen, whom the Belgian papers are never tired of praising up as honest folk, men of honour, and so forth, went even farther than that. They dispatched a certain M. Richard to the French officers now interned in Belgium, who gathered them together in the house of Taschard, the representative of MM. Gambetta and Favre in Brussels, and then urged and threatened them, to break the word of honour they had given the Belgian authorities, to make their way back to France, and to take service there once more against the Germans. Even in Silesia such emissaries seem to have over-persuaded some officers of low character. In the history of warfare cases like these are certainly not numerous. But the affair has another aspect; these disgraceful proceedings must give the German authorities great reason to question how far they can trust a government like that of the National Defence. When a government stoops to invite officers to break their word of honour: when it employs and makes use of officers who have done so, on its own initiative, proving by so doing that it shares and excuses these low conceptions of the value of solemn promises, we must, as a matter of course, treat it as in the last degree untrustworthy, so long as it goes on tempting its captive officers to break their parole, and employing and making use of them, after they have done so.

Dr. Lauer and Odo Russell were at table. The conversation was of no special interest, and almost no politics were talked at all. But we had some delicious wines from the Palatinate—Deidesheimer Hofstück and Forster Kirchenstück—the best blood of the grape, rich in every virtue, fragrant and fiery. "From fire man's spirit was created." Even Bucher, who usually drinks only red wine, did honour to this heavenly dew from the Haardt mountains.

In the evening, Consul Bamberg, the new editor of our Versailles journal—an elderly man, in a sort of sea-captain's uniform, flying the ribands of a couple of orders—paid us what is after this to be a daily visit. The recent inspection of the hospital in the château by the Chief has given rise to an inquiry, and if I understand rightly, he has had a letter from the war ministry informing him that everything is in perfect order, that the sick have been getting what was proper for them, and that the sentinel who told him about the alleged neglect has been suitably punished.*

Afterwards I wrote an article in which I expressed a polite astonishment at the brazen-facedness with which Gramont reminded the world of his existence in the Brussels *Gaulois*. It is through his unheard-of narrowness of vision, and his almost unprecedented incapacity for the office he then filled, that France has been brought to her present misery, and he ought, like his colleague Ollivier, to have hidden himself away in silence, and been only too thankful that people should forget his existence, or, as his ancient name required and obliged him—and his bodily robustness well enabled him to do it—he should have gone into some regiment, and done his best by hard fighting for her to atone, as far as lay in his power, for the injury he had done his country. Instead of which, he has the courage to remind the whole world that he is still alive,

* For details see a subsequent page.

and that he once directed the foreign policy of France. "A brazen-faced dunderhead." Naturally, one does not answer the statements of such people.

After the consul with the order, L. came in with the good news that Rouen was occupied yesterday afternoon by General von Goeben, and that the German troops operating in that region had now turned their attention to Havre and Cherbourg. I requested him also to write something for his paper about the employment of the officers who had broken their word of honour, and about Gramont's audacity.

According to English accounts from Paris things began, quite a fortnight since, to be very uncomfortable there. Several kinds of disease have broken out, and the death cases are considerably more numerous than in ordinary times. Anxiety and disheartenment, as well as want of food, have contributed. In the first week of September there were 900 deaths; in that ending the 5th of October, nearly twice as many; in the following week, 1900. Small-pox rages in the town, and is carrying off many victims; and a great number of people have died of bowel disease. Home-sickness has broken out like an epidemic among the battalions recruited from the provinces. An English correspondent who visited the hospital "du Midi" in the last week of October, noticed a placard above the entrance-gate, on which was printed, "Any person bringing in a cat, a dog, or three rats, will get his breakfast and dinner. N.B. It is absolutely essential that the animals be brought in alive." Similar placards are said to be quite common at the gates of the Paris hospitals.

It wants still five minutes of midnight. The Minister is already off to bed—very early for him. The candles in the bottles I use for candlesticks are nearly burnt out. Mont

Valérien thunders down a frightful salute into the valley below it. With what object? Perhaps it is only to tell the Parisians it is about twelve o'clock, a sort of night watchman calling the hour; otherwise all this shooting is much ado about nothing. During the last two days of battle, Abeken was told to-day that the forts threw about 6000 bombs and grenades, but only fifty-three of our men were hurt by them, and several of them only slightly wounded.

## CHAPTER XIV.

#### PROSPECTS BEFORE PARIS IMPROVE.

WEDNESDAY, *December* 7.—Disagreeable weather. Only now and then a shot fired from the forts or the gun-boats. The lies with which Gambetta and his people have been trying to stop up the hole which the defeat of the "red-breeches" at Orleans has knocked in the hopes the people cherished of a great victory over us, induced us to send the following note to the *Moniteur:*—" The members of the Government of Tours have published accounts of the defeat of the Army of the Loire which read like fragments of the tales of the 'Arabian Nights.' For instance, their telegram says, 'The retreat of the Army of the Loire was accomplished without loss, except that we left the heavy ships' guns spiked in the entrenched camp.' In reality, 12,000 unwounded prisoners fell into the hands of the German troops. The Tours despatch goes on to say, 'we lost no field artillery.' Forty-seven field-pieces, and several mitrailleuses, were captured by the conquerors. The German people, remembering the virtues of the Catos, Aristideses, and other Republicans of antiquity, were disposed to hope that the Republic would have wiped lying out of the list of its means of operation, and fancied that it would lie less, at all events, than the Empire. It was evidently wrong. These Catos of the present day have put to shame all previous attempts to substitute untruth for truth. When they have anything disagreeable to lie away, the advocates of Tours are much more unblushing than the generals of the Empire." Afterwards I telegraphed the new advances of our armies in the north, and the occupation of Rouen.

After three o'clock I went with Wollmann across the Place d'Armes towards the court of the château, where fourteen of the bronze guns taken at Orleans are ranged under the very eyes of the equestrian statue of Louis XIV., directly below the inscription, '*A toutes les gloires de la France*' (to all the glories of France), an ironical comment upon that expression of Gallic conceit and swagger. The guns were some of them twelve and some four pounders, and behind them were ranged gun-carriages and ammunition carts. The French guns have each a name—one, for instance, is called "Le Bayard," another, "Le Lauzun," a third, "Le Boucheron"; while others are "Le Maxant," "Le Repace," "Le Brisetout," or similar horrors. On several there is a scrawl, stating that they were captured by the 4th Hussar Regiment.

Counts Holnstein and Lehndorf were with us at dinner. We had the fine Deidesheimer again. The Chief began to talk, *inter alia*, of his recollections of Frankfort. "I got on well with Thun; he was an honest man. Rechberg was not bad upon the whole; at least, he was personally honourable, though he was very violent and effervescing—one of those furious very fair folks." He went on to say: "No Austrian diplomatist of the school of that day troubled himself very much about the exact truth. The third of them, Prokesch, was not at all the man for me. He had brought with him from the East the trick of the most miserable intrigues. Truth was a matter of absolute indifference to him. I remember once, in a large company, there was some talk of an Austrian assertion which did not square with the truth. Prokesch raised his voice, and said, so that I should hear him distinctly, 'If that were not true

I should have been *lying* (and he emphasized the word), in the name of the Imperial Royal Government.' He looked me straight in the face. I returned the look, and said quietly, 'Quite so, your Excellency.' He was obviously shocked; but when on looking round he perceived nothing but down-dropped eyes and solemn silence, which meant to say that I was in the right, he turned on his heel and went into the dining-room, where covers were laid. After dinner he had recovered himself, and came across to me with a full glass, for otherwise I should have supposed that he was going to call me out. He said, 'Come, now; let us make friends.' 'Why not?' said I; 'but the protocol must *of course* be altered.' 'You are incorrigible,' he replied, smiling. It was all right. The protocol *was* altered, so that they recognised that it had contained an untruth." Afterwards we spoke of Goltz, and the Chief once more told the Beaumont story of his unpopularity with his people, and asked Hatzfeld whether he had had anything to complain of from Goltz. Hatzfeld said " No; but it was quite true that Goltz did not get on well with the people of the Embassy."

After dinner, Consul Bamberg was with me, and received the article on the untruthfulness of the Tours people. I spoke to him also about L——, whose capacity I praised, while he said that he thought him a good patriot, and that he had formerly done some good work. . . . Later on, L—— himself turned up, and told us, among other things, that people were beginning to call the Hôtel des Réservoirs the Hôtel des Préservoirs—no very brilliant joke, I thought; but people may have their own ideas about it, and anybody who was at that time in Versailles will know well enough what they were.

Hatzfeld told us at tea that numerous prisoners had passed through to-day, and that there had been considerable disturbance and disorder because civilians, especially women, had pressed in among the people, so that the escort had been driven to make use of the butt ends of their muskets. ... We then spoke of the bombardment, and the gentlemen agreed that the King really wished it, and that there was a hope that it would begin very soon. ... Moltke, it was added, wished it too. He had recently received an answer from Trochu to the letter he had sent, the sum and substance of which was, " Many thanks ; but, for the present, we had better leave things as they are."

*Thursday, December* 8.—A great deal of snow fell, and it was tolerably cold, so much so that, in spite of the big beech logs which were burning in my fireplace, I could not get reasonably warm in my room. ... Prince Putbus was with us at dinner. Besides other good things, we had omelettes with mushrooms, and, as several times previously, pheasant and sauer kraut boiled in champagne. There was also Forster Kirchenstück and Deidesheimer Hofstück. The Minister said that he preferred the former. "The Forster," he said, "is undoubtedly a higher style of wine than the Deidesheimer." Finally, besides this and other excellent drinks, we had an admirable old corn brandy. Putbus suggested that sauer kraut was not wholesome, and the Chief said, "I do not think so. I eat it precisely because I believe it to be wholesome. But, Engel, give us a schnaps" (a drop of brandy). The Minister then showed Putbus the *menu*, and, during conversation about it, it was mentioned that a young diplomatist in Vienna had carefully collected all the *menus* of his chief, and preserved them in two finely-bound volumes, in which some most interesting combinations were to be found.

Later on, the Chancellor remarked that the French must now have got one or two very big guns in one of the forts nearest us. "One can make that out by the report, which is much louder, but they may very likely hurt themselves with them. If they use a very heavy charge, the gun will either turn round and shoot straight into the town, or blow itself to pieces, though of course it might sometimes go off right, and then the shot might reach us at Versailles."

Somebody asked what was the position of the Emperor of Germany question, and the Chief said: "We have had trouble about it, with telegrams and letters; but the most important were those which Count Holnstein brought us—a very intelligent person." Putbus asked what office he held. "Master of the Horse. He made a journey to Munich and back again in six days. In the condition of the railroads he must have made a great effort to manage it. Certainly he had a capital constitution to help him; and he went, not merely to Munich, but as far as Hohenschwangau. King Ludwig, too, contributed very much to the speedy settlement of the affair. He took the matter up at once, and gave a decisive answer without putting off time."

I do not know how it came about that the conversation happened upon the expressions, "swells, snobs, and cockneys," which were then discussed at length. The Chief called a certain gentleman in the diplomatic service a "swell," and went on to say: "It is a capital word, the force of which we cannot quite give in German. It is something like 'stutzer' (a dandy), but it includes, besides, a puffed-out chest, and a sort of general blown-up-ness.

"'Snob' is quite different, and we have no exact expression for that either. It signifies different things and properties, especially one-sidedness, narrowness and Philistinism, and that a man cannot get out of mere local or temporary views. The snob is a sort of bourgeois person. All this is not quite a complete description. He cannot get beyond the interests of his family; his circle of vision in political questions is extremely limited; he is shut in by the ways of thinking and the prejudices in which he has been brought up. There are snobs, and very decided snobs too, of the female sex. We may also speak of party snobs—those who cannot help placing the higher politics on the same basis as questions of individual rights, radical snobs (*fortschrittsnobs*).

"A Cockney again is different. The word is applied chiefly to Londoners. There are people there who have never got outside their walls and streets, their bricks and mortar—who have never seen a green thing, who have learned life only in town, and heard nothing beyond the sound of Bow bells. We have people in Berlin also who have never been away from it; but compared with London, and even with Paris, which also has its cockneys, though they have a different name there, Berlin is a little place. In London, hundreds of thousands of people have never seen anything beyond the city. In such big towns views sprout up, ramify, and harden into permanent prejudices for those who live in them. It is in these great centres of population, where there is no experience, and consequently no correct idea—in many cases not even a conception—of anything outside of them, that this simpleton sort of narrowness is born. A simpleton who is not conceited is tolerable enough, but a simpleton who is impracticable, and conceited besides, is not to be endured. People in the country districts have a much better chance of understanding life as it really exists and grows about them. They may have less education, but what they know, they usually *do* know. There are snobs, of course, in the country. Well, for instance" (turning to Putbus) "a first-rate huntsman, who is thoroughly convinced that he is the first man in the whole world, that hunting is really everything, and that people who understand nothing about it are worth nothing at all; and a man on an estate outside there, where he is everybody, and where all the people depend entirely upon him. When he comes in from the country to the wool-market, and finds that nobody in the town takes him at the value at which he is estimated at home, he gets low, sits down on his woolsack and sulks, and takes no interest afterwards in anything but wool."

The conversation dropped away soon after this into stories about horses and horsemanship. The Chief told us about his brown mare, which he had not at first thought much of, but which carried him for thirteen hours at Sedan—at least fifty-five English miles—and which was quite fit for service next day. Then he gave us other stories of horsemanship; telling us, for instance, how once, when he was out riding with his daughter, he had come up to a ditch which he himself certainly would never have liked to take, but which the Countess, her horse having got into his stride, took quite easily, and so forth.

In the evening I was summoned several times to the Chief, wrote several articles, and among them one on the approval which the French Consul, Lefaivre, in Vienna, had expressed of Bebel, the Socialist Member of Parliament, on account of his sympathies with the French Republic. The moral of my article was, "So Germany is to go on for the future, obedient and thoughtful as in the past, while France is to transact business and be master." The *Frankfurter Zeitung* is no longer to be looked at in Berlin for extracts, as the French nonsense which it advocates is not worth reading.

At tea Keudell said I was in future to get not merely the rough draughts and sketches of important political matters which the Chief gave me, I was to see everything; he would talk the matter over with Abeken, who holds the position of secretary of state here, a piece of news which I heard with much gratification. Bucher told me that the Minister had given them a very interesting discourse in the *salon* when coffee came on the table. Prince von Putbus had spoken of his wish to travel in very distant countries. "Yes, and we might help you," said the Chief; "we might send you to notify the establishment of the German Empire to the Emperor of China and the Tycoon of Japan."

Afterwards, in view of the future, and naturally with some reference to his guest, he had launched out into a long discourse about the duties of the German aristocracy. The higher nobility ought to have some feeling for the interests of the State, to recognise their mission, to protect the State from vacillation in the conflicts of parties, to maintain a firm attitude, and so forth. There is nothing to be said against this, but when they associate with Strousberg they may just as well become bankers at once. One wonders whether, at that time, the Prince understood the whole affair perfectly, and whether he was accommodating his language to what he knew to be the facts.

*Friday, December* 9.—I telegraph the victory, the day before yesterday, of our 17th Division at Beaugency over a French corps of about sixteen battalions, with six-and-twenty cannon, and I contradict the story of the *Gazette de France* about Galvez, the Ambassador of Peru.

At breakfast we were told that Prince Trubetzkoi, a relation of Orloff's, wanted protection for his villa from our army police, and had also asked the Chancellor that our troops should be taken away from the neighbourhood of his property, as their being massed there raises the price of the necessaries of life. His letter will go to the waste-paper basket. The Commandant of Versailles, General von

Voigts-Rhetz, was with us at dinner. I believe he is a brother of him who was governor-general in Hanover in 1866, and who has now won the battle of Beaune la Rolande, a long man, with dark beard and eagle nose. The conversation, which turned principally on the recent battles between Orleans and Blois, was of no particular importance. The Chief was absent, being unwell, and it is believed that he has pains in his leg. In the evening Bamberg came in, and after him L. who had heard from a good source that the bombardment would begin almost at once, that the King had burst out against Hindersin in a frightful fury, because there was not ammunition enough ready yet, and that he himself was now to take the matter in hand.

Later in the evening extracts were made for the King from the report in the *Observer* of the discourse of a certain M. de Fonvielle in London on the bombardment, the purport of which was that the speaker had laughed at the idea that it was from motives of humanity that King William was not allowing Paris to be bombarded. De Fonvielle had said that he was unable to do it, and that his batteries were kept at a respectful distance by the brave marines who were serving in the forts. His plan was to starve the city, in which, however, he would not succeed, as it was provisioned for more than two months, and as earnest study of the question of nourishment had shown them how to convert the skin, blood, and bones of slaughtered animals into food, Paris would not let itself be intimidated by the attempt to reduce it by famine. Its cry was "No surrender," its only wish to sweep the enemy out of France, and it had now got the broom in its hands with which it meant to perform this operation.

*Saturday, December* 10.—Mist in the morning, a great deal of snow fallen, and the sky still full of it. The Chief is not yet right. I telegraph more about the battle of Beaugency, in which the 1st Bavarian, and the 8th and 22nd North German divisions fought against two new army corps on the French side, and more than a thousand prisoners and six cannon fell into our hands. The *Militär Wochenblatt* again notifies the escape of seven French officers who have broken their parole, and I forward a note about it for further publication in the *Moniteur*. At dinner the Chief, Bismarck-Bohlen, who has been suffering for three days, and Abeken, who has had the good fortune to be commanded to dine with the Crown Prince, were all absent. In the evening I prepared for the King an article in the *National Zeitung*, which shows that they are speaking even in the Reichstag of the delay in the bombardment, and which also expresses a wish for some explanation of the reasons of the delay.

Having been sent for by the Chief, I took the liberty before leaving to ask how things were going on in the Reichstag about the treaties. He replied, "All right; the agreement with Bavaria will either be adopted to-day, or voted upon to-morrow, and the address to the King too." I then permitted myself to ask how he was in health. "Better," he said, "it is a varicose vein in the leg." I said, would it trouble him long? "It may go away in a day, or it may bother me for three weeks."

Keudell told us at tea that the Reichstag had decided to send a great deputation to Versailles, charged to present its congratulations to the King on the unity of Germany, and on the restoration of the dignity of Emperor. Abeken did not like this. He said, sulkily, "It is frightful for the Reichstag to send us thirty fellows here—a deputation of thirty people is really dreadful." He gave us no hint of his reason for being annoyed. Thirty wise Bonzes with the title of

Privy Councillors might possibly not have been frightful, but thirty Marshals of the Household are enough to excite one. Hatzfeld expressed himself anxious about our immediate future in a military point of view. He believes that there is room for anxiety about our position in the west. Von der Tann, he says, has only 25,000 left of his 45,000 men, and the armies which have sprung out of the ground at the stamp of Gambetta's foot, are continually growing in number. News has come in at the Bureau that the French have got together two very large armies, and that the seat of Government has been removed from Tours to Bordeaux.

It is doubtful, of course, how long this energy of Gambetta will meet with a response in the capacity for resistance in the country, and in its readiness to submit to further military drains. In the southern departments people appear to be very much discontented and thoroughly exhausted with this destructive war. The *Gazette de France* gives a letter dated " Tours, 1st December," in which the writer says, " I have seen nothing for a long time which can be compared with the misery which the last *levée en masse* has entailed upon our country districts. The compulsory contribution for the pay and equipment of the mobilisable national guard for the next three months has converted our ill-humour into rage, and our distress into despair. The reason is, that though our good peasants may be much less clever than they are represented by Balzac and Victorien Sardou, they are certainly not such simpletons as Gambetta would like them to be for the success of his Republican exhortations. An instinct which is all but infallible shows them that while a *levée en masse* of fathers of families might likely enough only take place on paper, a war contribution makes an immediate demand upon them, unless it is in the form of a loan, which would press still more heavily. The peasants say that on the day when our mobilisable men get their equipment, they will not have a shirt left for their own backs.

"This extraordinary tax, which bursts upon us like a bomb-shell, at the beginning of the worst season of the year, has no relation whatever to the resources of our unfortunate country communities. Only two of the four simple rules of arithmetic are left to us—addition to our losses and multiplication of the misfortunes which are overtaking us. The Germans have taken subtraction for themselves, and the demagogues division. In our south-easterly departments, among the people of the Ardèche, the Durance, and the Rhone, want and misery began before the war, the invasion, and the republic. A drought, which made water in many places an article of luxury; the complete failure of the grass and hay crops, which compels us to sell our cattle for a third of the usual price; the sickness among the silk-worms, which has ceased to be interesting, having become chronic; the grape louse, an agreeable change after the grape rot—like M. Crémieux, instead of Louis Bonaparte—the unheard-of depression in the value of our manufactures; all these taken together had thrown us upon the bed of sickness long before the day when infatuation, folly, frivolity, improvidence, bounce, and incapacity united to betray France to the Germans. We were already sick enough. The war gave us the finishing stroke, and the Republic is looking after our burial."

*Sunday, December* 11.—In the morning, at nine o'clock, we have five degrees of cold, the garden below is covered with hoar-frost, and the moisture is frozen in delicate thread-work on the branches of the trees and shrubs. I pay Bismarck-Bohlen a sick visit, his illness having taken another form. The Chief, too, has not yet quite recovered, but he must be better, for he drives out at about two o'clock. Half an hour later, I take a walk through the park of the château, where about fifty persons, some of them ladies of doubtful character, and three or four whose characters are not at all doubtful, are skating on the big central reservoir. As I came back, I heard somebody scolding furiously in French. Looking round, I noticed walking right behind me an elderly man, who limped a little, and who was abusing an over-dressed and over-painted female who was going mincingly past us. "Shameless women, who bring disgrace into our families, and ruin on our young people; they ought to be driven out of the town," he said, turning to me as if he wished to bring me into the conversation. Then he came close up, constantly scolding, and ultimately coming to a person of the male sex, whom he called the destroyer of France, declaring that the misery into which these men had plunged their country was a frightful spectacle, which cried aloud to Heaven. I said to him, "But France, you know, wanted the war, and must accept the consequences." He allowed that, but still burst out in furious abuse of the Republic and its leaders, especially Gambetta; Trochu, Favre, Gambetta, and the whole of them, were good-for-nothing blood-suckers. The Republic meant government in the interests of the dregs of the people, who looked askance at the comforts of their neighbours, and would like to distribute the plunder amongst themselves. He would rather see the King of Prussia master of France, and the country mutilated, cut up small, and broken into fragments, than the Republic. The Emperor, too, had been good for nothing. He was a mere usurper. Louis Philippe had pleased him just as little; he was not the right heir. But the Republic was the worst of all; and so on. I accompanied the enraged Legitimist as far as the Place Hoche, where I left him, after he had told me his name and address, and I had promised that I would pay him a visit soon.

In the Avenue of Saint-Cloud I met Hofrath and Major Borck, who asked me whether I knew what could have been the reason why the King had been so very much depressed yesterday after Abeken had had his talk with him. I could not help him in the least.

The Chief dined with us to-night, but spoke little, and complained of headache. Hatzfeld told us that Hartrott had just informed him that 4400 horses and 1000 waggons were on the way from Germany to be used in the transport of ammunition. The bombardment of Paris would begin in eight or ten days. The Chief answered, "It ought to have begun sooner, and, as for the eight days, that has often been promised us."

In the evening, I cut out for the King a number of articles from the German newspapers, expressing their views upon the situation, and an article in the Belgian *Echo of Parliament*. Abeken will bring them before him to-morrow.

Our *Moniteur* gives us another list of the French officers who have escaped by breaking their parole. There are no fewer than twenty-two of them, ten of whom escaped from Hirschberg. I see from the same paper that the *Pall Mall Gazette* has accepted as genuine coin, and passed into circulation, a joke in the manner of Baron Münchausen. Moved by the mischances that have happened to several of the air-balloons sent up from Paris, the French are supposed to have put their calculating finger to their nose, and to have solved the problem of guiding these conveyances in the following manner. It is as simple as the egg of Columbus. They harness eagles to them. The correspondent of the newspaper writes, "However extravagant the idea of making birds guide balloons to their destination may appear, people in Paris have gone into the matter seriously. It is said that satisfactory experiments have been made with eagles from the Botanic gardens, harnessed to the car. These experiments took place in the presence of the Postmaster-General Ramport, of M. Chassinat, of the chief of the postal service in the Department of the Seine, and of the Receiver-General Mattet. Four or six powerful birds were harnessed to the balloon, and were guided by an aeronaut by means of a piece of raw flesh fastened to the end of a long stick, which was held in front of their beaks. The greedy birds keep struggling in vain to reach it, as it moves through the air with the same velocity as they do. When the aeronaut wishes the balloon to move in a different direction, he turns the stick, with the beef-steak at the end, to the right or left. If he wants to go down, he drops it; if to ascend, he lifts it up." The editor of the *Moniteur* adds the remark, " We are afraid that these eagles were geese."

Hatzfeld told me at tea all sorts of interesting things about his experiences and observations in Paris. In 1866 Napoleon said to Goltz, that he could not allow a complete incorporation of Saxony with Prussia, but if only the name and a small portion of the kingdom—Dresden, for instance, with a few square miles in the neighbourhood—were left, he would be quite content. If that be true, I have reason to think that the Chief's advice was to take no advantage of this offer. At first, the Empress could not endure Goltz, for the following reason. During the interim between Goltz and his predecessor, Prince Reuss represented the embassy, and the Court was very much attached to him; he was in high consideration, especially as coming of a princely family. Eugénie would have liked him to have been ambassador, but he was sent off to Brussels, and the Empress attributed that to Goltz, disliked him for it, received him with marked coldness, never invited him to her select parties, and only saluted him, not speaking to him at all, upon public occasions. Goltz, who was supposed to have been much smitten with her, often went away in a regular fury. Once, however, when he happened to have been invited to such a select evening, she had been compelled to say something to him, and in her perplexity, nothing occurred to her but the question, "What is Prince Reuss doing now?" When Goltz went home, he is said to have been in a frightful rage, and to have used a disagreeable epithet. . . . Afterwards, however, the relationship between them improved, and Goltz ultimately stood so well with the Emperor, that he (Hatzfeld) was of opinion that if Goltz had been alive in 1870, there would have been no war between us and France.

I asked what sort of woman the Empress was. He said, "Very beautiful, not over middle height, splendid bust, fair, with much natural intelligence, but little acquired learning, and few interests in intellectual matters." She had once taken him, with other gentlemen, through her rooms, and even into her sleeping apartment, but he had nowhere seen a book, or even a newspaper. Hatzfeld is of opinion that things will come round in the end to Napoleon's restoration. After all, he was not so bad as people represented him; and certainly by nature, he was the very reverse of truculent, being rather soft. If the French should see that they cannot pull through with their Republic of advocates, through whom they are falling more and more into ruin, they would invite him back again some day. As a second time the Saviour of Society, he might venture to treat with us upon the basis of what we require in order to make peace. His services in securing order might then make up for the loss in power and authority, which would be the necessary consequence of his giving up Elsass and part of Lothringen.

\* \* \* \* \* \*

I insert here a letter which a sympathiser with the Legitimist whom I have already mentioned in this diary, wrote to Prince Bismarck in 1871. It was as follows:—

"PRINCE,—Since the capitulation of this accursed city of Paris, very extraordinary things have happened in our unfortunate France.

"Ah, Prince, I am not initiated into the secrets of Providence, but it appears to me, if you will permit me to say so, that you were too magnanimous to that miserable and despicable population of Paris. Your armies ought to have humbled them to the uttermost, entered their city in triumph, and occupied it completely.

"Woe to him who had dared to disturb so well-deserved a triumph. You thought it better, however, to show more moderation. Look at the results. I do not know what the future may have in store for us; but it appears to me that your Excellency ought, as speedily as possible, to interfere with, and put an end to, a condition of things which is becoming critical for France and dangerous for Europe, and which may involve serious consequences for the other states. Beware, Prince, of the propaganda of wicked passions. If you could listen to the expression of all the hopes of these revolutionaries of the newest sort, as I can, you would, perhaps, not be without some anxiety about the future. Be assured, Prince, that if the Republic establishes itself in France, it will soon cause disturbances in every monarchical state of Europe. It would be better that France should perish than that she should receive such a form of government, the consequence of which could be nothing but incessant miseries, vice, and revolution.

"When I see so many crimes and basenesses, and so deep a moral degradation, I despair, and cry for some strong and energetic hand to put an end to it all. Yes, Prince, the whole party of right-thinking people in France would greatly prefer the sovereignty of the foreigner to that of the demagogism with which we are threatened, and which will never be put an end to till it has been annihilated. That, Prince, is the mission which is laid upon you. I believe that the right moment has come. Do not neglect it. No feeling ought to restrain your Excellency, especially when you think of the past, and the horrible struggles which we are witnessing every day. The tiger is unchained, and, if he is left loose, he will devour everything. Chain up Paris! Annihilate it if necessary, or subject it to your domination, and you will have deserved well of mankind. Allow me, Prince, to go one step further, and suggest to you a partition of France on an early day. Let Italy have the piece along the course of the Rhone, from Geneva to the sea, with the island of Corsica. Give Spain the strip up to the line of the Garonne, from sea to sea. Give England Algiers, and take all the rest, Prince, for yourself. It is reasonable that you should have the largest portion. Then let Russia and Austria aggrandise themselves in the East.

"Oh, my country! thou hast willed it! And thou, O accursed Paris, arrogant city, sink of all corruptions, sole cause of all our sufferings, may an end be put at last to thy domination! To you, Prince, all this may appear strange, coming from a Frenchman; but I have been witness of so many deeds of shame that I am weary of such a country, where every crime has free scope, and where we never meet men of high sentiments. I always cherish the hope, Prince, that I may one day have the good fortune to see your Excellency here in Lyons, another city which stands much in need of chastisement. Permit me, most gracious sir, to express to you the deep respect with which I have the honour to be," &c., &c.

The diary may now proceed.

*Monday, December* 12.—The Chief appears to be worse again, and he is said to be in a very fretful temper; Dr. Lauer has been with him. The *Times* contains an article, which is all we could wish, the principal points of which I may note here. It is as follows: " In the present crisis it is not the duty of the Germans to show high feeling or sympathy, or magnanimously to forgive their defeated enemy. The question rather is of a simple piece of business and of prudence. What will the enemy do after the war, when he has recovered his strength? People in England have but a faint recollection of the numerous cruel lessons which Germany has had from France during the last four centuries. For 400 years no nation has had such bad neighbours as they have found in the French, who were always unsociable, irreconcileable, greedy of territory, not ashamed to take it, and always ready to assume the offensive. During this whole time Germany has endured the encroachments and usurpations of France. To-day, when she has won the victory and has conquered her neighbour, it would in our opinion be very foolish of her not to take advantage of the situation, and not to acquire for herself a boundary likely to secure peace for her in the future. As far as we know there is no law in the world entitling France to retain the territories which were formerly annexed by her, after the owners, from whom they were taken, have laid their hands upon the thief. The French complain bitterly to those who will listen to them that they are exposed to losses which threaten their honour, and they incessantly and earnestly entreat people not to dishonour poor France, to leave her her honour unstained. Will her honour, however, be preserved, if France refuses to pay for her neighbour's windows which she has broken? The real fact is, that she lost her honour when she broke her neighbour's windows, and only her deep repentance, and her honest determination not to repeat the offence, can restore it.

"We must say with all frankness, that France has never shown herself so senseless, so pitiful, so worthy of contempt and reproach, as at the present moment, when she obstinately declines to look the facts in the face, and refuses to accept the misfortune her own conduct has brought upon her. A France broken up in utter anarchy—Ministers who have no recognised chief, who rise from the dust in their air balloons, and carry with them for ballast shameful and manifest lies and proclamations of victories that exist only in their imagination—a government which is sustained by lying and imposture, and chooses rather to continue and to increase the waste of human life than to resign its own dictatorship and its wonderful Utopia of a Republic—that is the spectacle which France presents to-day. It is hard to say whether any nation ever before burdened itself with such a load of shame.

"The quantity of lies which France, official and unofficial, has been manufacturing for us since the month of July, in the full knowledge that they are lies, is something frightful and absolutely unprecedented. Perhaps it is not much after all in comparison with the immeasurable heaps of illusions and unconscious lies which have so long been in circulation among the French. Their men of genius, who are recognised as such in all departments of literature, are apparently of opinion that France outshines other nations in a superhuman wisdom, that she is the New Zion of the whole world, and that the literary productions of the French for the last fifty years, however insipid, unhealthy, and often, indeed, devilish, contain a real Evangel, rich in blessing for all the children of men."

The article concludes in these words: "We believe that Bismarck will take as much of Alsace, and of Lorraine too, as he chooses, and that it will be the better for him, the better for us, the better for all the world except France, and the better in the long run for France herself. Through large and quiet measures M. von Bismarck is aiming with eminent ability at one single object—the well-being of Germany and of the world. If the large-hearted, peace-loving, enlightened, and earnest people of Germany grow into one nation, and Germany becomes mistress of the Continent in place of France, which is light-hearted, ambitious, quarrelsome, and over-exciteable, it will be the most momentous event of the present day, and all the world must hope that it may soon come about."

It is an admirable article, and we shall bring it to the knowledge of our friends in Versailles through the *Moniteur*.

At breakfast we talked of the fact that a few officers still despaired of the success of a bombardment of Paris. Formerly, however, the general staff had no doubt on the subject; and if some of them now have changed their views, we can see what motives and influences explain the change, and one of the gentlemen expressed himself emphatically on the subject. The chief difficulty now seems to be this, that large bodies of troops must be massed in the neighbourhood to cover the redoubts and positions where the guns are to stand, and may then be fired upon with effect from the forts and gunboats. During this talk Hatzfeld had information that his ponies had managed to get out of Paris unslaughtered, and with their flesh on them, and were now on their way to his house here.

The Chief stayed a long time in bed to-day, and it was not till the afternoon that he was able to transact business. He was also absent at dinner. Hatzfeld told us there that he had talked with several of the diplomatists who had just come in from Paris—the Russian General-Adjutant, Prince Wittgenstein; the English Military Plenipotentiary, Claremont; and a Belgian. They left Paris yesterday morning early, and got here this afternoon by Villeneuve Saint-Georges, with the ponies and some other horses. Claremont, Hatzfeld said, impressed him as a sensible man, well acquainted with the condition of things in Paris. He said that he himself had not had to eat any horseflesh or to endure any hardships, that all the cabs and omnibuses seemed still to be plying in the city, that people were still playing pieces in the theatre at the Porte Saint-Martin, and that concerts were given twice a week at the Opera House. According to his account the gas lamps and street lanterns are still burning, though only one in five of the latter is lighted, as indeed is usual here in Versailles; and the only difference is—and it is only among the well-to-do classes— that people regularly go to bed about ten o'clock, whereas before the city was blockaded they used not to go till midnight. The villages inside the French lines have all suffered worse than those inside ours. He supposes they may have provisions for two months yet. Abeken, on the other hand, had learned from Voigts-Rhetz that Moblots had come out in crowds to surrender. They had been fired upon, but a number of them, not frightened by that, had forced us to take them prisoners, and when they were examined had declared that they had suffered great misery, as only the regular troops were properly supplied with food.

All the evening I was hard at work. I translated articles for the King from the *Times* and *Daily Telegraph*, expressing themselves forcibly in favour of the restoration of the German Empire and the Imperial dignity. I prepared for his perusal several press utterances about the bombardment, and sent out, for printing, the manifesto which Ducrot addressed to his troops before the last great sortie. The conclusion of this pompous discourse deserves to be put on record. It runs as follows: "As for myself, I am firmly determined—and I declare it in presence of the whole country—that I shall return to Paris either a dead man or a conqueror. You may see me fall, soldiers—you will not see me retreat; and if I should fall, do not halt a moment, but avenge me." Ducrot returned to Paris from the Marne neither a dead man nor a conqueror. His address to his soldiers was nothing but empty phrases. He is a play actor, and has broken his solemnly-pledged word of honour a second time. It is doing him no injustice for the *Moniteur*, after giving his address, to put a note to it, "Fortunately we know the value of General Ducrot's word of honour."

After avowing that it cannot help viewing with lively satisfaction both the fact of the restoration of the German Empire, and the way in which it has come about, the *Times* goes on to say:

"The political significance of this change in the situation cannot be estimated too highly. An immense revolution has been accomplished in Europe, and all our old-fashioned traditions have suddenly grown out of date. Nobody can foretell the relations which must establish themselves between the Great Powers, but it is easy to see what, in its broader features, is the tendency of the epoch on which we are about to enter. There will be a strong and united Germany, at the head of which stands a family representing the interests of the German Fatherland and its military reputation. On the one side this Germany touches

Russia, a strong and vigilant power; on the other France, which will either patiently bide the time when her destiny will once more change, or, burning with the thirst for vengeance, will lie in wait for the opportunity of an attack. She will certainly not be in a position for a long time to resume the great part she has played in Europe, and which was conceded to her during the splendid period of the Napoleonic Restoration. As far as we in England are concerned, instead of having two powerful military states on the continent, as hitherto, with a nation between them with its forces scattered and unprepared for a struggle, which might have been annihilated at any moment if these overwhelming powers had happened to unite, we should have a solid bar in the middle of Europe likely to strengthen the whole framework. The political hopes of previous generations of English statesmen have thus been fulfilled. They all wished for a strong central Power. They wrought for it in war as well as in peace, through negotiations and treaties —at one time with the Empire, at another with the new Power which was rising in the North. From this day forward Germany must make a reality of what has long been nothing more than a political idea."

We must not on that account forget the fact that English policy has for the last half century been more favourable to Austria than to the "power which was rising in the North."

L. came in after eight, and claimed to know "on excellent authority," as usual, that the King did not care for the assumption of the Imperial dignity, and that the arrival of the thirty-man deputation from the Reichstag especially had not been to his liking. He is supposed to have said, "I dare say I owe this dignity after all to Herr Lasker."

Afterwards I wrote an article for the press, by the Chief's direction, pointing out that we are now fighting, not merely against France, but against those cosmopolitan Red Republicans—Garibaldi, Mazzini (who is now with Garibaldi, acting as his adviser), and the Polish, Spanish, and Danish members of the same party. The object for which this agreeable company is striving is set forth in a letter from the son of the prefect Ordinaire, who describes himself as an officer of Garibaldi's general staff. This letter, dated Autun, November 16, and directed to the editor of the journal *Rights of Man*, says :

"From the postmark you will see where we are—in the worst den of priestcraft in all France. Autun is one of the chief centres of the monarchical reaction. It looks more like an immense monastery than a town, with its great blank walls and its iron-barred windows, behind which monks of every description are praying and conspiring for the true cause and its right divine. Everywhere in the streets the red shirt comes in contact with the priest's black gown; and even the shop people, like everything else in the place, have a mystic look of having been saturated with holy water. We are on the 'Index' here, and slanderous stories are told about us—too many for even the waters of the flood to wash away. Every breach of discipline—and some are unavoidable with volunteers and free companions—is at once represented as a great crime. An outrage worthy of death will be manufactured out of nothing. The mountain often, of course, brings forth its mouse, but the bad effect produced on public opinion remains, notwithstanding.

"Could you believe it? The authorities themselves aggravate the situation. The authorities make themselves, I hope unwittingly, the echo of these slanderers, and regard us with evil eyes, so that our army almost seems to be considered by our fellow citizens a band of robbers. Yes, believe me, the

Monarchists of every shade have intermitted none of their pernicious activities, and hate us because we have sworn to leave none of those market-place stalls standing from which Kings and Emperors dictate their commands and caprices to the nations. Yes, we proclaim it openly, we are the *soldiers of the Revolution;* and, I will add, not merely of the French, but of the *Cosmopolitan* revolution. Italians, Spaniards, Poles, and Hungarians understood, when they hurried here to fight under the banner of France, that they were in reality defending the *Universal Republic.*"

"The significance of the struggle is already clear. It is between the principle of Divine right, of authority, of monarchy, and that of the sovereignty of the people, of civilisation, and of freedom. The *Fatherland vanishes in presence of the Republic.*

"We are citizens of the world, and we are ready, each according to his capacity, to fight to the death for the realisation of the grand idea of the United States of Europe, the brotherhood of all free peoples. The monarchical reactionists know this, and their enmity as good as doubles the Prussian armies. At our breasts we have the bayonets of the foreigner, and treachery at our backs! Why are all these ancient officials not chased away? Why are these former generals of the Empire, with their persons more or less decorated with their plumes, their orders, and their gold lace, not one and all cashiered without mercy? Can the Government of the National Defence not see that they will betray it; that with their hypocritical manœuvres, their shameful capitulations, their incomprehensible retreats, they are preparing the way for a Bonapartist restoration, or at least for an Orleans or a Bourbon ascending the throne?

"Let the Government which has undertaken to liberate

the soil of our country, polluted by the hordes of the foreigner, beware. Let it rise to the height of its own mission. Living in an epoch like ours, in the frightful circumstances in which we stand, it is not enough to be an honest man. One must show some energy, and must not lose his head, or drown himself in a glass of water. Let the Crémieuxs, the Glais-Bizoins, the Fourichons, recollect how men acted in 1792 and 1793. To-day we need men of the convention, a Danton, a Robespierre. Up, gentlemen, and room for the Revolution! She alone can help us. Great crises must be met by great means and great measures.

"Let us never forget that internal organisation must contribute to our defence against the outside world. It is a great matter to have nothing to trouble us when we march against the enemy; it is worth something to know that we are sustained by Republican officials, and that the army is not in the hands of men who are ready to sell it. What signify the formalities of the military hierarchy? Choose your generals, if necessary, from the ranks of your soldiers, and especially from among your young soldiers. Infuse a little fresh blood into the veins of the Republic, and the Republic will rescue herself and redeem all Europe from the yoke of the tyrants. Rise! A single effort, and long live the Universal Republic!"

The Fatherland vanishes in presence of the Republic! Use the same great weapons as Danton and Robespierre did; cut off everybody's head who differs from you in politics or religion; let the guillotine be declared a permanent institution. Generals Chanzy, Bourbaki, Faidherbe, Vinoy, Ducrot and Trochu, are to be sent about their business, and men from the ranks to take their places. This is what is preached by the son of a prefect, in the department of the Doubs, an officer of Garibaldi's general staff. I wonder how many will say Amen to these proposals when they read them a few days after this in the *Moniteur*.

*Tuesday, December* 13.—In the morning I wrote another article on the confession of faith of the cosmopolitan Republicans. Then I telegraphed the capitulation of Pfalzburg, and the commencement of the bombardment of Montmédy. The Chief's health is a trifle better, but he still feels himself very limp.

At breakfast the Chancellor's possible retirement was talked over; we amused ourselves over a Lasker Ministry, saying that "Lasker would turn out a kind of Ollivier," and, half joking, half serious, we discussed Delbrück as the probable Chancellor of the Confederation, "a very sensible man, but no politician." I thought it inconceivable that they could allow the Chief to retire, even at his own request. The gentlemen thought it not impossible. I said that if things here went on four weeks longer they would be forced to recall him. Bucher doubted whether in such a case he would come back, and said positively that from his knowledge of him he felt sure that he would never come back, if he once retired. He enjoyed Varzin far too thoroughly when he was away from business and bother of every kind. He was happiest in the woods and in the country. "Believe me," the Countess had once said to him, "a *wruke* (a turnip) interests him more than all your politics," a *mot* which one must accept with some reserve, and consider applicable only in his occasional moods.

At half-past two I went to him for business. He desired me to direct people's attention to the King of Holland's perplexity about new Ministers, and to point out that it was a consequence of the parliamentary system which forces the King's advisers to retire, whatever may be the circumstances, when the majority of the representatives of the people are against them on any single question. He remarked, "I remember that, when I was Minister, these people were having their twentieth or twenty-first ministry since the introduction of their parliamentary system. When people hold strictly to the principle that the Minister must be sent about his business if the majority goes against him, too many politicians get used up; they have then to go to the second-raters. In the end there is nobody left willing to devote himself to the kind of work. The moral is, either that the salary of ministerial offices ought to be raised, or that people must a little relax the severity of parliamentary practice."

The Chief drove out about three, after having Russell again with him, and he also came, God be praised! to dinner with us, where he drank a little beer and a couple of glasses of Vichy water with champagne. We had turtle-soup, and, among other delicacies, a wild boar's head and a *compote* of raspberry jelly and mustard, which was excellent. The Minister said, "Things were very bad with me this time. I was troubled with varicose veins in 1866 also. I lay full-length on the bed, and had to answer letters of a very desperate sort—very distracting for me—with a pencil. They" (he meant the Austrians) "then wanted to disarm on the northern frontier, but to keep their armies together farther down, and I had to convince them that that would not do for us at all."

He then spoke of his negotiations with Russell, and of Gortchakoff's demands. "The people in London," he said, "don't want to return a straightforward 'Yes' to the proposal to restore to Russia and Turkey the Black Sea, and complete sovereignty over their own coast lines. They are afraid of public opinion in England; and Russell returns perpetually to the idea that some sort of equivalent should be offered. He asked, for instance, whether we could not adhere *simpliciter* to the agreement of April 16, 1856. I told him that Germany had no real interest in it. Or whether we might not pledge ourselves to remain neutral, if it came to a conflict? I said I was no friend of conjectural politics, under which class such a pledge would come; and that it would all depend on the circumstances. At present we saw no reason to trouble ourselves about it. That ought to be enough for him. For the rest, I was not of opinion that gratitude was without its place in politics. The present Emperor had always shown himself friendly and well-disposed to us; while Austria had never shown herself trustworthy, and had occasionally been very uncertain. As for England, he knew well enough how much we had to thank her for. The friendliness of the Emperor, I said, was a relic of old relationships which originated partly in the family connection; but it rested also on the recognition of the fact that our interests were not in collision with his. Nobody knew how that might be in future, and it was better not to talk about it." . . . "Our position, I represented, was different from what it had been. We were the only power that had reason to be content; we had no call to do anybody a favour when we did not know whether he would do us a service in return."

"He came back to his equivalent, and asked me whether there was nothing I could propose to him. I suggested the opening of the Dardanelles and the Black Sea to all nations. It would probably be agreeable to Russia, as it would give her access to the Mediterranean from the Black Sea; and to Turkey, as she would then have her friends close to her; and to the Americans, who would lose one of the reasons which draw them towards Russia, in the realisation of their wish for the freedom of all the water highways of the world. He seemed to take that in." "The Russians," added the Chancellor, "ought not to have been so modest in their requirements; if they had asked for more, they would have had no difficulty in getting what they want about the Black Sea."

The conversation then turned on the four principles of the new law of the ocean: no fitting out of privateers; no seizure of goods except contraband of war; that a blockade is only to be valid when it is effective, and so on. One of these had been flagrantly infringed, the Chief said, by the French when they burned German vessels; and he closed our discussion of the subject, saying, "Yes, we must see how we can get rid of all this nonsense."

In the evening I extracted more articles for the King from the German papers, wondering and complaining about the delay of the bombardment. Afterwards L. came in to inquire whether I knew anything particular about a certain Heldig or Hillwitz. I told him I did not. L. went on to say, that he lived upon his means, was a democrat and a friend of Classen-Kappelmann's, had recently been here, and had had an interview with the Chancellor. On his way home he had been thrown into prison, but released, in consequence of a telegram from the Chief. He was supposed to be an agent for the restoration of Napoleon, whom he wanted to see set on the throne again, with a view to the final establishment of the republic, as an expedient *ad interim* which might ensure the peace of Germany during the inevitable struggle for the mastery among parties in France. If there is anything at all in this, the story is partly wrong, and certainly incomplete. I refrained, however, from remarks on the subject and contented myself with making a note of it.

*Wednesday, December* 14.—A cloudy sky, and mild weather. Yesterday and the day before there was little firing from the forts and gun-boats, and to-day there was none at all. In the morning, by the Chief's orders, I telegraphed the occupation of Blois by our troops and the capitulation of Montmédy. The Centralists in Germany are still expressing their dissatisfaction with the convention with Bavaria. T. in H. writes me about it almost in a tone of despair: " I quite understand that Count Bismarck could make no better of it, but it is a sorrowful business all the same. Bavaria has once more, as in 1813, through the convention of Ried, put a stick between our legs. As long as our leading statesman is left to us, we shall be able to get along in spite of it. But afterwards? I cannot feel the same unconditional confidence in the new empire as I had in the vital force of the North German Confederation. I can only hope that in spite of the seeming defects in the constitution of the state, the healthy forces of the nation may daily grow." I hope so too, though the deficiencies in our constitution do not strike me as so dangerous as they do our friend in H. For the rest, what is the use of complaining about things which it was impossible to arrange differently? What was possible has been done, and our watchword now must be, Accept what is to be had; with industry, patience, and good luck, more will come of it in time.

Before dinner, I again attended the funeral of two soldiers who had died in the hospital of the château. The procession crossed the Boulevard de la Reine and the Rue Adelaide on its way to the churchyard. This time the French saluted the corpse by lifting their hats. The music played through the streets the melody " Wie wohl ist mir, O Freund der Seelen," and outside of the big common cemetery, " Wie sie so sanft ruhn."

The Chief dined with us, and his guest was Count Holnstein. The conversation did not turn upon politics. The Minister talked in the kindliest and most good-humoured fashion of all sorts of things. He said, for instance, that as a young man he had been a fast runner and a capital jumper, whilst his sons had unusual strength in the muscles of their arms. He would not like to try them in a stand up-wrestle. He then brought out the case with the gold pen presented to him by Bissinger, the jeweller, to show to his guest, and he told us that the countess had written to know the truth about it, thinking it might turn out like the story about the clown at Meaux,—a story which I now heard for the first time, about the new-born child of a French soldier who had recently fallen, being deposited one morning on the Chief's bed, and which was, of course, an invention of the newspapers. Somebody said that the deputation from the Reichstag had got as far as Strassburg, and would be here the day after to-morrow. The Chancellor remarked, " Then we must think seriously what answer we are to give them. Simson will manage the thing very well. He has several times before had similar things to do on the first deputation about the Emperor and at the Hohenzollernburg. He likes to speak, and on such occasions speaks well and agreeably. Abeken remarked that the deputy Löwe had said that he had gone through this experience once before, and had the opportunity afterwards of reflecting on the matter, far from Madrid. " Really, was he there in 1849?" asked the Minister. "Yes," said Bucher, " he was President of the Reichstag." " So, then," said the Chief, " it was not on account of the Emperor's journey that he had to remain away from Madrid, but because of the trip to Stuttgart, which was a very different affair." At that time, according to him, he was first in the Hohenzollernburg, where all the branches of his family had separate apartments, then in another old castle in Pomerania where all the Dewitzes had formerly had a right of tenancy, but which had now become a picturesque ruin, the people of the next small town having made use of it for a quarry, and after that again with the owner of an estate in the country who had got his money in a peculiar way.

"He had always been apparently in difficulty and want, at one time up to the neck, the caterpillar having devoured his woods, a fire having burnt down a good part of them, and a hurricane finally levelling many of his trees to the ground. The wood had to be sold, and to his surprise he got a large sum for it—fifty or sixty thousand thalers—so that he was at once set on his feet again. It had never occurred to him that he had his wood to cut down."

The Chief then told us of another remarkable person, a neighbour of his own. "He had ten or twelve properties, but never any ready money, and often wanted to dispose of something. Whenever he gave a formal breakfast party, he used to have to sell one of his properties. At last there were only one or two left. His peasants bought one of them for fifty-three thousand thalers. They paid him fifteen thousand thalers down, and immediately sold off ship's timber to the amount of twenty-two thousand. He had never happened to think of that."

He talked next of the dragoon guards in Munich, whose bigness and whole style had given him the impression that they must be capital judges of beer. Then he talked of his son Count Bill, who was the first German to ride into Rouen. Some one said he would be a conclusive evidence to the inhabitants, that our troops had not so far been badly looked after, and the Chancellor again descanted on the strength of his "lads." They had uncommon strength for their age, he said, "though they had had no gymnastic training. I had no feeling against it certainly, but there had been no opportunity for it away from home." While we were smoking our after-dinner cigars, he asked whether the gentlemen of the office smoked. "They all do it," said Abeken. "Well," he said, "Engel must distribute the Hamburg cigars among them. I have had so many sent me that I shall still have some left to take home, even if the war lasts another twelvemonth."

After 9 o'clock in the morning I was twice called to the Minister. A note was sent for the press stating that Tarbé, the editor of the *Gaulois*, which now appears in Brussels, got out of Paris and through the Prussian lines by purchasing his passport from a Swiss for 10,000 francs. "Say nothing about the other Swiss (who we are informed sold his pass through the circle of our outposts to another Parisian for 6000 francs)," said the Chief. "It might look as if we wanted to worry Switzerland, which we have no intention of doing."

*Thursday, December* 15.—The weather was mild. Hardly any firing from the forts. Counts Frankenberg and Lehndorf were our guests at the beginning of dinner. Half an hour afterwards Prince Pless came in. The Minister was extremely chatty and good-humoured. We talked first about the question of the day, when the bombardment was to begin, and the Chief said he thought probably in eight or ten days from now, but that it would have little effect for a few weeks, as the Parisians had had time to make their preparations to meet it. Frankenberg said that people in Berlin, especially in the Reichstag, spoke of nothing so much as of the reasons which had made us put off the bombardment of Paris so late as this. Everything else fell into the background. "Well," said the Chief, "now that Roon has taken the thing in hand something will be done. There are a thousand waggons on the way here, adequately horsed. Ammunition for transport, and some of the new mortars have already arrived. We may look out for something soon now."

We then began to talk of the way in which the restoration of the German Empire had been brought before the Reichstag, and several of those present said that in their opinion it had not been managed as they should have liked. The thing had been badly arranged. The Conservatives had had no notice of the intended communication, so that it reached them just as they were at breakfast, and Windhorst, with his usual ability in turning circumstances to account, had been quite entitled to remark that he should have expected more sympathy from the Assembly. "Yes," said the Chief, "there ought to have been a more effective *mise en scène* for such a piece. . . . . Somebody might have come forward to express dissatisfaction with the Bavarian Convention. It wanted this, and omitted that. Then he should have said, that if any counterpoise for these defects could be found, anything in which the unity of Germany would find adequate expression, it might alter the case, and at that point the Emperor might have been brought out." "After all, the Emperor has more power than many fancy." "I don't for a moment deny that the Bavarian Convention has its faults and deficiencies; that is easily said by people who have no responsibility. How would it have been if I had refused to meet the Bavarians half-way, and nothing had come of the whole affair? It is impossible to realise the difficulties we should have got into, so that I was frightfully anxious about the freedom from prejudices of the centralistic party among the deputies of the Reichstag." "This is the first time for many a day that I have had a couple of hours' sound and satisfying sleep. I used at first to lie awake full of all sorts of thoughts and troubles. Then Varzin would suddenly come up before me, perfectly distinct in the minutest particulars, like a great picture with even all its colours fresh—the green trees, the sunshine on the stems, the blue sky above. I saw every individual tree. I struggled to shake the thing off, but it came back and worried me, and when at last I ceased to see it, other things came in—reports, notes, despatches, and so on, till I fell over about morning."

The conversation then turning on the fair sex in this country, the Chief said—" I have travelled a good deal through France, during peace, too, and I don't recollect that I ever saw anywhere a single nice-looking country girl, but I have seen frightfully ugly creatures often. I believe that there are a few, only the pretty ones go off to Paris to make their market there." Towards the end we talked of the enormous destruction the war had entailed on France, and the Minister said, " I can imagine that the country might become empty and masterless, and that after the emigration of the people we might have to let the estates out to deserving Pomeranians and Westphalians."

I was after dinner with H., who leaves to-morrow for the outposts of Bougival, where the incidents, at present, are a French grenade bursting into the house and hurting a lot of people, or a glass of beer at the Hôtel de Chasse. His cousin is there, and the doctor in the hospital at the château. He happened to speak of the visit the Chief had recently paid to the wards and said, that in the way in which the Chancellor had taken it up, neither the doctor, who was involved, nor the other officer complained of, had really been to blame, for the men not being properly looked after. The sentry who had been talking to our Count about the neglect of the sick was a sot, not in any way trustworthy. The thing really at fault was the close scrimped "form" for the dietaries of the Prussian hospitals. Men could neither live on it, nor die on it. The system would have broken down altogether but for the contributions of voluntary benevolence and the presents from friends, and that doctor's gruffness and irritability to people who brought presents, to French ladies, for instance, had often prevented the soldiers getting such things.

In the evening, at tea, Bucher was at first alone with me; then Keudell came in, who was a good deal troubled, and anxious about Gambetta's gigantic levies, which were estimated, as he had heard from the general staff, at 1,300,000 men. He had been told also by Moltke's people, that we were to get 80,000 or 90,000 new troops, but he thought we ought to have had half a million. What would happen if the French with 300,000 men from the south-east were to fall on the thin line of our communications with Germany? We might then easily be compelled even to give up Paris. Certainly this is too melancholy a view of the situation.

## CHAPTER XV.

CHAUDORDY AND FACTS—OFFICERS BREAKING THEIR PAROLE—FRENCH MISCONSTRUCTIONS—THE CROWN PRINCE ENTERTAINED BY THE CHIEF.

FRIDAY, *December* 16.—Weather mild and sky clouded. In the morning I wrote several articles on Chaudordy's circular despatch about the barbarous way in which we are represented to be carrying on the war. My line was as follows:

"To the slanders which the French press has been circulating for months in order to excite public opinion against us, we have now to add an official document emanating from the Provisional Government of France, the object of which is to induce foreign courts and cabinets to take part against us by exaggerated and distorted statements of our proceedings in this war. An official of the Ministry of Foreign Affairs, M. de Chaudordy, has taken occasion to complain of us in a circular letter to the neutral powers. Let us look at the main points of his indictment, let us then state the real facts of the cases he describes, and leave the world to judge whether the French or we are more open to the reproach of barbarism.

"He asserts that our requisitions are immoderate and that we demand from the towns and communes which have fallen into our hands exorbitant contributions. We are said even to have laid hold of the private property of individuals. We are accused of savagely wrecking and burning down towns and villages where the inhabitants have fought against us or even been helpful in the slightest way to the French who are defending their country. Our accuser says, 'To punish a town for the offence of a single inhabitant whose sole crime was that he rose against the foreign invader, superior officers have ordered it to be set on fire and plundered, thus shamefully abusing the unquestioning discipline exacted from their soldiers. Every house where a Franctireur had hidden or had a meal has been burnt down. What becomes of private property?' The circular goes on to say that in bombarding open towns we have introduced a practice which has no precedent in history. Finally, among other outrages of which we have been guilty, we have taken hostages with us in the railway trains to secure ourselves against the rails being lifted and other damage and injury done to the lines.

"We answer these charges thus: If M. de Chaudordy had known anything of war, instead of complaining of the sacrifices our operations require from the French population, he would have been astonished at our comparative reasonableness. The German troops respect private property everywhere, but it is not to be wondered at if, after forced marches or hard fights where they have been exposed to cold and hunger, they insist on getting lodged as comfortably as possible and on requiring of the inhabitants whatever is of immediate necessity—food, drink, and firing, for instance —or if they take them, in cases where the inhabitants have fled. There is evidence, that so far from attacking private property, as M. de Chaudordy says they do, they have often done the very opposite, and have, at the risk of their own lives, rescued for the owners objects of special or artistic value, exposed to injury from the French guns. We are charged with having burned down villages. Has our accuser never heard of the reason: of the Francs-tireurs, assassin-like, firing at our men in them, of the inhabitants helping these murderers and rendering them every possible assistance? Has he not heard how the Francs-tireurs, who went recently from Fontaines to Lyons, declared loudly and openly that the object of their march was to pay visits to those houses in the district, the plundering of which was worth their while? Can he give a single authenticated instance of horrors committed by our soldiers like those practised on them by the Turcos and the free companions of the French? Have they cut off the ears and noses of their enemies, either dead or alive, as the French did to the German soldiers at Coulours on the 30th of November? Eight hundred German prisoners should have been brought into Lille on the 11th of December. There were only two hundred. Many of them were severely wounded, but instead of offering them assistance the people pelted them with snowballs, and cried to the soldiers to run their bayonets into them. The number of times the French have fired on flags of truce is unprecedented, and the following incident, though all but incredible, is perfectly authenticated. On the 2nd of December Under-Sergeant-major Steinmetz von Villers wrote a letter to his lieutenant in Mirecourt by the express request of an officer of the Garibaldians, notifying that if our troops allowed reprisals against Vettel or any place in the neighbourhood, he would cut off the ears of fourteen Prussians who had fallen into the hands of the free companions.

"We have often refused to treat free companions as soldiers, but only when, by following the principles recommended to the country people of the department of Côte d'Or by the Prefect Luce Villiard on the 21st November, they failed to conduct themselves as such. He told them, ' The country does not ask you to embody yourselves in companies and march against the enemy. It expects you, every morning, to pick out three or four men to go to any place which the character of the ground renders suitable and fire at the Prussians wherever they can do so without danger. Above all things, fire at the enemy's cavalry, and give their horses up at the chief place of the arrondissement. I shall pay you a reward (the wages of assassination) and shall publish your heroic conduct in all the newspapers of the department and in the *Journal officiel*.'

"We have bombarded open towns, such as Orleans, but is M. de Chaudordy not aware that at the time they were in the occupation of the enemy? Has he forgotten that the French bombarded the open towns of Saarbrücken and Kehl? Finally, about the hostages, who are taken with our railway trains, they accompany us, not to interfere with the heroic deeds of the French, but to prevent malignant crimes. The railways carry other things besides soldiers, ammunition, and war materials. They are not a mere means of war, assailable, like others, by armed violence. Crowds of wounded, doctors, nurses for the sick, and other altogether peaceable persons, are conveyed on them. Is any peasant or free companion to be allowed to tear up the rails or lay stones across, so as at one blow to endanger the lives of hundreds of these people? Let the French see to the safety of their trains, and their hostages will only be taken little pleasure excursions, or, if they prefer it, we shall make Germans accompany them to re-establish order along the lines. We need say no more in answer to M. de Chaudordy's complaints. The European cabinets know the humane spirit in which we carry on war, and people here will have little difficulty in rating the assertions of our French accuser at their real worth.

"After all, war is war. Silk gloves are not in place, and perhaps the iron gloves with which we have had to handle them would have been worn less frequently had the Government of National Defence not passionately proclaimed a people's war, which inevitably leads to greater cruelties than one between regular armies."

In the afternoon I again visited the magnificent bronze deities behind the château, and the moss-grown marble statues on the main road through the park. Besides Bohlen, who was still sick, we missed at dinner Hatzfeld, who had turned unwell, and Keudell, who had been commanded to dine with the King. This time Count Holnstein and Prince Putbus were our invited guests. The conversation turned first on the Bavarian Convention, and Holnstein expected that it would be approved by the second Chamber, in which a two-thirds majority is necessary, as it is already known that only about forty votes are to be recorded against it. It is also as good as certain that it will not be rejected by the Chamber of the Royal Councillors. The Chief said, "Thünger will surely be for it." Holnstein said, "I believe so, for he voted for our taking part in the war." "Yes, said the Minister, "he is one of the honourable Particularists, but there are others who have different ends in view." Holnstein said, "Certainly some of the patriots have shown clearly enough that they leave out the "For God and Fatherland," and hold only by the "With the help of God."

Putbus then turned the conversation to the approaching festival, and said that it was nice that the men in the hospitals were also to have their Christmas trees. A collection had been made for that object, and 2500 francs had been gathered. "Pless and I signed," he went on to say. "Then it was taken to the Grand Duke of Weimar, who subscribed 300 francs, and the Grand Duke of Coburg 200." "Of course he would have to subscribe neither more than Weimar nor less than Pless." Putbus said they proposed to lay the list before his Majesty, and the Chief asked, "Won't you allow me to have a share in it?"

It was then mentioned that a French air-balloon had come down at Wetzlar, and that Ducrot was said to be in it. "Well, he will be shot at last," said Putbus. "No," said the Chief, "if he comes before a council of war, it will not shoot him, but a council of honour, the officers tell me, would condemn him quickly enough."

"Is there anything else new in military matters?" said Putbus. The Minister said, "The general staff may know something, but we don't. For our much asking, we get the crumbs they let fall to us, and they are not many." Somebody then said he had heard that another great sortie of the Parisians was expected to-morrow: and one of those at table added, that there was a report that a dragoon had been shot on the road to Meudon, and an officer in the wood between this and Ville d'Avray. (Hence the notice yesterday ordering that no civilian is to be allowed in the woods near the town between three in the afternoon and nine next morning, and commanding sentries and patrols to fire on any non-military man who shows himself there during these hours.) "They appear to have air-guns," the Chief conjectured. "Probably they are the old poachers of the neighbourhood."

Finally we spoke of the report that the Government of the National Defence was proposing to issue a loan, and the Minister turned to me and said, "It might be worth while to point out in the papers the risk people run who lend their money to this Government. It may turn out that its loans may not be taken up by the Government with which we conclude peace, and we may make it one of the conditions. You might get that specially into the English and the Belgian papers."

After we left table, Abeken told me that Count Holnstein had asked who I was (probably because I am now the only person at the Chancellor's table in civilian costume); was I, perhaps, the Minister's personal medical attendant, as people called me Doctor? In the evening L. told us that a Conservative of high position, who sometimes favoured him with communications, had told him that, in his circles, people were anxious to see what the King would say in reply to the deputation from the Reichstag. He was supposed not to like their visit, for it was only the first German Reichstag, and not the North German Reichstag which would be entitled to offer him the Emperor's crown. (The King thinks much less about the Reichstag, which does not propose to offer him the crown on its own account, but to come, along with the princes, asking him to accept it, than of the princes, some of whom have not yet sent their answer to the proposition of the King of Bavaria.) For his own part, L.'s high-placed Conservative would rather have seen the King made Emperor of Prussia (which is a matter of taste), in which case Prussia would merge in Germany, and about that he confesses he has his scruples. L. told us also that the Crown Prince was indignant at certain correspondents in the German papers, who had compared Châteaudun to Pompeii, and had otherwise drawn lively pictures of the desolation of the country by the war. I suggested to L. to work on the subjects: "A new French Loan" and "Chaudordy and Garibaldi's ear-slitters" for a Belgian paper, to which he has access, and he promised to do so to-morrow.

After he left I wrote an article on the former subject for a German paper, which went into our letter-box, and ran much as follows:

"The reckless 'devil-may-cares,' who are now attempting

to guide the destinies of France from Paris and Tours, want to coax another loan for themselves out of the pockets of foreigners. This measure has for some time been unavoidable, and there is no reason to be surprised at it. But we may point out to the financial world that, besides the advantages which will be offered them, there is a very intelligible risk, which we need only mention to show how serious it is. The Government which raises the loan has neither been accepted by France nor recognised by any state in Europe. It will be remembered too that the Germans notified that they would take care that certain loans which it was tried to raise from the French Communes for war purposes, should never be paid. That declaration may serve as a hint that the principle may receive a wider application. Possibly, indeed probably, the French Government will have to conclude a peace with Prussia and her allies—but to all appearance it will not be the existing Government—and that Government of the near future may not unlikely be required, as one of the conditions of peace, to decline to be responsible for the responsibilities undertaken by Messrs. Gambetta and Favre, either by paying principal or interest. It would certainly be entitled to do so, as these gentlemen are going to borrow in the name of France indeed, but without being commissioned or charged by her. Forewarned is forearmed."

After tea Wollmann came in, and told us that the deputation from the Reichstag had arrived, and that Simson, their speaker, was already below with the Chief, who would clearly explain to him the King's disinclination to receive them before the arrival of letters from all the princes agreeing to what is proposed. These letters have to be sent first to the King of Bavaria, and he forwards them to our King. All the princes are believed to have already answered in the affirmative by telegram—only Lippe seems not yet to have quite got to the bottom of his meditations. To account for this delay, probably a couple of the members of the deputation will have to be taken ill. W. tells us also that the last telegram, notifying the passage of the Convention with Bavaria through the Reichstag, contained the words: "Even the district magistrates were powerless to obstruct the march of universal history."

*Saturday, December* 17.—A yellowish-red as we looked out at our windows on rising in the morning, and beautiful weather outside. About nine, while I was taking a walk with Abeken through the pleasure-grounds of the park, a thick fog gathered suddenly, spreading itself over a small amphibious world. At present it is half winter, half summer. The ground is covered with snow; but the trees in the park, with their branches intertwined with ivy, one side of the enclosure wall also overgrown with it, and the plain round the little waterfall, where the tender foliage of young ferns is coming out—are all quite green. Violets are blowing under the fallen leaves on the beds with their box borders, and we gathered a charming bouquet for Abeken's wife. It was not till about twelve that the fog dispersed.

In the course of the morning I wrote a second article on the new French loan. During breakfast we were informed that Vendôme had been occupied by our troops. The secretaries told us that when he is dictating, the Chief's custom is to walk up and down the room, every now and then giving a knock on a table, a chair, or a commode, sometimes with the tassel of his dressing-gown, which he keeps swinging about. He seems not to have had a good night last night, for about half-past eleven he had not breakfasted, and an hour afterwards he was still not to be spoken with. There is to be a great council to-day of the military authorities at the King's—perhaps about the bombardment? In the afternoon I read a paragraph giving increasingly numerous instances of French officers who have broken their parole, and run off from the places where they were "interned" to take service against us afresh. There are already more than fifty of them, among whom are officers of all grades, including Generals Ducrot, Cambriels, and Barral. After the battle of Sedan, it was in our power, by annihilating it, to have rendered the French army shut up there harmless. Humanity, and our faith in promises, induced us to refrain. The capitulation was concluded, and we were entitled to suppose that all the officers had accepted it, and were prepared to live according to the conditions imposed upon them. Wherever this was not the case, we were entitled to be warned of the fact. We should then have dealt with these exceptions as exceptions, and not have given such officers the privileges which we gave the others : in other words, we should not have allowed them that freedom of movement of which they now take such shameful advantage. Certainly the majority of the captive officers have been true to the word they gave, so that we might pass the matter over with a mere shrug of the shoulders. The thing looks differently the moment the Provisional Government of France condones the breach of an officer's word by restoring him to his position in a regiment in active service against us. Has anyone ever heard of a case in which such a deserter has been refused restoration to his former place in the French army? Or of one where French officers have made any remonstrance against the readmission to their ranks of comrades who have broken their words in this way? It is not merely the Government, therefore, but the entire body of French officers, which considers such dishonourable conduct perfectly *en règle*. The German Governments are consequently compelled to ask themselves whether the ameliorations of their captivity hitherto granted to French officers are in harmony with the interests of Germany. We must ask ourselves this further question: whether we are justified in trusting the engagements by which the present French Government binds itself, in dealing with Germany, without material securities or pledges in pawn for their full performance.

Herr von Arnim-Kröchlenburg, the brother-in-law of the Minister, was at dinner, a gentleman with an energetic expression of countenance and a full reddish beard, apparently going into fifty. The Chief was in excellent humour, but the conversation this time had no special significance. It turned chiefly on the bombardment and the position which a certain party at head-quarters had taken up with respect to it. The Chief suddenly asked Bucher, "Have you a pencil and paper beside you?" "Yes."—"Then telegraph" (I suppose to Delbrück): "The King will receive the deputation from the Reichstag about two o'clock to-morrow afternoon. Details to follow.'" (Probably he means to signify to them that he is prepared to assume the dignity of Emperor, as they wish him to do, but that he considers that he owes it in the first instance to the requisition from the King of Bavaria and the agreement of the other German princes with him, and that that agreement has not yet been formally expressed by everybody.) Arnim said he could eat no more, as he had already had too much sausage, and the Chief smiled and said, "Where did they come from? I hope not from Paris, for in that case they might perhaps contain rat." We learn, in fact, that they are now very short of fresh meat there; and it is said that in some parts of the city a regular rat-market has been established, which is abundantly supplied with good stock from the sewers.

L. came in after eight o'clock, as usual, to exchange news.

He told us that there was considerable excitement at present among the English in Versailles. Several sons of Britain, who are acting here as newspaper correspondents, and among them a Captain Hosier, had had the misfortune, on a journey from this to Orleans, to be arrested as spies and kept prisoners in an inn, by German soldiers who did not understand their English. They made an exception in favour of Hosier only, who spoke some German. In spite of their correct papers all the rest were kept in charge, put into a conveyance and brought to Versailles. The Crown Prince was very angry at the behaviour of the soldiers, and the London papers would storm frightfully, and try to turn the affair into a national insult. L. seemed a little warm over it. I thought to myself, that he who thrusts himself into danger must abide the consequences, and that the man who goes a journey is likely to have something to tell. Bucher, too, when I told him the story, seemed to think it rather enjoyable than serious, and said that it was a continuation of the well-known comic narrative of Brown, Jones, and Robinson, who undertook their famous journey to foreign parts without knowing any language but that of the London Cockney, and who had fallen into all sorts of trouble.

Afterwards Bucher told us that the Chief was a great lover of nature and of picturesque places. He had several times rambled through the country near Varzin with him, and about the close of the walk he often said, "You are wearying for your dinner no doubt, but there is that one hill for us to climb yet, to get the view from the top."

In the evening after ten there were repeated discharges from the forts.

*Sunday, December* 18.—The weather is cloudy, but without fog. In the morning a few shots were again to be heard from the big guns. In the forenoon I wrote several letters for Germany. About two the Chief went out to the prefecture for the presentation of the people from the Reichstag. In the interval before his probable return, I took a walk through the Park with Wollmann, ending by way of the Avenue de Paris, where the ceremony at the prefecture seems to have been got through very simply. The Princes present here went, I believe, to the King, as did also the delegates of the Reichstag. After two o'clock the King came into the audience-room, accompanied by the Crown Prince and Princes Karl and Adalbert. The Grand Dukes of Baden, Oldenburg, and Weimar, the Duke of Coburg and Meiningen, the three actual Hereditary Grand Dukes of Mecklenburg, Weimar, and Oldenburg, Prince William of Würtemberg, and a number of other princely personages were present, and the rest of the audience was grouped round the Chancellor of the Confederation. Nobody was, it seems, in full uniform. Simson made the address to the King, who answered pretty much as had been expected. About five o'clock, a dinner of eighty covers closed the ceremonies.

This afternoon I dined with Dr. Good,* and met there another Kentuckian, Mr. Bowland, MacLean, and the English newspaper correspondent Conningsby. The Americans were charming people. They were much astonished at the accuracy with which I described to them Falmouth, Bowland's birthplace, and the way to it from Cincinnati. They wanted to know my opinion about the United States, and especially what I thought about the great Civil War, in which Good had been a long time engaged. My answer,

* An unusually agreeable young doctor from Louisville, Kentucky, who, being a complete master of German, had devoted himself to the care of the sick at headquarters, and whose acquaintance I had made through MacLean. Some time afterwards he was himself the victim of a long and fatal illness, caused by the fatigues he had undergone during the American Secession War.

in which I did justice also to the Secessionists, seemed to please them greatly. Then Conningsby brought up the incident with Hosier and his friends, and wished to know what I thought about it. I told him that the gentlemen had added a fresh chapter to the adventures of Brown, Jones, and Robinson. It could not reasonably be expected that our soldiers and subaltern officers should understand English, and the thing appeared to me to be founded on a misunderstanding. He replied that Hosier had certainly spoken German, and that the papers which all the four gentlemen had on their persons were written in German and signed by Roon and Blumenthal. "In that case," I said, "it is in all likelihood an instance of military over-conscientiousness; too much zeal and precaution." Mr. Conningsby replied that he could not see it in that light; he thought that the soldiers had ill used the correspondents, because they were inoculated with the bitter feeling in Germany about the English supply of arms. We should see, however, what would come of it.

I did not want to say that what he called embittered feeling was probably more like distrust, or that I thought it quite intelligible. So I merely said, "Most likely it will make a great noise, an angry effervescence in the newspapers, and nothing more." I added that I could not imagine that more could come of it. He replied that I should not be too sure of that, and talked about the British lion and *civis Romanus*. I answered that if the lion roared, we should say, "Well roared, lion;" "Roar again, lion." As for the *civis*, times had a little altered since he used to be the fashion. "People have their own thoughts about these matters," I said. He replied that we were quite intoxicated with our success, and that if the British Lion were not satisfied he could fight as well as roar. The least that could be asked would be the cashiering of the officer in command when his countrymen had been arrested. I begged him not to get excited, to look at the matter in cold blood. It could not in any circumstances be serious. We should certainly not throw our people over at once as a sop to the Lion, however that animal might rage. If injustice had been really done to the correspondents, a point which an inquiry would settle, they would undoubtedly get satisfaction. As for our intoxication with our success, I must point out to him that throughout this war we had as a nation shown ourselves most modest, very free from conceit or vaingloriousness, especially when contrasted with the unmeasured lying and boasting of the French. I ended by saying that I repeated that I considered the whole affair a trifle, that it was impossible that England should quarrel with us, or, as he seemed to expect, declare war against us, about trifles. But I continued to believe that the matter would make a great noise in the newspapers, and that nothing serious would come of it. In the end he calmed down, and confessed that he had himself been arrested during the engagement near Bougival and Malmaison, and harshly used by the Prussians, but even more harshly by his own countryman, Colonel Walker, to whom he had appealed. Walker is the English military plenipotentiary at headquarters. He had received him gruffly, and told him in plain words that he had no business in battlefields. He then described Walker to us as a man of no ability. I suppressed the remark I thought of making, that in that instance Colonel Walker seemed to have shown himself a man of better judgment than some other folks. The discussion at last dropped away peaceably enough. Throughout, the American sided with me and the Germans.

I told the Chief about the Hosier affair in the evening about eleven. He had heard nothing whatever about it, would not at first quite believe it, and to the last was unable to take anything but a humorous view of the affair. He then told me to despatch a telegram about a fresh victory of trifling importance over Chanzy's army, and a notice of the King's reception of the deputation from the Reichstag.

*Monday, December* 19.—In the morning Abeken and I again gathered violets in the garden, and found three bunches, which I sent home. Afterwards I answered the article on cold steel in the *Kölnische Zeitung*, in which the French doctors are said to infer, from the circumstance that they have seen very few Frenchmen wounded with bayonet and sabre, that the Germans do not like hand-to-hand fighting. I made the remark, that if these gentlemen really judge from their own experience, their opinion must be due to the fact that, in the first place, they never had the opportunity of seeing the bodies of those who fell at Spicheren, Gravelotte, and Le Bourget, pierced by German bayonets or felled by German muskets; and that, in the second place, the French usually do not wait for the bayonet, but take to flight before we can come up to them with cold steel. Afterwards I again spoke of the international revolution which has brought so many free companions and heroes of the barricades to fight against us. My line of argument was something like this: At first we imagined we had only France against us, which was the case up to Sedan. After the 4th of September, however, another power appeared to oppose us,—the Universal Republic, the International Union of fanatics, without a native country, in the interests of the United States of Europe—the Cosmopolitan Revolution. To the devotees of this idea from every point of the compass the standard of France is a centre and a gathering-point. They troop together to fight us, who are supposed to be soldiers of the monarchy, Poles, Irishmen, Spaniards,

Italians. Even a few casuals from Turkey have joined themselves, like brothers, to the French Republicans. Everybody who wants the universal conflagration, in which the old states are to be destroyed, and the Cosmopolitan Democracy, and all the Red Republicans who appear in congresses at Basle and Geneva, look upon the France of the present day as the hearth on which the great Revolutionary fire is to be lighted. Mazzini, the forerunner of the Christ in the Red Republican Evangel, looks for the beginning of the bankruptcy of existing states and of society, not from his native country, Italy, but from France, to which we owe the Revolutions of 1789, 1830, and 1848. The power of expansion which she has shown in these Revolutions gives her a right to begin the "final war" demanded and proclaimed by the Peace Congress. The German Democrats of all shades bow down before the Parisian spirit, recognise in France their mother Republic, and consider the German armies, with their loyalty to duty and their love of country, as hordes of barbarians, from the hour when the Republic was proclaimed in France.

We believe that France is not to be envied the tribute paid her by these professional revolutionists. Nobody considers her fortunate because these desperate men have selected her soil as the battlefield on which they seek to realise their dreams. The great majority of the French people themselves have no wish for a triumph, which would mean the annihilation of their nationality, the destruction of their political and social arrangements, the abolition of church and faith, the Revolution *en permanence*, and universal anarchy, which usually ends in despotism.

"God preserve us," says the *New York Tribune*—the Republican convictions of which are above suspicion—" God preserve us from wishing to see such a Republic established in unfortunate France, or anywhere in Europe!" I shall deal with the matter in this spirit in the *Moniteur*.

After two o'clock I made an excursion through the park, meeting the Chief twice, with Simson beside him in his carriage. The Minister was invited to dine with the Crown Prince at seven, but half an hour or so before, he ate a little with us. He told us about his drive with Simson. "The last time he was here was in 1830, after the July revolution. I thought he would have taken an interest in the park and the beautiful views there, but he seemed to do nothing of the sort. Apparently the feeling for landscape is completely wanting in him. There are many people in whom it is so. As far as I know there are no Jewish landscape painters, and, indeed, hardly any Jewish painters of any kind." Somebody mentioned Meierheim and Bendemann. "Meierheim," he said, "yes; but Bendemann had only Jewish grand-parents. There are plenty of Jewish composers—Meyerbeer, Mendelssohn, Halévy; but for painters, a Jew paints indeed, but only when he does not need to do it."

Abeken then told us about Rogge's sermon yesterday in the church of the château, and said he had talked too much about the deputation here from the Reichstag. The Chief replied, "I am not at all of that mind, certainly not. These people have once more voted us a hundred million thalers (fifteen million pounds), and they have approved the Versailles Conventions in spite of their own *doctrinaire* views, and much to the disgust of many people. We ought to recognise all that. No; I cannot entertain such an opinion of them. I am only cross with Delbrück, who disturbed my mind greatly by saying that they were not likely to agree to the Conventions."

The privy councillor talked of the incidents at Ems, shortly before the war broke out, and told us that after a certain despatch the King had said: "Well, even he (Bismarck) will be pleased with us." "And I believe," added Abeken, "that you were." From the Chancellor's reply, it must have been a "partial satisfaction." "I remember," he said, "how I received the news in Varzin. I had gone out, and I found the first telegram waiting for me when I came home. I went off at once, driving by our pastor's house at Wussau. He stood right before his door, and saluted me. I said nothing to him, but merely made this cut (marking the crossing of swords in the air). He understood me, and I went on." Then he told us how the thing changed back and forward up to the point when the declaration of war came. The Minister then said that he had meant at first to go to church yesterday, "but I was anxious," he said, "not to catch cold in the procession. I caught a most frightful headache once before in it; and, besides, I was very much afraid that Rogge would say too much."

Afterwards, in what connection I do not remember, he began to speak of the "nut war," which was the result of the battle of Tannenberg, in which the combatants are said to have lost themselves in a large wood, which at that time stretched from Bütow far into Poland, and consisted entirely of walnut thickets and of oaks. In connection with something else, though I do not remember this connection either, he mentioned the battle of Fehrbellin, which brought him to talk of old people who had outlived so-and-so. "We had an old cowherd called Brand at home, who may very likely have spoken to people who were at the battle of Fehrbellin. Brand was one of those ancient pieces of furniture with which the recollections of my youth are inseparably bound up. When I think of him I seem to be smelling heather and meadow flowers. Yes, it is possible; he was 91 or 93 years old, and died in 1820 or 1821. He had seen King Frederick William the First in Cöslin, where he had served with his father as a post-boy. If, then, he was born about 1730, it is quite possible that he may have known people who fought in Fehrbellin, for that is only fifty or sixty years farther back."

Abeken had also his remarkable recollections of youth. He had seen the poet Göckingk, who died in the course of the last twenty years, from which we made out that the old man was born in 1809. The Chief then said that he might himself possibly have seen pig-tails when he was a child. Turning to Abeken, he continued: "It is more likely that you did, as you are five or six years older than I am." Then he returned to Pomerania, and, if I do not mistake, to Varzin, where a French Piedmontese had settled down after the last French war. The man interested him, as he had worked himself up to a respectable position, and although originally a Catholic, had become one of the churchwardens. As another instance of people settling and becoming prosperous in some chance locality, he mentioned other Italians, who during the war of 1813, had got into this back region of Pomerania, remained there, and founded families, distinguishable from those of their neighbours only through the cast of their features.

Finally, we spoke of Mühler, a friend of Abeken's, whom he had that day, contrary to Keudell's opinion, declared to be quite unreplaceable. From the influence of that minister's wife upon his decisions, and his whole political attitude, the conversation turned on the influence which energetic wives usually exercise over their husbands. "Yes," said the Chief, "in such cases one usually cannot tell to whom the merit or demerit of a thing is to be attributed—*quid ipse fecit et quid mulier fecit*" ("which is his part and which his wife's"); a remark which he illustrated by many examples which cannot be given here. It was after ten o'clock before the Minister came back from the Crown Prince, and he then went out to take the Crown Prince's Marshal of the Palace, who returned with him ten minutes later, for a short walk in the garden. Afterwards, when I was having tea in my own room, Engel whispered me up the staircase, "Do you know, doctor, that the Crown Prince is to dine with us to-morrow evening?"

*Tuesday, December* 20.—Mild, broken weather. I telegraph again several small military successes, and I prepare for the King the paper in which the *National Zeitung* has expressed its opinion of Moltke's letter to Trochu, in its leading article of the 15th of December. Afterwards I write, on the Chief's instructions, two articles, to be manifolded: one on a misunderstanding, or perversion, of the King's proclamation after he entered French territory, and the other upon Trochu's relations with the remaining members of the Provisional Government.

The first said something of this kind: "We have had occasion several times to expose a misunderstanding, or intentional falsification, of the words which King William addressed to the French people in his proclamation of the 11th of August. It appears once more, and this time, to our astonishment, it comes from a usually estimable French historical student. M. d'Haussonville has made an assertion in his pamphlet, 'La France et la Prusse devant l'Europe,' not very creditable to his love of truth, or perhaps to his scientific thoroughness. The entire pamphlet is shallow and superficial, full of exaggerations, errors, and assertions founded upon nothing better than groundless reports. Among other gross mistakes of the author—who is obviously blinded by patriotic passion—let us content ourselves with mentioning one. According to him, King William was on the throne during the Crimean war. But this by the way.

"We have to deal here only with the falsifying of the proclamation addressed to the French in August, and printed usually both in German and French, to prevent any misunderstanding. According to M. d'Haussonville, the King said in it, 'I make war with the Emperor, not at all with France' ('Je ne fais la guerre qu'à l'Empereur et pas à la France'). In reality, what was said in the proclamation was this: 'The Emperor Napoleon has attacked the German nation, which wished, and still wishes, to live in peace with the French people both by sea and land. I have taken the command of the German armies to repel this attack. Military reasons have induced me to enter French territory to make war on French soldiers, but not on French citizens.' ('L'Empereur Napoléon ayant attaqué par terre et par mer la nation allemande, qui désirait et désire encore vivre en paix avec le peuple français, j'ai pris le commandement des armées allemandes pour repousser l'agression, et j'ai été amené par les événements militaires à passer les frontières de France. Je fais la guerre aux soldats et non aux citoyens français.') In order to make any misunderstanding impossible it went on to say: 'These' (viz., the French citizens) 'will accordingly continue to enjoy full security in their persons and property, so long, at least, as their hostile action against the German troops does not deprive me of the right to extend my protection to them' ('Ceux-ci continueront, par conséquent, à jouir d'une complète sécurité pour leurs personnes et leurs biens, aussi longtemps qu'ils ne me priveront eux-mêmes, par des entreprises hostiles contre les troupes allemandes, du droit de leur accorder ma protection.') The contrast between d'Haussonville's quotation and the original of the proclamation is manifest, and certainly no ambiguity is to be discovered in it which could excuse the mistake."

The other article ran in this way: "The delegation of the Government of the National Defence, at present in Bordeaux, has convinced itself of the uselessness of further resistance to the German arms, and would be willing, according to the view of M. Gambetta, to conclude peace with Germany upon the principles required by the latter. General Trochu, on the other hand, is said to have decided to continue the war. In reality, the delegation at Tours, which is now in Bordeaux, pledged itself to General Trochu from the beginning, not to treat for peace without his consent. According to other accounts, General Trochu is supposed to have accumulated provisions for several months on Mont Valérien, so as to go there with whatever troops he can gather after the capitulation of Paris has become a necessity, in order to influence the destiny of France after the conclusion of peace. The object of this proceeding is believed to be to safeguard the interests of the Orleans family, one of whose adherents General Trochu is said to be."

Whilst I was preparing this article in the Bureau, Keudell told me that the Chief had decided that all State documents as they came in and went out were from this time forward to be open to my inspection on my request. He gave me a telegram to read from the Minister himself, referring to Luxemburg, and afterwards he sent me, through Wollmann, the authority required for my better information.

After three o'clock the Minister went to the King, and I took a walk with Wollmann through the town, and afterwards through the Avenue de Saint-Cloud. On the main road, a peculiar dark blue mass appeared in the distance coming to meet us. They looked like soldiers, and yet not like soldiers. They marched in close column and in regular step. There were muskets without bayonets; there were neither caps nor helmets; and there was no white leather. It was only when the procession came nearer that I recognised the black glazed hats of the sailors of our Marine, their black belts and main braces, their shiny knapsacks, their pea-jackets, and their cutlasses. There were some hundreds of them, with five or six officers, from whom, when the troop halted, we learned that they were the crews of four of the Loire steamers which have been captured by Prince Frederick Charles's troops. It appears that they are quartered in the Rue de la Pompe, and in the Rue Hoche. There were many strapping and good-looking fellows amongst them. Numbers of French gathered round to watch these mysterious foreigners, the like of whom they had never seen. "They are German sailors," I heard somebody say; "they can speak many languages (*ce sont des polyglottes*), and are to serve as interpreters for the Prussians."

Shortly after six o'clock the Crown Prince, with his adjutant, came to dine with us. He wore the ensigns of his new military rank, a large cross and a field-marshal's *bâton*, upon the shoulder-plates. He sat at the top of the table, with the Chief at his right and Abeken at his left. After soup, we spoke first of the subject that I had been that morning preparing for the press, namely, that according to a communication from Israel, the secretary of Laurier, the provisional government's London agent, Gambetta no longer believes in a successful defence, and is inclined to make peace upon our conditions; that Trochu alone of the present rulers of France wants to go on fighting, and that the others pledged themselves, when he undertook the conduct of the defence of Paris, to act always in harmony with him. On that point the Chief remarked, "He is said to have provisioned Mont Valérien for two months.

so as to retire there with the regular troops who stay by him, when the city is given up, probably in order to influence the settlement of the terms of peace. I believe for my own part," he continued, " that France will in future break up into several fragments. It is broken up into parties already. In the different districts people are of very different parties. They are Legitimists in Brittany, Red Republicans in the South, Moderates elsewhere, and the regular army is still attached to the Emperor, at least the majority of the officers are. Each of these parts of France may follow its own convictions: one Republican, one for the Bourbons, one where the Orleanists have most supporters, and Napoleon's people—tetrarchies of Judea, Galilee, and so forth."

The Crown Prince said that it was believed that Paris must have underground communication with the outside world. The Chief supposed that it must be so, and said, "They can't get provisions in that way, but they might get news. I have already thought whether we could not fill up the sewers with water from the Seine, and so flood at least the lower-lying quarters of the city. These sewers go right under the Seine." Bucher confirmed this statement, and said that he had been in the sewers and had noticed their side entrances at different points, where nobody, however, was permitted to go. Somebody said that if Paris were now taken it would have an effect upon opinion in Bavaria, the accounts from which were again not quite satisfactory. The Chief said, "The King remains always the most thorough-going German in these exalted regions." The conversation then turned on another princely personage, who was described as very hostile to Prussia, but is too old and frail to be very dangerous. "There is very little that is natural left in him," somebody said. "That reminds me of Gr——," said the Minister, "who had pretty much everything about him false—his hair, his teeth, his calves, and one of his eyes. When he wanted to dress in the morning, the larger and the better half of him lay round his bed on chairs and tables. It was like the picture of the newly-married man in the 'Fliegende Blätter,' whose bride, when she undressed, put her hair in one corner, her teeth in another, and other parts of her elsewhere, and the bridegroom asked, 'But what is there left for me?'"

The Chief went on to tell us that the sentry at the house of the person he had been speaking of, who is a Pole, refused, one evening recently, to allow him to go into the house, and it was only when he made himself understood in Polish that the man was persuaded to do so. "In the hospital," he added, "I tried, a couple of days since, to talk with the Polish soldiers, and they seemed quite to brighten up when they heard a general using their native tongue. It was a pity that I could not go on, and had to leave. Perhaps it would be well if their commander could talk to them."

"Ah, Bismarck, you are going to attack me again on that point, as you have done several times before," said the Crown Prince, smiling. "No, I really cannot do it; I am not going to learn any more languages."

"But they are really good soldiers, your Royal Highness," replied the Chancellor, "and brave fellows, only the majority of the priests' party are against us, as well as the aristocracy and their retainers, and those who hang on to them. A nobleman, who is nobody himself, maintains a whole crowd of persons and servants of all kinds, who have nothing particular to do, but who act as his house-servants, stewards, writers, and so forth. If he is inclined to rebel, he has these fellows on his side, as well as his day-labourers, the

Komorniks. The free peasants do not go with him, even when the priest, who is always against us, stirs them up. We saw that in Posen, too, where the Polish regiments had to be withdrawn, solely because they were too rough with their own country people. I remember not far from our place in Pomerania, there was a market where many Kassuben* had established themselves. There was a fight there once, because a German had said to a Kassube that he would not sell him a cow because he was a Pole. The other took this very ill. 'You say I am a Polack,' he said; 'No, I am a Prussack, like yourself.' A famous cudgelling ensued, other Germans and Poles mixing themselves up in the affair."

In this connection, the Chief added that the Great Elector was able to speak Polish quite as well as German, and that the later kings had also understood Polish. Frederick the Great was the first who had not taken the trouble to do so, but he had understood French even better than German. "I don't deny that, but I am not going to learn Polish. Let them learn German," said the Crown Prince, and the subject dropped.

Excellent new dishes every now and then came in, and the Crown Prince remarked, "You are really *gourmets* here. How well fed the gentlemen in your office look! all but Bucher, who has not been here so long." "Yes," said the Chief, "it all comes from love offerings. These contributions of Rhine wine and pasties, and smoked goose-breast, and goose-liver, are a speciality of the Foreign Office. Our people are quite determined to fatten their Chancellor."

* A tribe of Wends in East Prussia, near Cöslin, on the Lieber and the Baltic, who are almost entirely distinct from the Germans, who maintain their own customs and language, and whose preachers address them both in German and in their native tongue.

At this point the Crown Prince turned the conversation round to ciphering and deciphering, and asked whether it was difficult. The Minister explained to him the trick of it in detail, and went on to say, "If, for instance, I want to cipher the word 'but' ('*aber*'), I write down the group of numbers for Abeken, and after that the group signifying 'Strike out the two last syllables." Then I put the cipher for Berlin, and tell the writer again to strike out the last syllable. Thus I get 'aber.'"

At dessert the Crown Prince brought out of his pocket a short tobacco-pipe, with a porcelain bowl with an eagle on it, and lighted up, whilst the rest of us lighted our cigars.

After dinner, the Crown Prince and the Minister went into the drawing-room for coffee with the Councillors. After a while we, viz. myself and the secretaries, were brought out of the office by Abeken, to be officially presented to the future Emperor by the Chief. We were kept waiting perhaps a quarter of an hour, as the Chancellor had got deep into conversation with the Crown Prince. His distinguished guest sat there in the corner, between Madame Jessé's cottage piano and one of the windows, and the Chief spoke low to him, for the most part keeping his eyes down, while the Crown Prince listened with an earnest and almost gloomy expression. In the presentation Wollmann came first, and the Crown Prince remarked to him that he knew his handwriting. Then I came; the Chief introducing me as Dr. Busch, for the Press. The Crown Prince: "How long have you been in the service of the State?" "Since February, your Royal Highness." The Chief: "Dr. Busch is a Saxon —a Dresdener." The Crown Prince said, "Dresden is a fine city; I always liked to go there. What was your previous occupation?" I answered that I had been editor of the *Grenzboten*. "I have often read it, so that I know you," he replied. And then I had also been a great traveller, I told him. "Where have you been?" he asked. "I have been in America, and three times in the East," I answered. "Did you like it?—should you like to go back again?" "Oh yes, your Royal Highness, especially to Egypt." "Yes, I understand; I myself had a great desire to go back there. The colours in Egypt are splendid; but our German meadows and woods are far dearer to me." He then presented Blanquart; then Willisch, and finally Wiehr, who mentioned to him, among other things, that he had studied music for several years under Marx. Wollmann says that he was formerly a music-teacher, after which he became a rifleman, in which capacity he had come forward at the time the attempt of Sefelog on the life of the former King had been baffled. Then he was employed as telegraphist in the Foreign Office, and when there was no more direct telegraphing to do, as copyist and decipherer.

After the presentation, I read over in the Bureau the diplomatic reports and minutes of the last few days: the minute, for instance, on the King's speech to the deputation from the Reichstag, which was drawn by Abeken, and very much altered by the Chief. At tea Hatzfeld told me that he had been trying to decipher an account of the condition of Paris, which had come out with Washburne's messages, and that he was doubtful only about a few expressions. He then showed it me, and by our united efforts we managed to make out the sense of some of them. It appeared to be based throughout upon excellent information and to be in conformity with the facts. According to it, the smaller tradesmen are suffering severely, but the people below them not very much, as they are looked after by the Government. There is great want of firing, especially of coals. Gas is no longer burned. In the last sorties the French suffered considerable loss, but their spirit is not yet broken. Our victory at Orleans has produced no marked impression upon the Parisians.

I was called to the Chief about half-past ten. He wanted an account of Gambetta's being disposed to give in, and of Trochu's plan about Mont Valérien, to be inserted in the *Moniteur*.

*Wednesday, December* 21.—In the morning I again looked for violets, and found some. Then I turned over the recent publications. Afterwards I read a tract which I found among them, of the treaty between Charles the Bald and Louis the German, at the time of the partition of Lothringen, in the year 870, exactly a thousand years ago, establishing the first Franco-German boundary. I made extracts from it for the press.

In the afternoon the Chief rode out, and I took a walk with Wollmann. There was a keen cold wind, and several degrees of frost. We wanted to go to the garden of the château, but the railings in front of the reservoir of Neptune were closed, and the sentry at the post near the chapel would not let us pass through. We learned that a domiciliary visitation was being made in the town. We were told, also, that a search was being pursued for hidden weapons, and some said for certain persons who had managed to get into the town with the intention of making a dash at us, which is hardly credible.

We take a turn accordingly through the streets. The sailors are drawn up on the Avenue de Saint-Cloud, and we notice our Chief talking to their commander. In the Rue de la Pompe, on the right hand, infantry posts are planted before every house, and in the Place Hoche a company of dragoons is stationed. All the roads out of the town are barred. We see men in blouses arrested, and a gunsmith in the Avenue de Paris, behind whom a soldier is carrying a number of fowling-pieces. A priest is also marched in. Lastly, about a dozen guilty or suspected persons are brought in together, and taken across to the prison in the Rue Saint-Pierre, where they are ranged in the courtyard. There are some very desperate-looking fellows among them. It is said that forty-three fowling-pieces were found in the gunsmith's shop, and a gun-barrel, which he had most likely not come by in a good way.*

At table Dr. Lauer was the Chief's guest. We talked about the report that in Paris the people had already swallowed all the eatable animals in the Jardin des Plantes, and Hatzfeld told us that the camels had been sold for four thousand francs (one hundred and sixty pounds) each, that the elephant's trunk had been eaten by a company of gourmands, and that it made an admirable dish. "Ah," said Lauer, "that is very likely; it is a mass of muscles woven together, which accounts for its flexibility and for the force with which it can apply it. It is something like the tongue, and must taste like a tongue." Somebody remarked that the camels' humps were probably not bad either, and another said that the humps were a great delicacy. The Chief listened to him for a while, and then said, thoughtfully, first a little stooping, then taking a long breath and lifting himself up as he usually does when he is joking, "H'm! The hump-backed men, what about their humps?" Loud and universal laughter interrupted him. Lauer remarked, dryly and scientifically, that men's humps were due to a perversion of ribs or bones, or a sort of curvature of the vertebral column, so that they could not be very good for eating, whereas camels' humps were flexible growths of cartilage, which possibly might not

* The man's name was Listray, and as probably only concealment of weapons could be proved against him, he got off tolerably easily. He was only compelled to take an involuntary journey into Germany.

taste badly. This thread was spun out a little longer, and we talked of bear's flesh, then of bear's paws, and, lastly, of the gourmands among the cannibals, about whom the Minister wanted to tell a pleasant story. He began: "A child, a fresh young maiden, certainly, but an old grown-up tough fellow cannot be good for eating." Then he went on: "I remember an old Kaffir, or Hottentot woman, who had long been a Christian. When the missionary was preparing her for her death, and found her quite ready for glory, he asked her whether there was anything she particularly wished. 'No,' she said; 'everything was quite comfortable with her; but if anybody could oblige her with a pair of a young child's hands for eating, she would regard them as a great delicacy.'"

We then talked about sleeping, about to-day's domiciliary visit, and about the sailors whom we met yesterday. The Chief said, that if they could have brought the captured gunboats into the Seine, great services might have been expected of them. He then began to speak once more of the recollections of his youth, again mentioning the cowherd Brand, and telling us about an ancestor of his, who, if I understood him rightly, had fallen at Czaslen. "The old people near us," he said, "had often described him to my father. He was a mighty hunter before the Lord, and a heavy drinker. Once, in a single year, he shot 154 red deer; after which Prince Frederick Charles will scarcely come up to him, though the Duke of Dessau may. I remember how I was told things went in Gollnow, where the officers ate together, and the colonel managed the cooking. It was the fashion there for five or six dragoons to march up and down in a sort of chorus, and fire their carbines when the toasts were given. People certainly went on curiously in those days. For instance, instead of riding on a rail they had a wooden donkey with a sharp back, on which dragoons against whom any fault had been proved had to sit, often a couple of hours together—a very painful punishment. Every now and then, on the birthday of the colonel and of some others, they took this donkey out to the bridge and pitched him over it; but there was always a new one made. They had had a new one about a hundred times over. The burgomaster's wife (I could not quite make out what her name was, but it sounded like Dalmer) told my father . . . I have the portrait of this ancestor of mine in Berlin. I am supposed to be his very image, at least I was when I was young, so much so that when I looked upon him it was like looking at my own face in the glass."

We went on in this way about old stories and people, and ultimately agreed that many fashions of old days had come down to the present time, especially among folks in the country districts. Somebody spoke of the children's song, "*Flieg, Mai-Käfer, flieg!*" ("Fly away, maybug") which, along with the *abgebrannten Pommerland* (fire-ravaged Pomerania), recalled to one the Thirty Years' War. "Yes," said the Chief, "I know that expressions used to be common with us which manifestly took us back to the beginning of last century. When I had ridden well, my father said to me, 'He is just like' (the name was not quite distinct, but sounded like Pluvenel). At that time he always said 'He' in speaking to me. Pluvenel was a master of the horse of Louis XIV., and a famous rider. When I had ridden he also said sometimes, 'He really rides as if he had learned it at Hilmar Cura's,' who had been riding-master to Frederick the Great."

He went on to say that it was owing to a relation of his, whose opinion had great weight with his parents, Finance-Councillor Kerl, that he studied in Göttingen. He was sent there to Professor Hausmann, and was to work at mineralogy. "People at that time thought a good deal of Leopold von Buch, and fancied themselves going about through the world like him, chipping off bits of rocks with a hammer. Nothing of the sort happened with me. It would have been better if they had sent me to Bonn, where I should have met young men from my own district. In Göttingen there was nobody from Pomerania, so that I never came across some of my university friends again until I met them in the Reichstag." Somebody then mentioned one of them, Miers, from Hamburg, and the Minister said, "Yes, I remember, he was left-handed, but he was not good for much."

Abeken told us that a sortie of the garrison of Paris had taken place after the lively cannonade from the forts which we had heard in the morning, and that it had been directed especially against the lines occupied by the Guard. It had, however, resulted almost entirely in an artillery skirmish, and the attack had been known beforehand, and prepared for. Hatzfeld remarked that he would like to know how they managed to foresee a sortie. He was told that it must take place in open ground, that one could see the waggons and the guns which had to be brought out, that for any movement of great masses of troops nothing could be arranged in a single night. "That is true," said the Chief, smiling, "but a hundred louis d'or are often an essential part of our military previsions."

After dinner I read minutes and despatches. In the evening I suggested to L. to write an article for the *Indépendance Belge* upon the Gambetta-Trochu subject. He was also informed that Delbrück would come back here on the 28th.

*Thursday, December* 22.—It is very cold, certainly, perhaps fourteen degrees of frost. The ice flowers are all over my window pane in spite of the quantity of logs in my fireplace. In the morning, early, I studied my sketches and minutes, and then looked through the newspapers. The article upon the Black Sea question, and that defending the Luxemburg people against the complaint the Chief had made against them because of their support of the French, were of especial interest. There was a good deal said of the eclipse of the sun, which was to begin about half-past one. Abeken did me the honour to present me with the photograph of the Councillors and the secretaries, which is not very good, and the gentlemen propose accordingly to be taken over again, when I mean to go with them.

There was no stranger at table to-day. The Chief was in an excellent humour, but the conversation had no special significance. I may however indicate what I remember of it. Who knows to whom it may be agreeable? First the Minister said, smiling, and looking at the *menu* lying before him, "There is always a dish too much. I had already decided to ruin my stomach with goose and olives, and here is Reinfeld ham, of which I cannot help taking too much, merely because I want to get my own share,"—he had not been to breakfast. "And here is Varzin wild boar, too." Somebody mentioned yesterday's sortie, and the Chief remarked, "The French came out yesterday with three divisions, and we had only fifteen companies, and not four complete battalions, and yet we made almost a thousand prisoners. The persons who make these attacks, here one time and there another, seem to me like a French dancing-master, who is leading a quadrille, and shouting to his pupils, now 'Right!' now 'Left!'

"'Ma commère, quand je danse,
   Mon cotillon va-t-il bien?
Il va de ci, il va de là,
   Comme la queue de notre chat.'"

During the course of ham he said, "Pomerania is the land of smoked provisions: smoked goose-breast, smoked eels, and smoked ham. They only want nagelholt, as they have it in Westphalia, to make smoked beef. The name, however, does not explain itself very clearly—nails, I mean, on which things hang while they are being smoked, but the 'holt,' perhaps, ought to be written with a *d.*" Then we talked about the cold, and, when the wild boar came on the table, of a wild boar hunt which had taken place at Varzin during Count Herbert's illness at Bonn. Afterwards the Chief remarked, "That Antonelli should, after all, be making ready for a journey, and should be coming here must be quite bewildering to many people." Abeken remarked, "Antonelli has been very variously estimated in the newspapers; sometimes as a man of lofty and distinguished intellect, sometimes as a crafty intriguer, sometimes merely as a stupid fellow or a blockhead." "Yes," said the Chancellor; "but that is not done in the newspapers only; it is the same with the judgment of many diplomatists—Goltz, for instance, and our Harry. I shall say no more of Goltz; he was not that kind of man; but for ——, he is this way to-day and that way to-morrow. When I was at Varzin, and had to read his reports from Rome, his opinion about the people there changed twice every other week, according as they had been treating him in a friendly way or the reverse. Indeed, he changed with every post, and frequently he had different views in the same letter."

In the evening I read despatches from Rome, London, and Constantinople, and the answers to them.

*Friday, December* 23.—Another very cold day. People speak of twenty-two degrees of frost. The paragraph in the *Situation*, which makes the Empress Eugénie see reason to conclude peace with us, was sent to the editor of the

*Moniteur*. An article of the *Times*, about Luxemburg, defining our position, was forwarded to Germany. The beginning of Treitschke's pamphlet in the *Preussische Jahrbücher* was prepared for the King's reading. The article in the *Situation* is dated November 17, and is as follows: "Yes, we ask the reigning Empress to negotiate peace with Prussia; and we ask Prussia to negotiate with the reigning Empress. From the moment when the distinguished lady expresses her desire to put an end to the effusion of blood, King William will owe it to his own dignity to take a step to meet her, and neither the originators of war to the bitter end, nor the different pretenders each of whom wants to utilise the misfortunes of his country to set a crown on his own head, could expect him to do so to meet them.

"The Empress need not ask herself whether her idea is really an expression of the mind of France. Let her speak, and she will see that France never misunderstands heroic sentiments. As for the Prussian Government, it is not necessary for us that it should wish the return of the Napoleonic dynasty; it only needs to see that the greatest mistake it could commit would be not to promote an alliance between itself and a dynasty the destruction of which it can never contemplate if it reflects seriously on its own real interests. To mutilate us would be to kill it, and it cannot consent to mutilate us if by its doing so no power would be left in France strong enough not to be liable to be compelled to violate even its own solemn pledges. The Empire alone can relieve Germany, making it unnecessary for her to conquer the whole country, and permitting her to moderate her claims for a rectification of territory, because only the Empire can discuss with France those serious alterations in the map of Europe which the attitude of the neutrals renders indispensable, both for the repose of Germany and for the restoration of France."

About breakfast time a French lady, whose husband has been detected in treacherous relations with a band of Francs-tireurs in the Ardennes, and been condemned to death for it, is announced as waiting for the Chief. She is going to beg his life, and the Chief is to procure it for her. He will not see her, since, as he sends her word, the matter is not in his province. She must go to the War Minister. She goes off to him, but Wollmann believes that she will get there too late, as Colonel Krohn had received an order on the 14th to let justice take its course.*

In a cutting cold wind Wollmann and I drove out in the afternoon, while vigorous firing was going on in the North, in Rothschild's little coach, to the Villa Coublay, which lies on the road which brought us here from Ferrières, and where the park of artillery destined for the bombardment of the south side of Paris is collected. There were about eighty cannon, and nearly a dozen mortars, arranged in four long rows. I had pictured these instruments of destruction to myself as something frightful to look at. Somebody noticed clouds ascending in the north—perhaps the smoke of cannon firing, possibly only from factory chimneys.

When I got back I discovered, on reading over the newspapers, that one of the English reporters had already described this siege park quite accurately in his journal, and I marked the article for the Chief. Hatzfeld handed it to him, probably for forwarding to the general staff.

* This was a mistake. The letter may have gone off, but the person concerned, the notary Tharel, from Rocroy, in the Department of the Ardennes, was banished to Germany. In June 1871 he was still in Verden, where he was liberated shortly afterwards on the application of the French Government.

At dinner our guests were Baron and Deputy von Schwarz-Koppen, and my old Hannoverian acquaintance, Herr von Pfuel, who had in the meantime become district chief at Celle. They were both to be appointed to prefectures, or something of that sort. Afterwards Count Lehndorf, and an uncommonly handsome man, von Dönhoff, a lieutenant of hussars, who, if I am not mistaken, was an adjutant of Prince Albrecht's. To-day's *menu* may be given as a proof that our table was excellently supplied at Versailles. It included onion soup (with port wine), a haunch of wild boar (with Tivoli beer), Irish stew, roast turkey, chestnuts (with champagne and red wine, according to choice), and a dessert of excellent Caville apples and magnificent pears.

We were informed that General von Voigts-Rhetz had appeared before Tours, the population of which having offered resistance, he had been compelled to fire grenades at the town. The Chief remarked: "It is not as it should be, if he stopped firing as soon as they showed the white flag. I would have gone on firing grenades into the town till they had sent me out 400 hostages." He again expressed himself severely about the mild treatment that officers gave civilians who resisted. Even notorious treason is frequently not suitably punished, so that the French think they can venture to do anything against us. "That is how Krohn behaves," he went on. "He first charges an advocate with conspiracy with Francs-tireurs, and after seeing that he is condemned to death, he sends us one petition for pardon after another, instead of shooting him, and at last—though he gets the credit of being an energetic officer—he makes no difficulty about sending the man's wife on to me with a safe-conduct round her neck."

From this foolish indulgence the conversation turned to Unger, the chief of the general staff who had been sent home, his mind having given way. He usually sits quiet, brooding on vacancy, occasionally, however, bursting out into loud sobbing. "Yes," sighed the Chief, "the chief of the general staff is a sorely harassed man. He is incessantly at work, and always responsible; he can carry nothing through; he is perpetually cheated; it is almost as bad as being a Minister." "I know, myself, what that sobbing is," he said; "a nervous hysteria, a sort of feverish convulsion. I had it once at Inkolsburg, so badly that my gorge rose. If a chief of the general staff has a bad time, so has a Minister—every kind of vexation, gnat stings without end. The other office may suit some people, but good management is absolutely indispensable."

When the haunch of wild-boar from Varzin was set on the table the Minister talked with Lehndorf and Pfuel about hunting, about these denizens of the woods and marshes, and about his own exploits in the sport. Afterwards somebody mentioned the *Moniteur*, which appears here, and the Chief remarked, "During the last few weeks they have been printing in it a novel by Heyse about Meran (a watering-place in Austria). Such sentimental business is out of place in a paper which is published with the King's money, as this really is. The Versaillese don't want it. They want political reports and military news from France and England, —and I should like to see some from Italy—not this sugary-tasted tittle-tattle. I have some poetry in my nature, too, but I don't remember ever glancing at this *feuilleton* after I read the first couple of sentences." Abeken, who had induced them to publish the novel, stood up for the editors, and said that it had been taken from the *Revue des deux Mondes*, which was an eminent French paper, but the Chief adhered to his opinion. Somebody then said that the *Moniteur* was now writing better French. "That may be," said the Minister; "I don't care much about it. It is the way, however, with us Germans. We are always, even in the highest circles, asking whether we are pleasant and agreeable to other people. If they don't understand it, let them learn German. It is a matter of indifference whether a proclamation is drawn up in an elegant French style, so long as it speaks adequately and intelligibly. We can never be quite perfect in a foreign language. It is impossible that a person who uses it only now and then during, perhaps, two years and a half, should be able to express himself as well in it as one who has been using it for fifty-four." Somebody ironically praised Steinmetz's proclamation, and quoted some remarkable specimens of language from it. Lehndorf said, "It was certainly not elegant French, but it was quite intelligible." The Chief, "Yes, understanding it is what they have to do with it. If they can't, let them get somebody to translate it for them."

"Many people who are quite familiar with French are no good for us. It is our misfortune that anyone who cannot speak German decently is at once a made man, especially if he mangles English. The old man (I understood him to mean Meyendorff) once said to me, 'Never trust an Englishman who speaks French with a correct accent,' and I have found that generally right. But I ought to except Odo Russell."

He then told the story how old Knesebeck once, to everybody's astonishment, got up to say something in the State Council. After he had stood there a while, without saying anything, somebody coughed. "I beg," he said, "that you will not interrupt me," after which, and after standing another couple of minutes, he said, in a sorrowful way, "I have really forgotten what I had to say." and sat down.

The conversation turned on the subject of Napoleon III.

and the Chief said he was not a man of large views. "He is," he went on, "a far kindlier man than he usually gets credit for, but nothing like the clever fellow he used to be thought." "That reminds me," said Lehndorf, "of a criticism of the First Napoleon—a good fellow, but stupid." "No," said the Chief, seriously, "in spite of what we may think about the *coup d'état*, he is really kindly, a man of feeling, even sentimental; but neither his intelligence nor his information is much to speak of. He is especially poor in geography, though he was brought up in Germany and went to school there, and he lives in a world of all sorts of fantastic ideas. In July he kept buzzing round and round for three days without being able to decide on anything, and even now he does not know what he wants. His knowledge is of that sort that he would certainly be plucked in an examination for admission to the bar. Nobody would believe it when I said so, long ago. So far back as 1854 and 1855 I told the King so. He has absolutely no idea how things are in Germany. When I was Minister, I had an interview with him in Paris. He then said that things could not go on long as they were doing, that there would be a rising in Berlin, and a revolution in the whole country, and that the King would have everybody voting against him in a plebiscite. I told him that the people in our country were not barricade-builders, and that in Prussia revolutions were only made by the kings. If the King could stand the strain on him for three or four years, and I allowed that there was one—the estrangement of the public being very painful and disagreeable to him—he would certainly win his game. Unless he got tired and left me in the lurch, I would not fail him. If we were to appeal to the people, and put it to the vote, he would even now have nine-tenths of them in his favour. The Emperor, at the time, said of me, ' *Ce n'est pas un homme sérieux*' ("He is not a man of consequence")—a *mot* of which I did not think myself at liberty to remind him in the weaving-shed at Donchery."

Count Lehndorf asked if we need be in any apprehension about Bebel's and Liebknecht's imprisonment, and whether it would cause much excitement. "No," said the Chief, "there is nothing to be afraid of." Lehndorf said, "But Jacoby's case caused great disturbance and lamentation." The Chief said, "He was a Jew, and a Königsberg man. Touch a Jew, and a howl is raised in every nook and corner of the earth—or a freemason. Besides, they interfered in a public meeting, which they had no right to do." He spoke of the Königsberg people as always quarrelsome, and inclined to go into opposition, and Lehndorf said, "Yes, indeed, Manteuffel understood Königsberg well when he said in his address, ' Königsberg continues to be—Königsberg.'"

Somebody remarked that people began letters to Favre with "Monsieur le Ministre," and the Chief said, "Next time I must address him as ' Hochwohlgeborner Herr' (' Right Honourable Sir ')." Out of that grew a long Byzantine discussion about titles of honour, and the expressions, Excellency, Right Honourable, and Honourable. The Chancellor's views and opinions were decidedly anti-Byzantine. "We ought to give up the whole thing," he said. "In private letters I never use them at all now, and officially I call councillors down to the third class, Right Honourables."

Pfuel remarked that in legal documents also these high-sounding addresses were omitted. "You are to appear on such a day at such a place." "Neither are these legal addresses quite my ideal. A trifle would make them perfect. They should say, ' You are to appear, you scoundrel, on such a day at such a place.'"

Abeken, who is a Byzantine of the purest water, said that it had been already taken very ill in diplomatic circles that people sometimes were not given their proper titles, and that "Right Honourable Sir" was not proper below Councillors of the second class. "And lieutenants," cried Count Bismarck-Bohlen. "I shall quite do away with it among our people," said the Minister; "there is an ocean of ink wasted over it annually; and the taxpayer is justly entitled to complain of the extravagance. I am quite content when I am addressed simply as the Minister-President Count von Bismarck. I beg you," turning to Abeken, "to draw up a proposition on the subject for me. It is a useless pigtail, and I wish it to be dropped." Abeken the cutter-off of pigtails—what a dispensation!

In the evening I wrote another article on the perversion of the words which the King addressed to French non-combatants at the beginning of the war. The army order from Homburg also is now brought forward to show that he has not kept his word; and it is not merely the French but their good friends the Social Democrats in Germany who are circulating these slanders. In the first week of the present month, for instance, a meeting of the Workmen's Union in Vienna passed a resolution charging the King with a breach of his word of honour on the strength of these misrepresentations. But neither the army order from Homburg (dated July 8) nor the proclamation (dated on the 11th) contains any pledge to make war only against French soldiers. In the former document are the words, "We make no war upon the peaceable inhabitants of the country." The emphasis is on the word peaceable. But Francs-tireurs and all who support them or actively resist our operations in that or in any other way, are not peaceable inhabitants. And in the proclamation it is expressly stated that "the generals in command of separate corps will specify the measures, of which further notification will be given, which are to be taken both against communes and individuals who set themselves in opposition to the usages of war. They will also regulate everything referring to requisitions for what may be thought necessary to supply the wants of the troops." These notices were acted upon. The French certainly had no right to complain of the severity of the Germans. We never banished persons domiciled amongst us as they did, hunting them for no reasonable excuse out of house and home, into misery. We threw no crews of captured merchant ships into our prisons. We destroyed no private property except what was capable of doing us harm, and the Geneva Convention was nowhere broken by us as it was by them. It was perfectly regular, and it was not in contradiction to our promises, for us to use measures of constraint with recalcitrant localities, or to make reprisals to prevent further outrages against humanity and public rights. It is under this head of complaint that we are charged with throwing shells recently into Tours—but the inhabitants had received us with hostility—and with breaking down the railway bridge near the town—a fact which the Chief ordered me to telegraph shortly before midnight. War is war, but now that it comes home to themselves, the French do not seem able to apprehend the fact. They mastered it more rapidly in other countries, as, for instance, in Algiers, in the States of the Church, in China, or in Mexico.

*Saturday, December* 24.—Christmas Eve in this foreign land! It is very cold, as it was both yesterday and the day before. I telegraph that with two divisions Manteuffel yesterday defeated Faidherbe, the general of the French army of the North, which is reckoned at 60,000 men, and compelled him to retreat.

At dinner Lieutenant-Colonel von Beckedorff is the Chief's guest, so old a friend of his that they "thou" each other. On the table stands a miniature Christmas tree, a span high, and beside it a case with two cups, one in the Renaissance style and one of Tula work. They are both presents from the Countess to her husband. Each holds only two good drinks. The Count sent them round the table for inspection, and said, "I am really silly about cups, although there is no sense in such a fancy. As these come from home, if you bring them under my eye when I am away from the country, nothing in the town will trouble me any longer."

Then he said to Beckedorff that his promotion had surely been slow, and added, "Had I been an officer—and I wish I had been—I should have had an army now, and we should not have been stuck here outside Paris."

This remark was followed by further discussion of the conduct of the war, during which the Chief said, "It is sometimes not so much the generals as the soldiers themselves that begin our battles and take direction of them. It was the same with the Trojans and the Greeks. Two combatants launched words of scorn at each other, they came to blows, spears were thrown, others rushed up, who also threw their spears and dealt their blows, and out of all this came a battle. The fore-posts first fire at each other needlessly, others cluster up to them when things are getting brisk, at first a subaltern in command of a few men, then the lieutenant with more, after him the regiment, last of all, the general and his whole army. It was in that way that the battle of Gravelotte came about, which was meant for the 19th. It was different at Vionville. They had to fling themselves on the French lines there as a mastiff flies at a terrier."

Beckedorff then told us how he had been twice wounded at Wörth, once between the neck and the shoulder-blade, certainly he believed, by an explosive bullet, and another time in the knee. He had dropped off his horse on the ground. As he lay there a Zouave or a Turco, leaning against a tree, took deliberate aim at him, and the bullet grazed his head. Another of these half-savages, he said, had thrown himself into a ditch during the flight of the French, and when our men had passed by without finding him, he got out and shot at them from behind. Some of them turned back to run after him, and one of them, as it was impossible to fire on account of our own troops, knocked him down. In that way they mastered and killed him. "There was not the least reason for his firing, for nobody had meddled with him in his ditch," said the narrator; "it was the mere passion for murder."

The Chief recalled other stories of the barbarity of the French, and asked Beckedorff to write his case down for him, and to allow the doctors to examine medically into the evidence about the explosive bullet. Then he began to talk about country life, saying that he was not very fond of hilly country, both because of the usually confined prospect in the valleys, and because of the going up and down hill. "I like the level country better," he said, "though it need not be quite as flat as at Berlin; but little heights, with pretty trees in leaf, and swift, clear brooks, such as we have in Pomerania, and especially on the Baltic coast." From which he diverged to the different Baltic watering-places, mentioning some as extremely agreeable and others as dull.

After dinner I went out for a couple of turns in the

avenue made by the rows of trees before our street. Meanwhile they were getting up their Christmas tree in the dining-room, and Keudell was showering about cigars and ginger-bread. As I came back too late for the festivity, my presents were sent up to my room. I then read, as I do regularly now, all that has been done during the day in the way of minutes and despatches. Afterwards I was called to the Chief twice over, one time immediately after the other, and then a third time. There are to be several articles about the horrible way in which the French are carrying on the war, not merely the Francs-tireurs but the regular troops, who violate the provisions of the Convention of Geneva almost daily, and appear to remember and claim the execution of only so much of it as seems advantageous to the French. I am to dwell on the firing on flags of truce, on the ill-usage and looting of doctors, sick carriers, and hospital assistants, on the killing of the wounded, the misuse of the Geneva band by the Francs-tireurs, the use of explosive bullets (as in Beckedorff's case), the treatment, contrary to the law of nations, of ships and crews of the German merchant navy, captured by French cruisers. I am then to add, that the present Government of France is chargeable with a great deal of the blame of these things. It was they who let loose on us a people's war, and who are now unable to control the passions they have kindled, which carry people beyond all public rights, and all custom of war. On them, therefore, rests the responsibility for all the severity with which we have been compelled to act in France upon our rights as combatants, against our own wishes, and, as the wars in Schleswig and Austria prove, contrary to our natural inclinations.

In the evening, about ten, the Chief receives the Iron Cross of the first class. Abeken and Keudell had been already made happy in the afternoon by the second class of the same Order.

*Sunday, December* 25.—In the morning it is again cold, but Abeken goes notwithstanding to hear sermon in the chapel of the château. Theiss pointed out to us his coat with the cross on it, and said, "The Privy Councillor won't certainly wear his cloak to-day." In the Bureau we learn that Cardinal Bonnechose, from Rouen, proposes to come here. He and Persigny want the summoning of the whole Legislative Body, and, perhaps even more urgently, of the Senate, which is made up of calmer and maturer elements, to deliberate on peace. It appears, moreover, to be certain that people are in earnest about the bombardment of Paris, which will take place in a very few days now. So at least we understand the King's order, just issued, appointing Lieutenant-General von Kameke, at present commanding the 14th Division of Infantry, to the supreme command of the Engineers, and Major-General Prince Hohenlohe-Ingelfingen to the supreme command of the siege artillery.

To-day we had nobody at dinner, and during the conversation almost nothing was said worth noting. I may perhaps mention, that Abeken remarked, I forget now in what connection, that I was keeping a very exact diary. Bohlen confirmed this, and said in his lively way, "Yes, he writes, 'At 3.45, Count, or Baron So-and-so said this or that to me,' as if he expected some day to have to swear to it." Abeken was of opinion that it would one day be a valuab'e source of historical knowledge, and he hoped he might live to read it. I said that it certainly would be, and trustworthy, too, even if it were thirty years before it appeared. The Chief smiled, and said, "Yes, people will then say, 'Cf. Buschii cap. 3, p. 20.'"

After table I read documents, and found in them that the

idea of pushing the boundaries of Germany farther westward was first laid before the King officially on August 14th, at Horny. On September 2, the Government of Baden had sent in a memoir pointing in a similar direction.

*Monday, December* 26.—That on Boxing-day of the year '70, I should be eating genuine Saxon Christmas cake in a private house in Versailles is what I should have refused to credit, if all the twelve minor prophets had told me of it beforehand. Yet this morning I had a large slice of one, a gift from Abeken's liberality. He has received a box with these sorts of baked things from Germany.

Except for indispensable work, to-day was a complete holiday. The weather was not so cold as it had been, but as clear as yesterday. About three there was brisk firing again from the forts. Perhaps they have had a note of the fact, that we are pretty nearly ready to reply to them? Last night they certainly fired fiercely for a while out of their big mouths of thunder.

Waldersee was with us at dinner, and the subjects spoken of were almost wholly military.

At length the conversation turned on the power of drinking a good deal, and the Minister said: "Once I never thought of the amount I was drinking. What things I used to do—the heavy wines, especially the Burgundies!" The conversation then turned on cards, and he said that he used formerly to do a great deal in that way, and that once, for instance, he had played twenty rubbers at whist, one after the other, "equal to seven hours of time." He only took an interest in it when the play was high, but high play was not for the father of a family. The discussion rose out of the Chief's happening to say that he had called somebody a "Riemchenstecher;" and after asking whether any of us understood it, he explained the word as follows:

"Riemchenstechen is an old game of soldiers; and a Riemchenstecher is not exactly a rogue, but a crafty and subtle sort of person."

In the evening I wrote another article on the barbarous way in which the French are carrying on the war, and pre-prepared for his Majesty's perusal a paper in the *Staatsbürger-Zeitung*, which recommends less tender dealing with the French.

## CHAPTER XVI.

#### FIRST WEEKS OF THE BOMBARDMENT.

AT last, at last! On *December* 27 the long-desired bombardment of Paris began on the east side of the city. As what follows will show, we knew nothing at first about it, and even afterwards our fire made an impression of great power only on certain days. One very soon got used to it —it never distracted our attention from trifles, and never long interrupted the course of our talk or the flow of our thoughts. The Diary will tell us more about it in due time.

On Tuesday, from early morning till well into the day there was a heavy snowfall with tolerably hard frost. In the morning the man-servant attached to the Chancellor's office, who attended on Abeken and me, told me about our old privy councillor, whom he evidently considered to be a Catholic: "He reads his prayers in the morning. I believe they are in Latin. He reads them quite loud out, so that I hear them often in the ante-room. Probably it is the Mass." He added that Abeken was of opinion that the heavy thundering of cannon which had been going on in the distance since seven o'clock was probably the beginning of the bombardment.

I wrote several letters with instructions for articles. After twelve I telegraphed, by the Chief's command, to London that the bombardment of the outworks of Paris began this morning. Mont Avron, a work near Bondy, seems to be the first point aimed at by our artillery, and the Saxons have had the privilege of firing the first shot. The Minister stays the whole day in bed, not because he is particularly unwell, but, as he says, because he cannot keep himself reasonably warm in any other way. He did not come to dinner. Count Solms dined with us. The only thing to note in the conversation was that Abeken said that there was a very good poem on the Duke of Coburg in *Kladderadatsch*—probably a eulogy.

The Bonapartists appear to have become very active and to have great plans. Persigny and Palikao want us to neutralise Orleans, to let the Corps Législatif be summoned there, to put the question to it, Whether it wishes a Republic or a Monarchy, and if it votes for a monarchy which Dynasty it prefers. We shall wait a little yet before that, till greater dejection makes people even more pliable than at present. Bonnechose, the archbishop of Rouen, wants to make an attempt to negotiate a peace between Germany and France. He was at one time a jurist, and later in life became a clergyman. He is supposed to be an intelligent man, and is on terms with the Jesuits. For himself, he is a Legitimist, though he holds Eugénie in great respect for her piety. He was an eager champion of the Infallibility dogma, and expects to be Pope, and so indeed he has some prospect of being. According to what several people say, he hopes to induce Trochu, with whom he is acquainted, to agree to the surrender of Paris, provided we renounce our territorial claims! In place of making them we might, the archbishop thinks, require that Nice and Savoy should be given back to Victor Emmanuel, and then compel him to restore their territories to the Pope, the Duke of Tuscany, and the King of Naples. Thus we should acquire the credit of being the champions of order and the restorers of right all over Europe. What a comical plan!

The Chief has given orders for the most stringent measures against Nogent-le-Roi, where a surprise by the Francs-tireurs was supported by the population; he has also refused to receive the petition of the mayor and municipality of Châtillon, for a remission of the fine of a million francs, imposed on them because something of the same sort happened there. His principle in both cases is, that the people in the country districts must be made to realise what war is, so as to incline them to think of peace.

I was called to the Chief about eleven. He gave me several Berlin newspaper articles for "my collection" (made by his order, of instances of the barbarous way in which the French carry on the war), and two other papers which are to go to the King.

*Wednesday, December* 28.—A snowfall, and moderate cold. The Chief does not leave his room to-day either. He gives me a letter in French to do what I like with, which "an American" lady had sent him on the 25th December. It says: "Count von Bismarck,—Enjoy the pleasant climate of Versailles as much as you can, Count, for one day you will have to endure the flames of hell for all the misfortunes you have caused France and Germany." That is all. It is not easy to see the lady's object in writing the letter.

At breakfast, his Excellency Delbrück is again with us. He is convinced that the Second Bavarian Chamber will ultimately adopt the Versailles Convention just as completely as the North German Reichstag did. Before their final decision he had really had some very anxious days.

The French papers make out that nearly every German soldier is uncertain about the duties imposed on him by the eighth commandment. According to a notice issued by the prefect of the Department of the Seine and Oise, there must be exceptions, and very splendid exceptions, even to this rule. It says: "The public is informed that the following objects have been found by the soldiers of the German army: (1) In the house of the notary Maingot, at Thyais, which is now standing empty, at the corner of the street leading to Versailles and to Grignon, a packet containing aluables estimated at 100,000 francs (£4,000). (2) At Choisy-le-Roi, in a house in the Rue de la Raffinerie, No. 29, deserted by one of the inhabitants, a packet with valuable papers. (3) On the road from Palaiseau to Versailles a purse of money with ten Prussian thalers (thirty shillings), and several small French and German coins. (4) In the deserted house of M. Simon, at Ablon, two packets with nearly 3000 francs in them. (5) In the garden of M. Duhuy, adjunct at Athis, a box with railway shares and other valuable papers. (6) In the deserted house of M. Dufossé, at Choisy-le-Roi, Rue de Villiers, No. 12, papers of the value of 7000 francs. (7) In the convent at Hay 11,000 francs worth of valuable papers. (8) In a house deserted by its owner, on the bank of the Seine, at Saint-Cloud, a packet with valuable papers. (9) In a deserted house at Brunoy a small mantelpiece clock." (A kind of thing which, according to the assertions of the French journals, we are particularly fond of packing up and carrying away with us.) "(10) In the garden of the house near the church, at the corner of the street between Villeneuve-le-Roi and the churchyard of Orly, several articles of jewellery of antique and of modern workmanship. (11) In the garden near the conservatory of the Château Rouge, at Fresnes-les-Rungis, a milk-pail containing articles in gold and silver, drafts payable to bearer, and other things."

*Thursday, December* 29.—Much snow, and not much cold. The Minister remains in bed as he did yesterday, but continues to work, and there does not seem to be very much wrong with him. He tells me to telegraph that the First Army, in pursuit of Faidherbe, has pushed forward to Bapaume, and that Mont Avron, which was under fire yesterday—thirty or forty guns were employed in bombarding it—has ceased to reply. At breakfast we learn that the Saxon artillery had four men killed and nineteen wounded during yesterday and the day before.

In the afternoon Granville's despatch to Loftus about the Bismarck circular on the Luxemburg affair was translated for the King. I then studied official documents. About the middle of October a memorial was sent from Coburg to the Chief, proposing a new constitution for Germany. Among its suggestions is one pointing to the restoration of the dignity of Emperor, and to the ultimate substitution for the Confederation Council of Confederation Ministries, and the creation of a United Council of the Empire out of representatives of the Governments and delegates from the district Parliaments. The Chief answered that it had long been contemplated to carry out one of the ideas involved in these proposals. He must guard himself against the suggestion about Confederation Ministries and the Council of the Empire, as he considered that it might stand in the way of any other new arrangements. . . . From Brussels we are informed that the King of the Belgians is well disposed to us, but that he sees no way of interfering with the press in his own country, which is hostile to Germany. The Grand Duke of Hesse has gone so far as to say that Elsass and Lothringen must become Prussian provinces. Dalwigk, on the other hand, who is as much against us as ever, wants the provinces which are to be taken from France to be incorporated with Baden, which could give the district of Heidelberg and Mannheim to Bavaria, so as to restore the connection with the Palatinate on the left bank of the

Rhine. In Rome the Pope will undertake "mediation" between us and France.

In the evening I gave Bucher, for action on the subject, my collection of newspaper accounts of the inhuman way in which the French are carrying on the war contrary to the laws of nations. About ten the Minister sent for me. He was lying on a sofa before the fire, covered with a blanket. He said, "Well, we have it." "What, your Excellency?" "Mont Avron." He then showed me a letter from Count Waldersee, to say that the fort was occupied this afternoon by the troops of the Twelfth Army Corps, who had found there numerous gun-carriages, rifles, and munitions of war, and many dead bodies. The Minister said, "I hope there is no mine there to blow up the poor Saxons." I forwarded the account of this first success by telegraph to London, in cipher, for fear the general staff might take offence.

Afterwards the Chancellor sent for me again, to show me a paper in the *Kölnische Zeitung*, reproducing an article from the Vienna *Tageblatt*, in which it was said that Bismarck had been completely wrong about the French capacity for resistance, and, in consequence of this over-confidence, to which hundreds of thousands of men (they might as well have said millions) had been sacrificed, he had advanced demands far too extravagant as conditions of peace. The answer on our side was, that nobody could tell the Chancellor's peace conditions, as he had not yet had any opportunity to formulate them officially, but that they were certainly not so exacting as those of public opinion in Germany, which was almost unanimous in demanding back the whole of Lothringen. Neither could anybody be sure of his views as to the capacity of Paris for resistance, as he had never had an opportunity to state them either.

Firing, several times renewed, was carried on all day from

heavy ordnance, and also through the night up till midnight.

*Friday, December* 30.—The bitter cold of the last few days continues. The Chief still keeps his room, on account of illness, and is mostly in bed. In the morning, at his request, I telegraph fresh details about the occupation of Mont Avron, and about the shameful bribe offered, according to official admissions, by the Government of Tours to tempt the captive French officers to break their word of honour. I wrote articles also. for the German press, and one for the *Moniteur* here, on this subject, much as follows:

We have several times taken occasion to point out the depth of degradation in the ideas certain statesmen and officers of the French army entertain on the subject of military honour. A communication which reaches us from a good source, proves that we had not yet realised how deeply this evil is seated, and how widely it has spread. We have before us an official decree issued by the French Ministry of War, from the 5th bureau of the 6th division, and which is headed *Solde et revues*, dated Tours, November 13, and signed by Lieutenant-Colonel Alfred Jerald, and by Colonel Tissier, the chief of the general staff of the 17th army corps. This document, which refers also to another issued on November 10, promises a reward in money to all French officers without exception, who, being now prisoners in Germany, can make their escape. We say without exception—that is, to those officers even who have given their word of honour not to attempt to escape. The bribe offered for such a shameless proceeding is 1750 francs (£70). This fact needs no comment. It will probably excite indignation throughout France. Honour, the most precious possession of every German officer—and, duty and justice compel us to add, in old days of every French officer also—is regarded by the men whom the 4th of September raised to power, as a matter of sale and purchase, and at a very moderate rate too. In this way French officers will be driven to see that France is no longer directed by a Government, but by a business house of loose principles in the matter of honesty and decency, trading under the name of Gambetta and Co. "Who will buy our goods: any words of honour for sale?"

Afterwards I sent off a short article on a mistake which cropped up again in the *Kölnische Zeitung* on the occasion of the despatch sent by the Chancellor to Vienna. The great Rhenish newspaper says: "Since 1866 we have been among those who have incessantly entreated Vienna at one time, and Berlin at another, to be done with their mutual jealousies, which then became meaningless, and to draw as close as possible one to the other. We have often regretted the personal rivalry between Bismarck and Beust, which appeared to be an obstacle to this reconciliation," &c. My answer was: "We have already had occasion repeatedly to notice that the *Kölnische Zeitung* perpetually attributes what the Chancellor does and leaves undone to personal motives, personal likes or dislikes, inclinations, or ill-tempers, and we find here a new proof of this unjustifiable prejudice. We cannot make out how people can keep coming forward continually with such suspicions. We know this, however, that there is no personal rivalry between the Chancellor of the North German Confederation and the Imperial Chancellor of Austro-Hungary; that the two statesmen were on a very good footing with each other before 1866, when they often came into personal relationship, as Count Bismarck has mentioned several times in the North German Reichstag. Since that they have had no private intercourse to create bitterness, for the simple reason that they have had none at all. If they have been hitherto more or less opposed to each other as statesmen, the reason is no secret. They have been the representatives of different political systems, endeavouring to realise different political ideals between which it is not easy to find a point of reconciliation, though it may not be absolutely impossible. This and nothing else is the explanation of what the *Kölnische Zeitung* tries to explain through personal motives, by which no statesman of the present day is less influenced in feeling or action than the Chancellor of the Confederation. Let us take the opportunity to remark that Count Bismarck has never been utterly wrong, as the Rhine paper, echoing the opinion of a Vienna paper, says he has, and that indeed he has never been wrong at all about the resistance of Paris. He was never asked about it, but we know from the best sources that he considered the taking of the city in less than several months a very difficult thing, and that he was against investing it before the fall of Metz."

In the evening I read documents in the Bureau, and among them interesting reports from Bavaria. Afterwards a hint was sent to Elsass that the chief point at present was not to alleviate the misery of the country, or to reconcile the population to their approaching incorporation with Germany, but to secure the object of the war, which is to be attained by a speedy peace, and by looking to the security of the troops. Accordingly, all French officials who will not place themselves at our disposal, and judges who are not willing to act under us, are to be sent into the interior of France. For the same reason, pensioners are not to be paid their pensions. Let them go to Bordeaux, and they will be much more eager for the conclusion of peace.

In the evening at ten I telegraphed the successes of the first army against the Mobiles and the Francs-tireurs. After eleven I was again called to the Chief. Then I corrected a false representation of the situation before Paris, which had appeared in the *Kreuz-Zeitung*. The people there seem to think that we are already bombarding the city. It is a mistake, and this generally well-informed paper is in error through its defective knowledge of the lie of the country round Paris. Our first business is with the forts, which are a good way outside Paris. To try to bombard the town across the forts would be as if somebody on the Müggelsberg had forts of the size and strength of Spandau before him at Köpnik, and on the hills near Spandau, and were to try to bombard Berlin away across these fortifications. We must take the forts first before we can fire into the town. Till that time only the suburbs, or parts of the city which it is no use to fire at, are within the range of our guns.

After tea, when I make my last entries in the diary, till nearly eleven, there is tolerably brisk firing from Mont Valérien or from the gun-boats.

*Saturday, December* 31.—Everybody here is out of sorts. I myself begin to be languid, and will have to cut down the nightwork my diary requires, or to break it off altogether for a couple of days. The severe frost, too, from which the fire protects one only partially, disinclines me to sit up long after midnight, as I have been in the habit of doing.

Gambetta and his colleagues in Bordeaux grow every day more violent in their capacity of dictators. The Empire itself, against the arbitrary action of which they used to protest, was scarcely so despotic, and would hardly have set aside lawful institutions or arrangements as summarily or autocratically as these republicans of the purest water. MM. Crémieux, Gambetta, Glais-Bizoin, and Fourichon, issued a decree on December 25, in which, with reference to previous notices, it is summarily enacted that "the General Councils and Councils of Arrondissement are dissolved, as well as the departmental commissions, where they have been established. For the general councils departmental commissions are to be substituted, which are to consist of as many members as the Department contains cantons, and are to be appointed by the Government on the proposal of the prefect." Where *we* are, naturally nothing of the kind will happen. I send the decree to be printed to the editors of the *Moniteur*.

*Monday, January* 2.—The languor and the cold both continue. The Chief is still unwell. So are Hatzfeld and Bismarck-Bohlen. Gambetta's war, *à outrance*, is to be carried on now with the assistance of a sort of Arabian Francs-tireurs. What will M. de Chaudordy, who recently complained of us as barbarians to the Great Powers, say to the article in which the *Indépendance Algérienne* explains the views these savage hordes entertain of what is permitted in war, or which it tries to inspire in them? Several journals in France itself openly approve, for they have reprinted this absolutely brutal article without a word of remonstrance, and if they can venture to do so, we may assume that they reckon on the approval of their readers. I quote it as an evidence of the boiling heat which passionate hatred has reached in the hearts of a great number of our enemies. This outburst of fury of the African journalist, which many of his French brethren adopt, is as follows:—

"'The moment has come! Let each of our provinces raise ten Gums of 200 men each! They will be commanded by their Cadis and some officers from the Arabian bureaux. As soon as they are ready, these Gums will sail for Lyons, where they will be used as flying sharpshooters and scouts, a service which our light cavalry does not understand.

Their first service will be to annihilate the Uhlans, or at least to frighten them, by cutting off a few heads. In two or three bodies, each of which must be supplied with a few German-speaking officers and subalterns, these brave children of the desert will throw themselves on the Grand Duchy of Baden, where they will burn down all the villages, and set fire to all the woods. It will be easy at present, as the leaves are dry. The Black Forest will light up the Rhine Valley with its flames. The Gums will then push forward into Würtemberg, where they will lay everything waste. The ruin of the countries in alliance with Prussia will doubtless precipitate the defeat and ruin of Prussia herself.

"The Gums carry with them nothing but their cartridges. Wherever they go they will take what they need to live upon. If they starve and suffer thirst for several days they will burn down towns and villages. We shall say to these valiant sons of the prophet, ' We know you, we esteem your courage, we recognise that you are energetic, enterprising, vehement. *Go and cut off their heads; the more heads you cut off the more highly we shall value you.*'

"When the news of the invasion of these Africans is carried into the enemy's country, a universal terror will run through all Germany, and the Prussian armies will rue the day they left their wives and daughters to pay the debts of their fathers and their husbands. Away with pity! Away with feelings of humanity! Neither pity nor mercy for our modern Huns! This burst into Germany is the only thing to raise the siege of Paris. The Gums will rise to the height of their task. It is enough for us to lay the reins loose on their necks, and say to them, '*Murder, pillage, burn!*'"

The writer must be a pleasant person. Agreeable suggestions, especially as French officers are, it is proposed, to lead these savages to the murder, pillaging, and incendiarism they are to commit. And such Gums appear in reality to have already disembarked on French soil, for we saw a notice recently of the fortunate arrival of reinforcements from Africa.

*Tuesday, January* 3.—The idea that the wide dispersion of the German armies over the North and South-West has its dangers, and that concentration is called for finds supporters elsewhere also. The Vienna *Presse*, for instance, has just published a memoir from a military critic, which represents a concentration of our troops at present in France as essential if we want to avoid their being broken in detail, so as to hinder and diminish our offensive power. The author points to a concentration of our troops within a circle of from seventy to ninety miles round Paris. Then the French armies, gathering together from all quarters to raise the siege, would be met and shattered by the whole force of the German armies. Even the gigantic and hitherto uninterrupted streams of force which Germany has sent out, are not sufficient, says our military critic, simultaneously to do all the work which the Germans have undertaken. The wish to accomplish it all at the same time must lead to a dispersion of the army corps full of all kinds of risks, a state of affairs the more serious as long marches in severe winter weather weaken and waste the men. The article accordingly warns us against large-looking military enterprises like advances on Havre and Lyons, and recommends the establishment of entrenched camps at a suitable distance from Paris, and the destruction of the railroads outside the circle of these camps, so that the districts of France in the circumference not yet occupied by us should become incapable of communicating with each other except by shipping.

This renunciation of any farther advance and concentration of the German fighting power is recommended also by the *National Zeitung*, in an article which expresses even better than that I have quoted, the ideas of certain people here in Versailles. It is said there (in the number for December 31) "The evacuation of Dijon and the non-occupation of Tours, to the very gates of which, it is well known that a division of the Tenth Army Corps had advanced, may, perhaps, indicate the views which ought to be decisively adopted on the German side, especially in the case of the war being continued. Perhaps it is not to be expected that France will give up her resistance after the fall of Paris, and accept the German conditions of peace. Certainly, we cannot reckon on it as assured, so that we must be prepared what to do in the opposite event. In any case, there cannot, after the fall of the city, be any regularly recognised Government supported by the representatives of the nation with which conditions of peace can be settled with adequate guarantees of permanence. If the war is to go on, it is impossible that its object can be the complete subjugation of a country so extensive as France. Our armies might be as victorious as ever, and might destroy the fighting power of the enemy, but that would not suffice. We should have to establish a new civil government in every one of the conquered districts, and to see that it was obeyed by the inhabitants. In the strip of country between the Loire and the English Channel our troops are hardly numerous enough now to make intercourse everywhere secure, to sustain the dignity of a foreign administration in every town and village, to guard against assassinations and surprises, and, above all, to collect the taxes, as well as the contributions and levies which are the unavoidable consequences of war. To spread this net out immeasurably farther would overtax our military power, highly as we may think of it; and we at home should find the strain on the strength of our civilian staff which such an attempt would necessitate too considerable. If peace, therefore, is not to be obtained immediately, our military authorities must see clearly what they are aiming at, and resolutely confine themselves to it. They must settle on a well-defined portion of French soil, which they must occupy in such force that we are able to hold it thoroughly in hand, and to keep it under our authority as long as we choose. This portion would include the capital and the best provinces, with the ablest and most warlike populations of France; and it would naturally have to bear all the burdens and expenses of the war until a peace party grew strong enough throughout the country to impose its will on the authorities of the moment. The district to be held in military occupation would have to be so bounded as to be militarily defensible with the least possible difficulty. Across this line there would naturally be expeditions every now and then for temporary objects; but the intention ought to be to abstain from permanently overstepping it. In the districts which Germany requires for the security of her frontier, the process of incorporation should go steadily forward without waiting for the conclusion of peace."

*Friday, January* 6.—Till yesterday the cold was very intense, I believe as much as nine or ten degrees below zero. With it there was generally fog, which was particularly dense on Wednesday. The Chief has been unwell almost the whole week. Yesterday he drove out a little in the afternoon for the first time, and again to-day. Hatzfeld and Bohlen are ill. My own depression of spirits and disinclination for work have only begun to diminish to-day, probably because I have had two nights of abundant sleep, and perhaps also on account of the improvement in the weather; for the mist, which changed this morning into hoar frost and hangs in sparkling crystals on the branches of the trees, has been followed by a fine day, though portions of its withdrawing veil still hang about the wooded heights between this and Paris. Thus we commence a new life, like our guns, which have been doing little work these last few days on account of the mist, but which have begun to shoot away briskly enough. I may best insert here, perhaps, a few notes for my diary, which have been omitted. In the interval the Upper Governmental Councillor Wagner has been my fellow-worker in the office, and a Baron von Holnstein, who is, I believe, a secretary of legation, also came in. Among the articles I sent out during the last six days there was one on the measure which detached great numbers of railway carriages from the objects and necessities of German industry for the purpose merely of bringing up provisions for the time when Paris, after being really starved out, will be compelled to surrender. I described such a proceeding as humane, but impracticable and impolitic, as the Parisians, when they learn they are provided for outside, will hold out till their last crust of bread or joint of horse, so that all our humanity will end only as a kind of contribution towards the protraction of the siege. It is not our business, by establishing magazines or supplying means of transport for re-provisioning the city, to avert the danger of famine which menaces the Parisians. It is their business to do so by capitulating at the proper time. Yesterday I translated into German for the King two English protests against the sinking of English coal vessels at Rouen, which our troops had considered a necessary measure. Early this morning I telegraphed, according to advices from the general staff, to London, that the result of the bombardment directed for three days past against the forts on the Eastern front, and since yesterday also against those on the Southern front, has been very satisfactory, and that our loss is quite inconsiderable. Yesterday I again visited the officers of the 46th, who have established themselves in the farmhouse of Beauregard, and made themselves extremely comfortable with furniture which they have sent in from Bougival. To-day I visited with Wagner the point of view I have several times spoken of at Ville d'Avray, and from it we watched the bombardment. Wagner has found accommodation not far from us at the corner of the Rue de Provence and the Boulevard de la Reine, in the main door flat of a Frenchman, under all sorts of oil paintings. Paris seemed to be on fire in two places and white clouds of smoke were rising. In the evening I read despatches and also minutes. It appears that 2800 axles have been required from the German railway for waggons for collecting provisions for Paris. The Chief protested energetically against this measure as politically disadvantageous, seeing that the Parisian authorities, knowing that provisions have been collected for them outside, can delay their surrender till the very last possible moment, by using up every scrap in the city. Bonnechose has, at the suggestion of the Pope, written a letter to King William, from whom he wants peace, an "*honourable*" peace, one that is to say, without any surrender of territory, such as we might have had twelve weeks since from M. Favre if the Chief had not preferred one that was *advantageous*. Prince Napoleon is to come to Versailles to mediate. He is a talented and estimable man, but not of much consideration in France. In the London Conference on the Black Sea question we are to support the Russian claims with all our strength.

*Saturday, January 7.*—We have now—perhaps have had for the last few days—a body-guard of bright green Landwehr riflemen, oldish men with long wild beards. They are said to be all admirable shots.  On the suggestion of H. that there might possibly be something found of political importance in Odillon Barrot's house at Bougival, Bucher and I took a carriage there this morning.  The weather was dull and cold.  Mist drizzled down on us.  We first sought out H. at Beauregard to get him to describe to us the exact position of Barrot's villa.  Our drive took us by all sorts of defence preparations, walls pierced with loop-holes for shot, half-wrecked country houses, a ruined nursery garden, and so on, down the hill of Saint-Cloud into the valley under La Celle, where the long street of Bougival lies with its pretty church. On the way through the town we were told we should see soldiers, as no civilian had been allowed to peep behind the windows of the houses, the population having had notice to quit after the last sortie, or the last but one, in this direction.

In the middle of the village, where two streets cross at the little square, and where the Prussian sentry stood, we left the carriage, and asked the sergeant-major in command to supply us with a soldier as guide and companion. We first passed the druggist's shop, frightfully wrecked ; near it a sentry had been posted to protect the entrance to the immense deposit of wines discovered here some weeks ago. We then crossed a strong barricade which bars the outlet of the street in this direction towards the Seine.  It consists of barrels and casks filled with earth and stones, and all sorts of house furniture.  Then we looked for the house of which we were in search, in the narrow street leading to Malmaison.  In it also there were several barricades with ditches, and the side lane which leads down from the middle of it to the left towards the river contained several more.  The houses here, too, all of them unoccupied, and most of them damaged by shells, were prepared for defence.  There was very little furniture left.  We managed to pass the first barricade in the street by going in on some boards, turning to the left through the window of the house next it, and out through the house door on the other side of the ditch of the barricade. We passed a second small fortification to the right in a similar way.

Where the street opens on the high road by the river, the pavement of which was torn up, we saw before us a third system of barricades and ditches. It was the "musical" barricade, described so frequently by the correspondents of German and foreign newspapers, with no fewer than six cottage pianos stowed away in it. We could not look after them particularly, as at this point we dared not show our heads outside for fear of the Gauls on Mont Valérien, who would have been ready for us immediately with half-a-dozen of their shells. Here I discovered, three or four houses further on, the little green balcony which H. had mentioned as indicating Barrot's house, for which we were looking, but we were not allowed to approach it in front, the sentry who was posted here allowing nobody to pass. So we had to work round by the back, and a narrow foot-path between the houses and gardens enabled us to do so. In the steeply-sloped gardens behind the row of houses, all sorts of pieces of furniture were standing or lying about, and among them a desolate-looking chair in red plush, soaked through and through with snow and rain, with only one leg left. Books and papers were strewn plentifully round. After entering several houses, every one of which was terribly wrecked, we found the one we were looking for. A board across a deep ditch conducted us first into a room for flowers. From it we passed into the library, which consisted of two rooms. There might be a couple of thousand volumes, most of them lying on the floor in confused masses, possibly the work of the Mobiles and the

Francs-tireurs, who wrecked the surrounding neighbourhood before the investment of Paris. Many of them were torn or trodden under foot. Looking through the books, we saw that it had been a well-selected library, with books of history, politics, belles-lettres, and some English books; but there was nothing of the description of what H. had conjectured we might find.

When I got back to the Rue de Provence, I wrote two articles, at the Chief's direction, one of them a statement referring to a passage in the *Kreuz-Zeitung*, which is comforting itself in a straggling sort of fashion about the delay in the bombardment.

In the evening the Minister again dines with us. We learn that the fortress of Rocroy has fallen into our hands, and that the Saxon Minister, von Fabrice, has been appointed governor-general of a district of country including six departments. At tea we learned that the bombardment of Paris, or rather of its forts, had begun on the North side, too, and with good results. There had been conflagrations in Vaugirard and Grenelles, which, perhaps, might account for the smoke we saw rising yesterday from the hill-tops between Ville d'Avray and Sèvres. Keudell said that I should mention it to the Chief. At a quarter past ten I went up to him. He thanked me, and asked, "What time is it now?" I said, "It will soon be eleven, your Excellency." He replied, "Tell Keudell, then, to prepare the writing for the King about which I spoke to him."

*Sunday, January* 8.—In the morning I telegraphed the victory at Vendôme, and an account of the progress of the bombardment, and then wrote for the *Moniteur* a note on the lying spirit of boasting in which Faidherbe had once more claimed a victory over our troops, the fact being that he had been again compelled to retreat.

These last few days the Chief appears to be allowing his beard to grow. Delbrück tells us at breakfast that, in 1853, he was in North America, and got as far as Arkansas. In the afternoon Prince Hohenlohe was with the Chief, to inform him of the progress and success of the bombardment, probably on account of his remonstrances.

In the afternoon I read a report of *La France* on the state of health of Paris and sent it to the *Moniteur*. According to it, the deaths in the week, from the 11th to 17th December, rose to the enormous number of 2728. Smallpox and typhus especially, had carried away many people. Mortification is extending in the hospitals. The doctors complain of the bad effects of alcoholism on the sick, which makes slight wounds serious, and which appears to be dreadfully common among the soldiers in Paris. Their statement concludes with these words : " On this occasion we must remark, as we have done so often, that the crime of drunkenness, in its grossest form (*Ivrognerie Crapuleuse*), is on the increase in Paris, and neither the doctors nor we need an order of the day signed by Trochu and Clément Thomas to prove it, or to make us groan over it. Yes, we must say once more that the blush mounts to our foreheads when we see men every day, to whom the country has entrusted its defence, lowering and disgracing themselves by shameful potations. Can we wonder at all the unfortunate accidents which have happened through the careless use of guns, at the disorders, the insubordination, the deeds of violence, the plunderings and wreckings, which are reported every day by the public newspapers, at a time when the country is in mourning, when a hostile fate is heaping defeat after defeat on this unfortunate land, and visiting us with redoubled blows without intermission and without pity? People are indeed of a frivolous kind, who are simple enough to believe that this frightful war will infallibly reform our manners and make new men of us."

At dinner the Chief again spoke of his youth, especially of his earliest recollections, one of which related to the burning of the Berlin theatre. "I was then hardly three years of age. It was in the Gendarmes Market, on the Mohrenstrasse, opposite the Hôtel de Brandebourg, at the corner of the street, one story up, that my parents then lived. I myself remember nothing of the conflagration, which I must have seen, but I know, perhaps only because I have often heard the story told, that we raised ourselves on the chairs and on my mother's sewing-table, a step or two in front of the windows. As the fire progressed I mounted up there, putting my hands on one side of the window-panes and pulling them back at once, because they were so hot. Afterwards I went to the right window, and it was just the same. I remember, too, that I once ran away because my elder brother had used me badly. I got as far as the Linden, where they caught me. I ought to have been whipped for it, but somebody interceded for me, and I got off."

He then told us that from his sixth to his twelfth year he was in Plahmann's Institute, one of the educational establishments on the principles of Pestalozzi and Jahn, and that he had nothing but unpleasant recollections of the time he wasted there. At that time an artificial Spartanism was the rule. He never had enough to eat, except when he was occasionally invited out. At the Institute they always got "elastic" flesh, not exactly hard, but so that the teeth could not easily manage it, and parsnips. "I would have been glad to eat them raw, but they were boiled; and there were hard potatoes in the dish, four-cornered bits."

The conversation next turned on the luxuries of the table, and the Chief expressed himself vigorously about his likings for different kinds of fish. He always liked fresh lampreys. He was very fond of snipe-fish and Elbe salmon, just the proper mean between Baltic salmon and Rhine salmon "which is too fat for me." He then spoke of the dinners given at bankers' houses, where nothing is counted good unless it is dear. "They won't have carp, because in Berlin it is a moderately low-priced fish. They prefer perch, which cannot be brought there without difficulty." For my own part I don't care for perch, and I never liked Pomeranian salmon (*Maraenen*), the flesh of which is flabby. On the other hand, he could eat sea lampreys (*Muraenen*) every day : "I like them almost better than trout, and I don't care for any trout but those of moderate size, say half-pounders. The big ones, which are common in Frankfort at these dinners, and which usually come out of the Heidelberg Wolfspring, are not worth much, but they are dear enough, so that they must be on the table."

The conversation then turned on the Arc de Triomphe at Paris, which was compared with the Brandenburg Gate. The Chief said that the latter was very fine in its way. "I have, however, advised them to remove the sentry-boxes at the side, so as to show it. It would then be reckoned even a finer thing than now, as it is shut in and partly hidden."

While we were smoking our cigars, he said to Wagner, speaking of his old journalistic experiences : "I remember that my first newspaper article was upon hunting. I was then nothing more than a rough country squire. Somebody had written a spiteful article on hunting. My huntsman's blood warmed at this, and I set myself to and wrote an answer, which I forwarded to the editor, Altvater. It was unsuccessful. He answered me very politely, but said it did not suit, and he could not take it. I was in a rage that anybody should claim the right, or be allowed the privilege of attacking sportsmen without their being allowed to contradict him; but that was the way at the time."

In the evening I was told to send the following article from the *Français* to the English press and to the *Moniteur*: " From different quarters we are informed of acts of violence by certain battalions of the Mobilised National Guard, the proofs of which we hold at the disposal of General Clément Thomas. According to our accounts, these battalions have allowed themselves, at Montrouge and Arcueil, to wreck private houses, to break the window panes, to plunder the cellars, and needlessly to burn expensive pieces of furniture. In Montrouge a collection of rare copper-plate engravings was committed to the flames. Acts of this sort demand the interference of the authorities. General Trochu's proclamation of the 26th December, in which he announces the establishment of courts-martial, was placarded all over the neighbourhood of Paris. That threat of repressive measures ought surely not to be allowed to lie dormant in view of such plundering and insubordination." The article finally expresses a wish for an inquiry into the following incident : " On the 16th December the men of a battalion of the National Guard, then stationed at Arcueil, are said, on their way back to Paris, to have sold to shopkeepers in the neighbourhood a number of objects, the results of their plundering in that town. They were mostly copper kitchen-vessels." It would be well that people in Versailles and its neighbourhood, as well as in England, should know these facts, so that after the peace they may not charge these disorderly proceedings on our soldiers.

Similarly, in the *Moniteur*, we have the report of an attendant on the sick from Thorn, who was made prisoner, contrary to the provisions of the Geneva Convention, and who was afterwards spat upon in Lille, and threatened with death. I telegraphed to Berlin afterwards that our newspapers should remind the public that the elections for the Reichstag were to take place this month.

The defence of the Luxemburg Government against the complaint we made of their breach of neutrality is not sufficient. It proves only that they are not themselves in a condition to maintain their neutrality. Accordingly they are again warned, and new proofs to support our complaints are forwarded to them. If this is not sufficient, we shall certainly be compelled to occupy the Grand Duchy.

*Monday, January* 9.—The weather was cold and foggy, and a good deal of snow fell. There was very little firing, either from our side or the enemy's; but during the night our fire was very violent. We learn from London that Prince Napoleon is going about with a plan, proposing to sign a peace on his own authority, which we might accept, and after the capitulation of Paris to summon the Senate and the Legislative Body, to lay the treaty of peace before them for ratification, and to ask them to vote upon it, on the form of the future Government, and ultimately on the future dynasty.

Vinoy and Ducrot are said to be in favour of this plan. On the other hand, the Orleanists are moving, and they hope to win Thiers to their side.

In the afternoon I sent a telegram about the further successful progress of the bombardment. When I laid it before the Chief, he struck out the passage in which I had mentioned that our shells had fallen into the garden of the Luxembourg, as "impolitic."

The following pleasant story is going the round of the newspapers. It first appeared in the *Leipziger Tageblatt*, as taken from a private letter of a German officer. "One day Adjutant-Major Count Lehndorff paid a visit to Captain von Strantz, at the outposts in Ville d'Avray in Paris. He asked him how things were going with him, and von Strantz answered, 'Capitally; for I have just come from my dinner, where I have been eating my sixty-seventh leg of mutton.' The Count laughed, and after some time went away. Next day the guard brought the captain the following communication: 'As his Excellency Chancellor Count Bismarck has been informed that Captain von Strantz is about to have his sixty-eighth leg of mutton this afternoon, he takes the liberty to send him four ducks for his dinner, as a little variety.'" This anecdote has the advantage over others in the newspapers, that it is substantially true, only the Count did not appear quite the next day. Lehndorff was dining with us some days before Christmas.

The Chief again appeared at dinner, shaven as usual. He spoke first of Count Bill having received the Iron Cross, and he seemed to think that it would have been better to have given it to his elder son, who was wounded in the cava'ry charge at Mars-la-Tour. "That was an accident," he remarked; "others who were not wounded may have been quite as brave, but it is a sort of compensation to the wounded. I remember when I was a young man, that a certain von R., who had received the Cross, used to go about Berlin. I wondered what he could have done, but I learned afterwards that he was the nephew of a Minister, and that he had been acting as equerry to the general staff.

Delbrück remembered the man too, and told us that he had afterwards cut his throat, in consequence of an inquiry about difficulties in some bill transactions.

"In Göttingen," the Chief went on, "I once called a student a 'Dumme Junge' (a 'stupid fellow'). He demanded an explanation, and I said that I had no wish to insult him, but merely intended to express my conviction as to the fact."

When the venison and sauer-kraut were on the table, somebody remarked that the Minister had not gone out shooting for a long time, though there was plenty of game in the woods between this and Paris.

"Yes," he said; "but something always happened to interrupt me. The last time was at Ferrières, when the King was away. He had forbidden us to shoot in the park. We went out accordingly, but not in the park, and there was plenty to shoot, but not much was shot, as either the cartridges or the fowling-pieces were poor." Holnstein, who usually shows himself an uncommonly estimable, most industrious, and serviceable person, thereupon remarked, "This is the way, your Excellency, that people tell the story. They say that you were well aware of his Majesty's command, and naturally anxious to respect it. You had gone out for a walk, when you had the misfortune to have three or four pheasants suddenly flying at your head, so that you were compelled to shoot them in self-defence."

The French Rothschild was mentioned, and then we spoke of the German Rothschild, of whom the Chief told us a diverting story from his own experience.

The conversation turned ultimately upon elegant literature. Somebody spoke of Spielhagen's *Problematische Naturen*, which the Chancellor had read, and of which he thought not unfavourably, remarking, "I will certainly, however, not read it a second time. I have no time here for that." But even a much-occupied Minister may take a book in his hand, and allow himself the luxury of a couple of hours with it before he has to go back to his documents. Somebody then spoke of Councillor Freitag's *Soll und Haben*, and praised the description of the Polish disturbance, and the accounts of the balls with the young girls, but the guests appeared to think his heroes insipid. Somebody said that they had no passion, somebody else that they had no soul. Abeken, who took eager part in the conversation, made the remark that he could not read any of these things twice, and that most of the better known new writers had published only one good book. "Well," said the Chief, "I will allow you that three-fourths of Goethe's works are good; I do not care for the rest, but I should not mind being shut up a long while on a desert island with seven or eight of his forty volumes." Finally, somebody spoke of Fritz Reuter. "Yes," said the Minister, "*Aus der Franzosenzeit* is very pretty, but it is not a novel." Somebody then mentioned the *Stromtid*. "H'm," said he, "that is as one finds it; that is certainly a novel—plenty that is good, much that is middling—but the country people are exactly as they are described there."

In the evening I translated a long article from the *Times* for the King, going into full details about the situation in Paris. Afterwards, at tea-time, Keudell spoke cleverly—and indeed, charmingly—about certain qualities in the Chancellor which reminded him of Achilles—his genial, youthful nature; his easily excited temperament; the deep sympathies which he not infrequently manifests; his inclination to take himself away from the pressure of business, and his victorious way of carrying things through. Certainly, we had Troy still with us, as well as Agamemnon, the shepherd of the people.

After eleven I was again called to the Chief, and telegraphed further results of the bombardment.

*Tuesday, January* 10.—The cold was moderate, and it was cloudy, so that one could not see far; sky and earth were filled with snow. Only now and then a shot was to be heard from our batteries, or from the forts. Count Bill was with us, and about one o'clock in the day General Manteuffel. They were passing through to the army which is to operate in the south-east against Bourbaki, and which Manteuffel is to command.

In the afternoon I telegraphed twice to London—the retreat of Chanzy upon Le Mans, with the loss of 1000 men in prisoners, and Werder's successful resistance against the overwhelming forces of the French, who were pressing forward to the relief of Belfort, and attacked him at Villersexel. At dinner we spoke first of the bombardment, and the Chief said that most of the Paris forts, with the exception of Mont Valérien, were little worth, hardly better than the fortifications at Düppel. The fosses, for instance, were only of moderate depth, and the *enceinte*, too, used to be very weak.

The conversation then turned upon the International Peace Association, and its connection with the Social Democracy, the head of which, for Germany, was Karl Marx in London. Bucher said that he was a very able man, with a good scientific training, and was the real leader of the International Workmen's Society. Speaking of the International Peace Association, the Chief said that its efforts were of very serious importance, and that its real objects were altogether different from peace. Communism was hiding behind it.

The conversation then turned to Count Bill, and the Chief remarked, "He appears at a distance like an elderly staff officer, he is so stout." Somebody spoke of his luck in being ordered to accompany Manteuffel. It would only be a temporary position for both of them, but he would see a great deal of the war. "Yes," said the Chief, "He is learning something for his age. In our days not much could be learned at eighteen. I would have needed to have been born in 1795 to have had the chance of fighting in 1813. Since the battle at —— " (I could not catch the name, but it was some battle during the wars of the Huguenots that appeared to be meant), "there is not one of my ancestors who has not drawn sword against France: my father, for instance, and three of his brothers, and my grandfather at Rossbach. My great-grandfather fought against Louis XIV., and his father also against Louis XIV., in the battles on the Rhine, in 1672 or 1673. Several of us fought in the Thirty Years' War, on the Emperor's side, and others for the Swedes. Finally, there was one who was with the Germans who fought for the Huguenots as hired troops. One of them — his portrait is at Schönhausen — was an original. I have a letter from him to his brother-in-law, in which he says:—'The cask of Rhine wine has cost me thirty reichsthalers. If my brother-in-law thinks it too dear, I will, so may God preserve me, drink every drop of it myself.' Then again, 'If my brother-in-law asserts so-and-so, I hope I may, so may God preserve me, get some day closer to him than he will like,' and in another place: 'I have spent 12,000 reichsthalers on the regiment, and I hope, so may God preserve me, to get it back in time.' As for this getting back, he probably meant it in this way, that people used then to be paid for the soldiers who were absent with leave, and for those who had not yet presented themselves with their regiments. Certainly the commander of a regiment was in a different position in those days." Somebody said that the same thing, perhaps, happened nearer our own time, as long, in fact, as the regiments were levied, paid, and clothed by the colonel, and only hired by the Prince, and the practice might possibly still prevail here and there. The Chief answered, " Yes, in Russia, for example, in the big cavalry regiments in the southern districts, which often consist of sixteen squadrons. There were there, as there still are, other sources of revenue. A German once told me this. He had been appointed to a regiment, I believe somewhere in Kursk or Woronesch, one of those rich districts. The farmers came to him with carts laden with straw and hay, and hoped their 'little father' would graciously receive them. 'I did not know,' said he, 'what they wanted, so I sent them away, and told them to leave me quiet and go about their business.' Surely their 'little father' would be reasonable. His predecessor had been quite contented with this; they could not give more; they were poor people. At last I took the whole of it, especially as they pressed me. They fell on their knees, and entreated me most graciously to keep it, and then I drove them away. When others came, with waggons laden with wheat and oats, I understood them, and took the present as others took it, and when the former people came back with more hay, I told them that they had misunderstood me, that what they had given me before was sufficient, and that they had better take home what they now brought. In this way, as I charged the hay and the oats to the Government for the troops, I made my 20,000 roubles yearly.' He told me this quite openly and unblushingly in a company at Petersburg, and I had nothing to do but to wonder at him." "Yes, but what could he have done to the farmers?" asked Delbrück. "Done?" said the Chief, "he could have done nothing; but he could have let them be ruined in another way; he had only to allow the soldiers to do anything they liked."

The conversation came back to Manteuffel, and somebody said that he had broken his leg at Metz, and made himself be carried into the battle. He had wondered a good deal, somebody remarked, that nobody knew anything about it here. Certainly, he must have thought how badly we were informed about the chief events of the war. "I remember," said the Chief, in the course of further conversation, "once sitting with Manteuffel and——" (name unintelligible) "on the stone before the church at Beckstein. The King came past, and I proposed to greet him as the three witches did: 'Hail, Thane of Lauenburg! All hail, Thane of Kiel! All hail, Thane of Schleswig!' It was at the time I concluded the Treaty of Gastein with Blome. That was the last time in my life that I played piquet, though I had given up play a long while before. I played so recklessly that the rest could not help wondering at me, but I knew quite well what I wanted. Blome had heard that piquet afforded the best possible opportunity for discovering a man's real nature, and he wanted to try it on with me. I thought to myself, You shall have your chance. I lost a couple of hundred thalers, which I would have been honestly entitled to have charged as spent in the service of his Majesty. I put him all wrong; he considered me a reckless fellow, and gave way."

The conversation then turned to Berlin, and somebody remarked that it was growing year by year more of a great city, even in its ways of thinking and feeling, and that that must have some effect upon its representatives in Parliament. "During these last five years they have certainly changed greatly," said Delbrück. "That is true," said the Chief. "In 1862, when I first had to do with these gentlemen, if they had known the degree of heat to which my contempt for them rose, they would certainly never have forgiven me."

The conversation then turned to the subject of the Jews, and the Minister wanted to know why the name Meier was so common among them. It was of German origin, and signified landowner in Westphalia, whereas the

Jews formerly had no land anywhere. I replied, " I beg your Excellency's pardon, but the name comes from the Hebrew. It is in the Old Testament, and in the Talmud, and signifies properly Meïr, something connected with gold, light, splendour, so that it signifies something like the enlightened, the illustrious, the magnificent." The Chief went on to say, "Then there is the name Kohn, which is very common among them; what may that mean?" I replied that it meant a priest, which was originally Kohen. "From Kohen came Kohn, Kuhn, Cahen and Kahn, and Kohn or Kahn sometimes got transformed into Hahn" (a cock), a remark which occasioned some merriment. "Yes," said the Minister; "but I am of opinion that they are improved by crossing. The results are not bad." He mentioned several noble families, and remarked, "All of these are clever and cultivated people." After a little musing, and omitting something he had said between, which probably referred to the marriage of Christian girls of distinguished families, German baronesses and so on, with rich or talented Jews, he proceeded to say: " Probably it is better the other way, when, for instance, the Christian horse of the German breed is mated with a Jewish mare. The money then circulates, and the race produced is not a bad one. I do not know what I may advise my sons to do some day."

The Roumanians appear to be in the greatest perplexity, but the Powers will not help them. England and Austria are at least indifferent. The Porte is not convinced that the union of the principalities would not be injurious to it. France is at present out of the question. The Emperor Alexander has a very kindly feeling to Prince Charles, but will not meddle in the business, and there is certainly no interference to be expected from Germany, which has no vital interest in Roumania. If, therefore, the Prince cannot help himself out of his trouble, the best thing he can do will be to draw back before he is compelled.

Beust appears to have entered into a new phase of his political way of looking at things in the despatch in which he replied to the notification of the impending union of the German South with the North, and it is possible that under his advice satisfactory relations may be developed and maintained between the two newly organised powers of Germany and Austro-Hungary.

About half-past ten the Chief comes down to tea, which Count Bill also drinks with us. Abeken returns from Court, and brings the news that the fortress of Péronne has capitulated, with its garrison of 3000 men. The Chief, who was at the time looking at the *Illustrirte Zeitung*, sighed, and said, "Three thousand more! they might at least have drowned the commandant in the Seine, remembering the fact that he broke his word of honour." The remark gave rise to a conversation about the numerous prisoners in Germany, and Holnstein said it would be a good thing if they could be let out to Strousberg for the railways he is constructing. "Or if," said the Chief, "the Emperor of Russia could be induced to settle them in military colonies in the Empire on the other side of the Caucasus. They would become admirable properties. These crowds of prisoners will certainly cause us serious perplexity after the peace. They will then have an army ready made, and soldiers who have had time to rest. We can do nothing more for them but present them with Napoleon, who needs 200,000 Prætorians to maintain himself in power." "Does he really then expect to come back as the governor of the country?" Holnstein asked. "Very much so," said the Chief; "extraordinarily so, enormously so. He thinks day and night of nothing else, and the English do the same."

Finally, somebody told us what had happened in Spandau, where people from the English embassy had behaved themselves improperly, and at last violently, in front of the place where the French prisoners were kept in charge, and had got badly out of the affair.

*Wednesday, January* 11.—The weather was again less foggy, and the cold moderate. During the night there was heavy firing. In the morning afterwards, and for most of the day, the thunder of the heavy guns on both sides was very loud; those on ours apparently from new batteries, one of which is between Saint-Cloud and Meudon. Several times I counted more than twenty shots a minute, but the echo might make the number seem larger.

The Minister got up before 9 o'clock. In the morning several telegrams were sent off about the bombardment of Paris, and the battles of Le Mans, and two articles were written, one defending Beust against the reproach of double dealing which the *Vaterland* in Vienna had raised against him, founded on a comparison between his despatch to Wimpffen and articles hostile to Prussia in the official newspapers.

It is said that Clément Duvernois, who was formerly one of Napoleon's ministers, is coming here to treat for peace in the name of the Empress. She is said to admit the principle of territorial compensation and of the boundary which we want. She will consent to pay the costs of the war, and allow us to occupy certain portions of France with our troops in pledge for the money, and she will promise to enter into no negotiations for peace with any power but Germany. Duvernois believes that though she is not popular, she will show energy, and as lawful regent will have a better position and will give us more security than any person who might be chosen by the representatives of the country and who would necessarily be entirely dependent upon them. Is he to be received or not? Perhaps he may, so that the authorities in Paris and Bordeaux may note the fact, and be more ready on their part to decide to give in.

After three o'clock we went to our post of observation on the roof of the country house between Sèvres and Ville d'Avray, to watch the bombardment. One sees there clearly the flashes of the guns in the French battery at the railway viaduct. We came back by a field way, which took us first over the ridge to the left from the valley of Ville d'Avray, and then past the frozen pond. Not far from the latter, where the road goes down the hill again, a herd of five roe-deer sprang up suddenly from a cover in the snow.

During dinner we spoke first, as we usually do now, about the bombardment, and somebody said that there was a conflagration in Paris. Somebody else remarked, that thick clouds of smoke could be distinctly seen there. The Chief said, "That is not enough; one must first smell it here. The conflagration at Hamburg could be smelt twenty miles off."

Somebody then mentioned the opposition of the "patriots" in the Bavarian Chamber to the Versailles Convention, and the Chancellor said, "I wish I could go there and speak with them; they have obviously lost their way, and cannot get either forward or backward. I should soon bring them right again, but one is so necessary here."

Afterwards he spoke of all sorts of hunting adventures of his own—one, for instance, in Russia, where Holnstein had scared away a bear which he had rashly shot at ninety paces. Afterwards the bear had come up to within twenty paces, and ogled the Chief. "I managed, however," he continued, "to shoot the brute so badly with a conical bullet, that he was afterwards found dead a little bit off."

*Thursday, January* 12.—In the morning, after seven o'clock, I went with Wollmann and MacLean to Ville d'Avray, but we saw little on account of the fog. We had fourteen degrees of frost. About midday it cleared up, and there was heavy firing again. The conversation at dinner turned first upon the performances of our siege artillery against the town. Somebody remarked, that the French complained that we aimed at their hospitals, but the Chief said, "Certainly that is not done on purpose. There are hospitals of theirs at the Panthéon, and the Val de Grâce, where a shot or two might have accidentally fallen. H'm! Panthéon? Pandemonium."

Abeken said he had heard that the Bavarians intended to storm one of the forts on the south-east, where our fire was very feebly answered. The Chief was pleased, and added, "If I were now in Munich among the deputies, I could easily put it before them so that they would make no more difficulties." Somebody said that it was believed that the King preferred the title "Emperor of Germany" to that of "German Emperor," and it was remarked that the former would be a new title which, at all events, had no historical basis. Bucher dwelt a great deal upon that point. He said that there had never been an Emperor of Germany, and, that indeed, there had been no German Emperor either, only a German King. Charles the Great had called himself "Imperator Romanorum," but afterwards the name given to the Cæsars had been "Imperator Romanus semper Augustus," Enlarger of the Empire, and German King. The Chief so expressed himself as to show that he attached little importance to the difference between the titles.

In the evening, after nine o'clock, it looked as if a great conflagration had burst out in Paris towards the North. There was a peculiar "shine" beyond the wood, and flames above the horizon in that direction. Several of the gentlemen came out to see it. Holnstein looked out of the window in the cook's room, and believed that the city was really burning; so did Wollmann, but it was probably a mistake, for the "shine" was not red, but whitish. The Chief, who called me up to him to give me an order, and whom I told about the appearance, said, "It is possible; I had already remarked it, but it seemed to me to be more like the shine from snow. One must first smell it."

Afterwards, I made an extract for the *Moniteur* from Braun's dissertation on France, and the rights of nations. It was something of this sort:

The war has been conducted on the German side with a desire to treat France with the greatest consideration. We have acted upon the Convention of Geneva, though the French have violated it in a frightful and horrible way, especially by their neglect and ill-usage of our wounded, and by plundering the sanitary columns. Sheridan wondered that the conqueror allowed himself to be plundered by the conquered, by paying patiently and readily the enormous prices demanded by the population for what he wanted. On the other side, English correspondents declare that the war is assuming more and more the character of a war of annihilation, like those of the Middle Ages. If it is so, the French alone are to blame. The King said at the beginning of the war in his proclamation, that he was going to wage it only against the armed power of France, not against its peaceful citizens. From these words it has been attempted to infer that we ought only to have fought against the Empire and not against the Republic, in presence of which it is supposed to have been our duty to lay down our arms. As for the peaceful citizens, the Francs-tireurs and those who support them are certainly not peaceable citizens. All the authorities on the law of nations, from Vattel to Bluntschli and Haller, agree in this, that the considerate treatment of the peaceable population rests on the assumption that an absolutely distinct line of demarcation is drawn between soldiers and civilians, and that the civilian abstains from those hostile acts which are the duty of soldiers. What the soldier must do the civilian must not do, and if he takes hostile action against the foreign troops invading his country, he loses the rights of a civilian without acquiring those of the soldier. When the soldier is no longer in a condition to do injury, he can demand to be treated mercifully, but the civilian who kills without being bound to do so, and who thereby wipes out the line of demarcation, cannot be disarmed except by death. The condition of a prisoner of war does not exist for him; he must be annihilated in the interests of humanity. At the very moment when King William was beginning the war with the declaration, "I wage war against the armies of the enemy and not against peaceful citizens," Prince Joinville published an appeal to the French peasantry, in which he called upon them to destroy our soldiers by assassination.

About eleven o'clock at night the King sends the Chief a bit of letter paper, with the words written in pencil that we have just had a great victory at Le Mans. The Minister, who was obviously touched and delighted at this attention, handed me the paper, so that I might telegraph the news, saying, "He thinks that the military authorities would not have sent it to me; that is why he writes himself."

Afterwards I prepared for the King an article from the *Norddeutsche Allgemeine Zeitung*, giving an account of Roon's jubilee. Before going to bed, we learned that a breach had already been noticed in Fort Issy.

*Friday, January* 13.—Mist in the morning, and blue sky after twelve o'clock. There was heavy firing. Harless applied to the Chief with a petition on behalf of the Lutheran church, concluding with a request, that in consequence of an illness which has again attacked him, he should be allowed soon to lay down his pilgrim's staff. He and his party want an orthodox Lutheran German National Church, that is to say, that he is an enemy of the union, and accordingly of Prussia, which is for the union. Recently he has taken part with the Catholic bishops. His object is a Protestant Pope, and he would like the place himself.

The delegation in Bordeaux has made an attempt to induce the Pope to offer his mediation for peace; and at ome they do not seem disinclined to take the matter up, s they believe they might give it such a turn that the Pope might come by his own again.

After three o'clock I took a walk with Wagner through the park. At dinner we had the Government president, von Ernsthausen, a large-built man, still young. The Chief, who had to dine later with the Crown Prince, stayed with us only till the Varzin ham came on the table, saying: "Give me a little; as I am here I must help you to eat it. It gives me home feelings." He said to Ernsthausen: "I am invited to dine with the Crown Prince. As I have an important discussion before me, I am strengthening myself for it. To-day is the 13th, and a Friday. Sunday is the 15th, so the 18th is Wednesday. That is the great day, and the proclamation to the German people about the Emperor and the Empire, on which Bucher is now at work, will then be issued."

Turning to Ernsthausen he said: "The King still has

his difficulties between German Emperor and Emperor of Germany, but he rather inclines to the latter. I cannot see much difference between the two. It is a little like the question of the Homousians and the Homoiusians, in the days of the Councils." Abeken corrected him : " Homöusians." The Chief said: "We call it '*oi*' in our parts. In Saxony they are provincials. I remember that somebody at our school from Chemnitz read in this way" (and he quoted a Greek sentence). " The master said, 'Stop. *No.* We don't speak here as you do in Saxony.'"

In the evening new despatches came in, and old minutes were read over. The Chief came back at 9.30 from the Crown Prince, and told me to telegraph that at Le Mans we had made 18,000 French prisoners, and captured twelve guns, and that Gambetta, who wanted to be present at the battle, nearly fell into our hands. He managed, however, to escape in good time.

Afterwards, Unruh's speech upon the deficiency of locomotives on the German railways was made ready for report.

## CHAPTER XVII.

#### THE LAST WEEKS BEFORE THE CAPITULATION OF PARIS.

SATURDAY, *January* 14.—Moderately cold; the weather in the morning somewhat foggy, tolerably clear towards midday, but so bad later on that one cannot see ten yards in front of one. The firing, both from the forts and the town, goes on without a break from morning till evening. At night we repulsed a sally of the Parisians, directed against the troops of the Eleventh Army Corps stationed at Meudon, the Bavarians at Clamart, and the Guards at Le Bourget. I despatched several telegrams, then wrote an official letter to M., and, as usual, read newspapers for the King and the Chief. After breakfast, where we heard that yesterday's sally had ended in places with the hasty flight of the French, and that the southern forts had well nigh ceased to reply to our fire, I took another walk with Wagner in the park behind the castle.

Count Lehndorf dined with us. The Chief told us he had heard from Jules Favre. He wished to go to the Conference in London, and declared he had only heard on the 10th that a safe-conduct would be provided for him. He would like to take out with him an unmarried daughter, a married daughter, with her husband, with a Spanish name, and a secretary. What he would like best would be a pass " for the minister and suite." He was not, however, to have any pass, but the military authorities were simply to be instructed to let him through. Bucher is to write to him that his best way will be to go by way of Corbeil, so as not to have to leave his Paris carriage, have to walk some way, and then take another carriage. He had also better go to Metz by Lagny, instead of Amiens. Should he not wish to go by Corbeil, would he say so? Other instructions should then be given to the military. "As for his wish to travel with his family," added the Chief, "one would almost think that he wanted to make his escape."

In the course of further conversation the Minister observed: "Versailles is just the most unfit place possible for the conduct of business. We had better have stayed in Lagny or Ferrières. But I know very well why: many people who have nothing to do would have been bored to death there. For the matter of that, such people are bored here and would be so, anywhere."

In the evening I wrote an article upon the difficulties of victualling Paris after its surrender, which was to appear in the *Moniteur*. "We find," so it runs "in the *Journal Officiel*, the following paper on the victualling of Paris: 'From a Bordeaux despatch, dated January 3, it appears that the Government of National Defence have collected considerable stores of provisions in view of the revictualling of Paris. Besides the articles comprised in the regulations, for which arrangements are being made, the stores of provisions already delivered, massed close to the transport waggons outside the range of the enemy's operations, and ready to be sent off at the first signal, consist of the following: more than 15,000 head of cattle, more than 40,000 sheep, which, thanks to the foresight of the authorities, are penned at the railway stations; and more than 300,000 (metrical) hundredweights of food of all kinds, which are stored in magazines and belong to the State. These supplies are destined solely for the revictualling of Paris.'

"When we come to consider this attempt at revictualling from a practical point of view, we encounter serious difficulties. If the assertion of the *Journal Officiel*, that the magazines stand beyond the range of the German operations, is well founded, one must assume a distance of at least one hundred and forty miles. But the condition to which the French themselves have reduced the railways which run into Paris is such that it would take at least several weeks to bring these provisions into the city. Nor must it be forgotten that besides the starving population of Paris, the German army has also a right to have its supplies recruited by means of the railways, so that with the best will in the world, the German authorities could not allow more than a portion of the railway material to be used for the revictualling of Paris. It follows, therefore, that if the Parisians, in view of the possibility of considerable stores of victuals becoming in the end available to them, should put off their surrender of the city till their last crust has been devoured, their inaccurate estimate of the state of matters would expose them to severe disappointment. The Government of National Defence should therefore give most careful consideration to the circumstances of the case, and not leave out of sight the grave responsibility they undertake in carrying out their principle of resistance to the uttermost. The distance between the armies raised in the provinces, whose approach is so impatiently expected, and Paris, utterly blockaded and cut off, does not diminish, but increases day by day. It is not lying reports that will save Paris. The calculation that to hold out to the last was feasible on the simple ground that neither the provinces nor the enemy would give over a city of two and a half millions of inhabitants to the pangs of hunger, might break down in the face of inexorable impossibilities, and the capitulation of Paris might at the very last moment (which God forbid) be the beginning of a really terrible calamity."

*Sunday, January* 15.—The weather is moderately clear and cold. Fewer shots are heard than during the last few days. The Chief passed a sleepless night, and had Wollmann awakened by four o'clock, in order to telegraph to London about Favre. Andrassy, the prime minister of Hungary, has declared that he not only shares the view of matters expressed in Count Beust's despatch on the New Germany, but has always been in favour of this policy and recommended it. The reservation in the preamble of that document might have been omitted, as the new organisation of Germany does not violate the treaty of Prague. The letters in which the German princes assent to the proposals of the King of Bavaria regarding the restoration of the Imperial dignity, express nearly the same sentiments. Only Reuss was inclined to explain his consent in a somewhat different way. On the side of Bavaria pretensions are put forward which cannot at all be admitted.

The Chief dines to-day with the King. In our party nothing worth notice was said at table.

Bamberg, who comes every evening after news for the *Moniteur*, explains to me the meaning of the branch of boxwood on the wall over my bed. It is consecrated in the church on Palm Sunday, and remains in its place all the year round. It serves, probably, as a safeguard against illnesses, evil spirits, and witches, and so plays its part in the popular superstitions of the French. . . . The Chief calls for me at nine o'clock. I am to make an article from the official reports on our position towards American ships laden with contraband of war. The point lies in the thirteenth article of the treaty of 1799. We cannot capture these ships, but can only detain them while the war lasts, or have the contraband goods handed over to us on our giving a receipt. In either case we must pay a moderate compensation. The paper was written forthwith and deposited in the letter-box of the office.

*Monday, January* 16.—A thaw, the sky cloudy, with a high south-west wind. The view is clearer again, but since yesterday evening not a shot has been heard. Has the bombardment ceased? or does the wind blow away the report of the shots?

In the morning I read Trochu's letter to Moltke, in which he complains that our fire in the south of Paris has struck hospitals and asylums, although these are distinguished by flags. He thinks this cannot be by chance, and refers to the international treaties, by which these establishments are inviolable. Moltke has defended himself stoutly against any idea of design. The humanity with which we have carried on the war, so far as the character which has been given to it by the French since the 4th of September allows us to be humane — protects us against such a suspicion. So soon as the air clears, and the distance between our batteries and Paris enables us to distinguish the Geneva flags on the buildings in question, even chance injuries will be avoided. Later on, we learn by telegraph of the pursuit of Chanzy by our troops. Before noon a telegram is despatched, telling of the capture of the camp at Conlie, and the successful resistance offered by General von Werder, south of Belfort, to the overwhelming superiority of four French corps.

Prince Pless and Maltzahn dined with us. We learn that the proclamation to the German people is to be read out to-morrow on the occasion of the festival, which will take place in the grand reception-room of the Palace here. The King will be hailed as Emperor in presence of a brilliant assemblage.  Deputations, with banners, from the army, the Generals, the Chancellor of the Confederation, and a number of Princes will be there.  We hear, too, that the Chancellor has changed his mind about letting Favre out of Paris, and has written him a letter, which is practically a refusal.  The Chancellor says : " Favre seems to me with his request to be allowed to attend the conference in London, just like children in the game of ' Fox in the hole.'  They shut the door to, and then contrive to come out at a place where you cannot do them any harm (like the ' pax ' in our Dresden game of ' Last man ').  He must eat the soup he has crumbled his bread in.  I have written to him that his honour requires it."  Possibly this change of mind may have been caused by an article in Gambetta's organ, *Le Siècle*, printed also in the *Nord-Deutsche Allgemeine Zeitung*, and marked for him.  It was to the effect that the permission to Favre to go to London amounted to a recognition of the present French government on our part.\*  The article went to the King and to London.

In the evening I saw the correspondence between Favre and the Chancellor.

I insert here a *résumé* of this affair, based on documents afterwards made public.

\* \* \* \* \* \*

On the 17th of November, Favre, as Minister for Foreign Affairs, learnt from a despatch dated Tours, November 11, and forwarded by Chaudordy, that news had come from Vienna that the Russian Government considered itself no longer bound by the Treaty of 1856.  Favre at once replied, recommending strict reserve until the arrival of official

---

\* This supposition was wrong.  The Chancellor changed his mind because of Favre's circular on January 12.

information, and pointing out how, without neglecting to assert the claims of France on every opportunity, she must be invited to the discussion of the Russian declaration. Communications on the subject, both by word of mouth and in writing, then passed between the different Powers and the Provisional Government of Paris, in which the French tried hard to induce the representatives of the other Powers to admit, that the French representative at the Conference would be bound to open a discussion of quite other importance (than that upon the Treaties of 1856), in respect to which they were not disposed to give any negative reply. The Delegation at Tours shared this opinion, though it thought that the invitation of Europe to the Congress, if one were to take place, must be assumed, even though neither a pledge nor an armistice had been obtained beforehand. Gambetta wrote to Favre on the 31st December: "You must be prepared to leave Paris to attend the London conference if, as is asserted, England has succeeded in obtaining for you a safe-conduct." Before these lines were received, Favre had told Chaudordy that the Government had decided that France, "if she were invited in regular form," should be represented at the London conference, provided that the Parisian deputy could procure from England, who had sent a verbal invitation, the necessary safe-conduct. This was undertaken by the English Cabinet, and Chaudordy informed Favre of the fact in a despatch which reached Paris on January 8, adding also that he, Favre, had been appointed by the Government to represent France at the conference. This communication was confirmed in a despatch written to Favre by Lord Granville under date December 29, which reached Paris on January 10. It ran as follows:

"M. de Chaudordy has informed Lord Lyons that your

Excellency proposes to represent France at the conference, and he has begged me to procure a safe-conduct for your Excellency through the Prussian lines. I at once requested Count Bernstorff to ask for this safe-conduct and to have it conveyed to yourself by the hands of a German officer sent under a flag of truce. Herr von Bernstorff yesterday informed me that a safe-conduct should be at the disposal of your Excellency, whenever it was applied for by an officer from Paris at the German headquarters. He added that it could not be conveyed by the hands of a German officer until satisfaction had been given to the officer who had been shot at when bearing a flag of truce. M. Tissot gives me to understand that it would take a long time for this communication to reach you through the Delegation in Bordeaux. I have, therefore, suggested to Count Bernstorff another means of conveying it to you. I hope your Excellency will allow me to take this opportunity of expressing the satisfaction I feel in dealing with you personally," &c. &c.

Favre saw in this letter a recognition of the existing French Government and an invitation which he might turn to account in opening the discussion upon the situation of France before the Powers in London. In the circular issued to the French Ambassadors on January 12, he said:

"Directly invited by this despatch, the Government could not refuse the invitation received in her name without neglecting the rights of France. It may no doubt be maintained on the other hand that the time for such a discussion of the neutralisation of the Black Sea is not well chosen. But the very fact that this formal step is taken by the European Powers towards the French Republic at the critical moment when the country is fighting single-handed for her honour and her existence, lends to it an exceptional gravity. It is a beginning, too long delayed, of the practice of justice, a pledge which cannot be recalled. *It consecrates our change of government with the authority of international rights;* and leaves on the stage where the fate of the world is being decided, the nation freed in spite of its afflictions, face to face with the power which has brought it to ruin, and with the pretenders who would fain hold sway over it. Who, moreover, does not feel that France, admitted among the representatives of Europe, has an indisputable right to raise her voice in their presence? Who will be able to hinder her, when, taking her stand upon the everlasting ordinances of justice, she shall vindicate the principles which assure her independence and dignity? Not one of these will she abandon. Our programme remains unchanged, and Europe, in inviting him who has laid it down, knows very well that he has both the will and the obligation to maintain it. We must hesitate no longer, and the Government would have committed a grave mistake if it had rejected the proffered opening.

"While recognising this, however, the Government thought, as I do, that the Foreign Minister could not, unless higher interests were at stake, leave Paris during the bombardment which the enemy is directing against the city." (Here follows a long sentimental lamentation over the damage which "the fury of the invaders" has, intentionally, "in order to spread terror," inflicted by their shells upon churches, hospitals, orphanages, and so on.) Then he proceeds: "Our brave Parisians feel their courage rise with the danger. Firm, animated, and determined, they are neither exasperated nor bowed down by their sufferings. They will fight and conquer more than ever, and we shall do so with them. *I cannot think of deserting them at this crisis.* Probably the protests we have addressed to Europe as well as to members of the diplomatic corps still remaining in Paris, will soon attain their object. *England will understand that till that hour my place is in the midst of my fellow-citizens."*

The same expression had been used by Favre in the following answer of two days before to Lord Granville's letter, but only in the first part, where he said: "*I cannot consider myself justified in leaving my fellow-citizens at a moment when they are the victims of this violence*" ("against an unarmed population" he had written in the lines immediately before, from a strong fortress with nearly 200,000 soldiers and militia!). Then, however, he proceeded: "Moreover, communication between London and Paris is, thanks to the commander of the besieging army (how *naïve!*) so tedious and uncertain, that I cannot, with all my goodwill, answer your summons according to the letter of your despatch. You have informed me that the Conference will meet on February 3, and probably last for a week. This information having reached me on the evening of the 10th of January, I could not have availed myself of your invitation in proper time. Besides, Herr von Bismarck in forwarding it to me did not accompany it with a safe-conduct, which is absolutely indispensable. He requires that a French officer should go to his headquarters to fetch it, and he bases this request on a reclamation addressed to the Governor of Paris, in consequence of an incident which a messenger with a flag of truce had to complain of on the 23rd of December. Herr von Bismarck adds, that the Prussian commander-in-chief has forbidden any communication by flag of truce until satisfaction for this has been obtained. I do not inquire whether such a decision, directly contrary to the rules of war, does not amount to an absolute denial of those higher claims of the amenities of warfare which necessity and humanity have always upheld. I content myself with remarking to your Excellency, that the Governor of Paris lost no time in instituting an inquiry into the incident indicated by Count von Bismarck; and that in announcing the fact to him, he brought very numerous cases to his knowledge, laid to the charge of the Prussian sentries, of which he had himself never taken advantage to interrupt the exchange of ordinary communications. Count von Bismarck seems to have admitted, partially at least, the justice of these observations, for he to-day asked the United States ambassador to inform me that, pending the reciprocal inquiries, he is re-establishing communications by parley. There can, therefore, be no necessity for a French officer going to the Prussian headquarters; and I will put myself into communication with the United States ambassador, in order to receive the passport which you have taken the trouble to procure for me. As soon as I have this in my hands, and *the condition of Paris permits me*, I will take the road to London, sure beforehand that I will make no vain appeal in the name of my Government to the principles of justice and morality which Europe is so vitally interested in seeing respected."

So far, M. Favre. The condition of Paris had not changed, the protests addressed to Europe had not yet put an end to the crisis. Indeed it was not yet possible that they should, when Favre, on the 13th of January, three days after his letter to Granville, and the day after the issue of his circular to the French representatives in foreign parts, sent the following despatch to the German Chancellor:—

"M. le Comte! Lord Granville has informed me, in a despatch dated December 29 of last year, which I received in the evening of the 10th of January, that your Excellency, by request of the English Cabinet, holds at my disposal a safe-conduct, which is necessary to enable the plenipotentiaries of France at the London Congress to pass the Prussian lines. As I have been appointed in this capacity I do myself the honour to request your Excellency to send this passport, made out in my name, *with the least possible delay.*"

My only object in quoting all this is to show the difference between the character and ability of Favre, and Bismarck as he really is. Compare the writings of the one, as they have been given in detail above, with the following utterance of the other. There we have indecision, ambiguity, conceits of pose and phrase, and, lastly, contradiction of what had been said emphatically a few lines before, and expressed with equal emphasis in other documents. Here, on the contrary, speaks a man who is sure, simple, natural, and always to the point. The Chancellor answered Favre on January 16 (I leave out the opening words) as follows :

" Your Excellency assumes that on the application of the Royal government of Great Britain a pass to enable you to attend the London Conference lies ready for you with me. This assumption, however, is not correct. I could not have entered upon an official negotiation resting on the supposition that the National Defence Committee is, by the law of nations, in a position to act in the name of France, so long as it has not been, in the least degree, recognised by the French nation itself.

" I presume that the commander of our outposts would have granted your Excellency the warrant to pass the German lines had your Excellency applied for it to the general of the besieging army. The latter would have had no occasion to consider your Excellency's political station and the purpose of your journey, while the fact of the warrant to pass our lines being granted by the military authorities to whom it would not have seemed, from their point of view, a matter for much hesitation, would have left the hands of his Majesty's ambassador in London free in regard to the question whether your Excellency's declarations could, by the law of nations, be regarded as the declarations of France, so that he could have taken up his ground, and on his part adopted some form by which prejudice might have been avoided. In addressing to me, by way of an official announcement of the object of your journey, an official request for a passport, in view of the representation of France at the Conference, your Excellency has debarred us from this course. Political considerations, in support of which I refer to the declarations published by your Excellency, forbid me to accede to your request by sending such a document.

"While making this communication I can only leave you to consider for yourself and your government, whether any other way can be suggested for removing the objections indicated, by which any prejudice arising out of your presence in London can be avoided.

"But even if such a way should be found, I venture to ask whether it is wise for your Excellency to leave Paris and your post as member of the Government there, to take part in person in a Conference about the Black Sea, at a moment when interests are at stake in Paris which are of far greater importance, both to France and Germany, than the 11th article of the Treaty of 1856. Your Excellency would also be leaving behind in Paris the diplomatic agents and *attachés* of the neutral states, who have remained, or rather been detained there, long after they received permission to pass through the German lines, and have therefore all the greater claims upon your protection and forethought as Minister for Foreign Affairs in the actual Government.

"I can therefore scarcely suppose that your Excellency, in the critical situation *which you have so essential a part in conducting to its issue*, will willingly deprive yourself of the opportunity of assisting in the solution, for which the responsibility rests on you."

\* \* \* \* \* \*

It is now the turn of the journal to speak again.

*Tuesday, January* 17.—The weather is warm, with much wind. No shots are heard. The bombardment, however, was carried on yesterday, satisfactorily, and with but trifling loss on the German side. I telegraph to this effect by command of the Chief, mentioning at the same time that the French loss during the six days' fighting at Le Mans has been far more considerable than was supposed. Nineteen guns and 22,000 unwounded prisoners have there fallen into our hands.

At dinner we had as guests the Saxon Count Nostitz-Wallwitz, who is to be appointed to the administration here, and a Herr Winter, or von Winter, who has been made Prefect of Chartres. On some one turning the conversation upon the future operations of the war, the Chief observed: "I think, if by God's help we take Paris, we will not occupy it with our troops. The National Guard might serve there under a French commandant. We should occupy only the forts and the outskirts. Every one would be let in, but no one let out. It would be a great prison until it came to be a small one on the conclusion of peace." He then spoke with Nostitz about the General Councils, and said that every attempt should be made to procure the goodwill of their members. Here would be a good field for further political operations. "As for the military side of the question," he went on to say, "I am for more concentration, not covering a certain quantity of ground, but so holding it in hand that the authorities can conduct the administration, and especially collect the taxes in a regular way. The military has a centrifugal plan of operations, I a centripetal." ... "If we cannot provide every place within our circle with garrisons, we can send a flying column from time to time to such places as prove troublesome, and shoot, hang, and burn. If that is done twice they will soon listen to reason." Winter thought that the mere appearance of the party to do execution in such places would produce the desired effect. "I don't know," said the Chief; "a moderate amount of hanging does much better; and if a few shells are thrown in, and a few houses burnt. That reminds me of the Bavarians, who asked the Prussian artillery officer, 'What think you, comrade; are we to burn this village to the ground, or only wreck it *in moderation?*' I don't know what the answer was."

He told us then that he had many well-wishers in Bremen. "They have lately made for me there a number of excellent cigars, very strong, but praised by all connoisseurs. In the press of business I have forgotten the name of the company"—(Bucher named, if I remember right, "Jacobi Brothers")—"and now they send me again a fine polar bear's skin. It is too good for the campaign; I shall send it home."

This led him to observe that, at St. Petersburg once, he wanted to go on a bear's hunt, down the Dwina to Archangel, but his wife would not let him; besides he would have been obliged to take at least six weeks' leave. In the woods up there, is an incredible quantity of game, especially blackcock and woodcock, which are killed in thousands by the Finns and Samoyeds, who shoot them with small rifles without ramrods, and bad powder, "A woodcock there," added he, "lets itself, I will not say be caught with the hand, but killed with a stick. In St. Petersburg they come to the market in heaps. On the whole a sportsman is pretty well off in Russia, and the cold is not so bad, for every one is used to struggling with it. All the houses are properly warmed, even the steps and the porch as well as the riding paths, and no one thinks of visiting with a tall hat in winter, but goes instead in furs with a fur-cap."

He came to speak again, I do not remember how, of his yesterday's letter to Favre, and said, "I have given him clearly to understand that it will not do, and that I could not believe that the man who helped to bring about the business of the 4th of September, would not wish to await its issue. I wrote in French, partly because I look upon it not as official, but as private correspondence, but also that it may be read, not only by him, but by everybody in the French army before it gets to him." Nostitz asked how diplomatic correspondence was generally conducted. "In German," said the Chief; "formerly it was in French, but I have changed this. Only with those cabinets, however, whose language we understand—England, Italy, and Spain; these can be read at a pinch;—not with Russia, for I am about the only man in the Foreign Office who understands Russian. Nor again, with Holland, Denmark, or Sweden, for their languages are not learnt as a rule. They write in French, and are answered in the same way." "The King has, moreover, given orders that the soldiers are only to converse with the French in German. Let them learn it. We have had to learn their language." "With Thiers (he meant Favre), at Ferrières, I conversed in French. But I told him that it was only because I was not dealing with him officially. He laughed at that. I said to him, however,

'You will see when we are discussing terms of peace that we shall speak German.'"

At tea we were told that the bombardment in the South had ceased, because one of the generals (who was supposed to have been always against it) had managed to get his own way. It is hoped, however, that the Crown Prince of Saxony will press rapidly forward, and keep up a sharp fire on the North. On our side we shall not then allow him to get in advance of us, for fear of giving justification for supposing that the Saxons have compelled the capitulation. This is clearly only a rumour. At least, Count Dönhoff, who came in just now, declared that our guns on the South side of Paris were not idle, only we do not hear the shots because of the south-west wind, and certainly there was not so much firing as on the previous days. Moreover, fire will probably be opened to-morrow upon the city from Saint-Denis, which will considerably astonish the Parisians in the Northern quarters.

In the evening, we find from the *Moniteur* that twenty-eight French officers, among them a major and seven captains, have recently broken their parole, and escaped from confinement. Altogether 108 of these men of honour have escaped already from the territories of the North German Confederation. Some of them, for example Lieut. Marchesau, who sneaked away in woman's clothes from Altona, have been caught a second time, and Colonel Saussier, who fled from Graudenz over the Russian frontier, was seized by the authorities there, and handed back again in Thorn.

*Wednesday, January* 18.—The sky is cloudy; the air clear. An extensive view; the temperature warm, with a little wind. In the morning I read letters and newspapers. Wollmann told me an order had come in promoting our Chief to the rank of Lieutenant-General. Hatzfeld and Bohlen have received the cross to-day. The others are expecting it, and the longing for it seems with some of them to be very great. What store even the lower officials set by it, and how useful the custom of decorations consequently is to the state, was shown by what our excellent T. said to me this morning, "God knows, doctor, I would gladly even give up all my extra pay, if you will believe me, if I could get the Iron Cross." I believed him, although it was hardly conceivable; for the extra pay to which he referred comes to one and a half times as much as his ordinary income.

Between twelve and half-past one there was the banquet of the knights in the great hall of the castle, and the proclamation in military splendour of the German Empire and Emperor. It must have been a very grand and imposing sight. Meanwhile I took a long walk with Wollmann. As we were on our way back, going from the railings of the Avenue de Saint-Cloud, up the alley, and through the Rue de Saint-Pierre, we heard the thunder-roll of loud hurrahs from the Place d'Armes; these were for the King, who was returning home from the ceremony. I should have said for the Emperor. At dinner the Chief was absent, as he was dining with the Emperor. Twice in the evening I was summoned to receive instructions from him; he spoke with an unusually weak voice, and seemed tired and exhausted.

The Minister has received a letter written by Kern, the Swiss ambassador, on behalf of a number of diplomatists remaining in Paris, requesting him to see that measures are taken to enable the protégés of the writers to escape, before the bombardment, to a distance from the town. This is to dispute our right to bombard Paris, and to infer that we purposely fire upon buildings which ought to be spared. In reply, we can say that we have repeatedly (as early as towards the end of September, and once more in October) drawn the attention of those of the inhabitants of Paris who are citizens of neutral countries, through their embassies, to the damage which the town must be exposed to from a prolonged resistance. For months, we allowed all neutrals who could show themselves to be such, and who wished to leave, to pass our lines without difficulty. On military grounds we can now grant this privilege only to members of the diplomatic body. If a number of neutrals have still not availed themselves of this permission to take themselves and their chattels to a place of safety, it is not our fault; they must either not have wished to go, or been hindered by the authorities of Paris.

If we bombard Paris, we are fully entitled to do so by the law of nations: for Paris is a fortress, nay, the principal fortress in France—an entrenched camp for a large army, which, after starting from it to take up the offensive against us, returns to it for shelter. Our general, therefore, could never be required to leave uncaptured this vantage point of his adversaries, or to touch it with velvet gloves. Our object in the bombardment is not to destroy the city but to storm the fortress. Allowing that our fire makes residence in Paris uncomfortable and dangerous, those who were warned of that should not have entered or remained in a beleaguered city, and their complaints should be addressed, not to us, but to those who have turned Paris into a fortress, and are using its fortifications as weapons against us. Lastly, our artillery does not fire intentionally upon private houses, or philanthropic establishments, such as hospitals and the like, and this ought to have been self-evident, from the careful respect we have shown to the stipulations of Geneva. Only by accident, from the great distance at which we are firing, have houses or persons, not concerned in the carrying on of the war, been hit. But Paris, from which the war was suddenly let loose upon us, and from which the war is now principally conducted, cannot be allowed to make use of such cases to prevent a severe bombardment, intended to make it untenable. I wrote an article in this sense.

*Thursday, January* 19.—The weather is dull. The post is delayed, and we learn on inquiry that at Vitry-la-Ville, in the neighbourhood of Châlons, the railway has been broken up. After ten A.M. we again hear a moderately brisk cannonade, in which field-pieces ultimately join. I write two articles upon a sentimental statement in the *Journal des Débats* to the effect that our shells have taken for their mark only ambulances, mothers and daughters, sick ladies, and cradles with infants in swaddling clothes—what horribly ill-disposed shells!

To-day's firing, Keudell tells us at breakfast, is due to a fresh and important sortie which the Parisians, with twenty-four battalions and numerous guns, have made against our positions between La Celle and St. Cloud. Towards two o'clock, when the whirr and rattle of the mitrailleuses are plainly heard, and the French artillery is at the most two miles in a direct line from Versailles, the Chief mounts to ride to the aqueduct of Marly, whither the King and Crown Prince have also gone. I set off thither likewise, with Wollmann.

On our way we meet, in Roquencourt, a musketeer coming back from the fight, who, on our asking how things are going, gives us to understand we are in a bad way, the enemy being already in the wood on the hills behind La Celle. We cannot believe it, because in that case there would have been more signs of life here, and we should have heard the firing more distinctly. Some way beyond we meet the Crown Prince returning to Versailles. There cannot then be any further danger. When we come to the heights in front of Marly we are not allowed to go further along the high road, which strikes north here, as straight as a line. We wait a while in a cutting wind and under a cloud, from which falls a dense shower of snow-flakes, among the long-bearded sons of Anak of the militia guard who are posted here. The King and the Chancellor are, I suppose, on the aqueduct. When the cloud lifts we see Mont Valérien deliver three shots in succession, and the redoubts beneath its walls fire eight times. Now and then too a flash comes from our batteries in the west beyond the Seine, and a house seems to be burning in one of the river-side villages. When the fire ceases we return home.

In Versailles, however, the situation must have caused uneasiness; for, as we pass through the town, we find that the Bavarians have entered it. Formerly one only caught sight of them here by ones and twos. They are posted, we are told, in dense masses in the Place d'Armes and the Avenue de Paris. The French, however, are encamped, they say, about 60,000 strong, under Mont Valérien, and in the fields east of it. They are supposed to have taken the Montretout redoubt, and to hold in their hands also the village of Garches, not much more than a couple of miles from here, and the western portion of Saint-Cloud. It was feared that to-morrow they might press on further and force us to evacuate Versailles. This cannot be true, or at least it is exaggerated.

The conversation at dinner seems to confirm this impression. The danger was not spoken of as imminent. We had as our guest Privy Councillor von Löper, who is to be

Under-Secretary of State in the Household. At first the purport of the talk was that the danger which had threatened our communications with Germany on the South-East had passed away, as General Bourbaki, who had pressed hard upon Werder for three whole days without being able to beat him back, had, probably on the news of Manteuffel's advance, given up the attempt to relieve Belfort, and was in full retreat. The Chief then alluded to a statement that the taxes could not be got in from different communities in the parts of France which we occupy, and said it was difficult, nay impossible, to plant garrisons everywhere, to compel the people to pay them. Then he went on to say, "That, however, is not at all necessary. The thing can be managed by flying columns of infantry, with some horse artillery and a couple of guns. They need not even enter a place, but simply send in a message, 'If you do not produce the outstanding taxes—in two hours shells will be thrown in.' Then they see you are in earnest, and they pay. In some instances a place will really be bombarded, so as to encourage the others. They must learn what war is."

Later on the conversation turned upon the indemnity that might be expected when peace was concluded, and this led the Chief to speak of that paid in 1866. He said, "We ought not to have made them pay in money. I at least resisted it for a long time, but at last I gave way to the temptation." "We ought to have been paid in land, as in 1815, and it would have been a good opportunity."

*Friday, January* 20.—The weather is rather cloudy, and no more firing is heard. In the course of the morning we hear that the Parisians have abandoned their positions of last evening, and marched back into the town with drums beating. Our losses in the fight are said to be trifling, while those of the enemy are very severe. From the West comes the news that Tours has been occupied by our troops, without resistance; from the North, that Goeben has beaten the French at Saint-Quentin, in a battle lasting seven hours, and taken 4000 unwounded prisoners. At twelve o'clock I am sent for by the Chief. He wishes his answer to Kern's memorial, and the letter in which he refused Favre his passport, to appear in the *Moniteur*.

At dinner, Bohlen was again present, as well as Lauer and von Knobelsdorff. The Chief was good-humoured and talkative. Among other things he told us that, when he was in Frankfort, he had constantly had invitations to the Grand-Ducal Court at Darmstadt, and accepted them. There was an excellent hunt there. "However," he went on, "I have reason to suppose that I was not a favourite with the Grand-Duchess Mathilda. She said once to somebody, 'He is always there, and looks as if he were as big a man as the Grand Duke.'"

As we sat over our cigars, the Crown Prince's Adjutant (Major von Hanke, or Kameke), came in suddenly, in a waterproof cloak, to tell us that Count ―― (the name was unintelligible) had come out, ostensibly in the name and by order of Trochu, to request a two days' truce for carrying away the wounded in yesterday's sally, and burying those who had fallen there. The Chief replied, that the French must not have this conceded to them, as it would only take a few hours to carry off the wounded and bury the dead; besides the dead would rest just as well above as beneath the earth. Soon after the Major reappeared and said the King was coming; and, true enough, scarcely a quarter of an hour afterwards his Majesty walked in, and the Crown Prince along with him. They went with the Chancellor into the drawing-room, where a refusal of Trochu's request was agreed upon.

About nine o'clock, Bucher sent me a few lines, in pencil, to say that, by the Chief's orders, the letter to Kern was to be printed in to-morrow's *Moniteur*, while that to Favre was to stand over till further notice. I at once sent instructions to that effect to Bamberg, who must by this time have received the letters through the office.

At tea, Wagner told us various anecdotes of the year 1848. He had made an agreement with the famous Müller, in the Linden, that if Müller's party would do the same when their turn came he would take care that his opponents did not get hanged when the Conservative party had the upper hand. "When, therefore, our side got quite the best of it," he went on, "I went to the head of the police, and asked him to allow me to have Müller's confinement somewhat abated; and I sent him, in memory of our agreement, a dozen bottles of wine and six smoked geese." This was another of his stories: "On one occasion when Held, who once played a leading part in Berlin, and was a great favourite with the lower classes, was having a public meeting, we had a handbill printed and posted up at the street corners, somewhat to this effect: 'Held, the father of the people, yesterday, at the meeting at' (such-and-such a place) 'made a collection for the sick and needy, which reached the considerable sum of 1193 thalers, so many silver groschen and so many pfennigs. Those in want should present themselves, therefore at his house' (such and such a number in such and such a street) 'and receive their share.' Of course he had made no such collection. But we had the satisfaction of bringing about his ears a number of people who would not believe a word of it."

*Saturday, January* 21.—A dense fog in the morning. No firing going on. At half-past nine the *Moniteur* comes in, and—contains the Chief's letter to Favre! Unfortunate; but my letter to Bamberg only reached him when the number was printed. About ten I was summoned to the Chief, who however said nothing of the mishap, though the paper was lying before him. He was still in bed, and wished Count Chambord's protest against the bombardment of Paris cut out for the King. I then wrote an article for the German papers, and an occasional note for the paper here.

At dinner in the evening, Voigts-Rhetz, Prince Putbus, and the Bavarian Count Berghem were the Chancellor's guests. The Bavarian had brought the pleasant news that the Conventions of Versailles had passed the Second Chamber in Munich by two votes to spare over the required majority of two-thirds. The German Empire then is formally established. The Chief accordingly proposed to the company to drink the health of the King of Bavaria, "who had really brought the matter to a satisfactory conclusion." " I always thought," he added, "that we should carry it through, if only by one vote; I had not hoped for two. The last good news from the seat of war probably contributed to it."

It was then mentioned that in the great sortie the day before yesterday the French had deployed against us more men than had been hitherto believed, probably over 80,000, and that the Montretout redoubt had actually been in their hands for some hours, as well as part of Garches and Saint-Cloud. They had, however, suffered frightful losses in storming them; as many as 1200 dead and 4000 wounded were talked of. The Chief observed, " The capitulation must soon come now; next week, I should imagine. After the capitulation they are to be supplied by us with provisions —that is understood—but, until they have given up 700,000 stand of arms, and 4,000 cannon, not a morsel of bread shall they touch, and no one will be let out. We occupy the forts and the suburbs, and put them to a little cost until they can bring themselves to agree to a peace that will suit us. There are still many intelligent and respectable people in Paris for us to deal with."

Afterwards we came to speak of a Madame Cordier, who stayed here some time ago, and had spent several hours each day walking up and down on the bridge of Sèvres, apparently with the intention of getting into Paris or conveying something in. She seems to be a pretty, somewhat elderly widow; and if I understood right, is a daughter of Lafitte and a sister of the wife of the Marquis de Gallifet, commander of cavalry, who was conspicuous among the elegant women of Napoleon's court. She seems to have been looked upon among us as a high-class spy, and the wonder was that she was tolerated here; but probably she had many friends and admirers among the higher officers.

The Chief remarked, "I remember when she came to Frankfort fifteen or sixteen years ago. There she undoubtedly expected to play the part of a beauty and a Parisian. But it did not succeed. She had common manners and but little tact, and was not so well-educated as the bankers' wives in Frankfort, who soon made out the fact. I know she went out one day in dirty wet weather with a rose-coloured satin cloak on, all covered with lace. 'If she got sovereigns sewn all over her dress,' said the ladies of Frankfort, 'we should see better what she wanted to show off.'"

The conversation then drifted into a learned discussion upon the difference between the titles "German Emperor" and "Emperor of Germany;" the possibility of an "Emperor of the Germans" being also mentioned. After the discussion had lasted for some time the Chief, who had hitherto remained silent, asked "Does any gentleman know the Latin for sausage?" "Farcimentum," replied Abeken. "Farcimen," said I. "Farcimentum or farcimen, whichever you please," said the Chief, smiling, "nescio quid mihi magis farcimentum esset." (I don't know which of the two I should consider the more made-up name.)

*Sunday, January* 22.—The weather is bright, but not cold. As yesterday, so to-day, only a few shots are heard. It is time for me that we should get away from here, for I feel quite tired and exhausted again. In the forenoon I wrote two articles for the German papers, and one for the *Moniteur;* and was twice with the Chief about them. At dinner there were present the Saxon von Könneritz— a handsome man with an aquiline nose and a large beard —General von Stosch, and Löper. There was nothing remarkable in the conversation but that the Chief again spoke of its being only fair to give the Iron Cross to the wounded. After dinner I read drafts and other documents, among others Heffter's extremely exhaustive report upon the Emperor's title. This conscientious scholar has studied a large number of documents bearing upon the point, which to the Chief is a question of sausages; but, if in the hurry of the moment I rightly understood his treatise, he has not come across any one of the titles put forward: German Emperor, Emperor of Germany, German King, or King of Germany.

In the evening I drew attention in two articles to a piece of cruelty on the part of the French, highly characteristic of the war set on foot by Gambetta, and, as the following statements show, thoroughly well attested:

"At the request of the battalion the undersigned states that on his march to Vendôme on the 1st of January, he received information that a dead cuirassier had been found in Villaria, with both his eyes gouged out. The undersigned saw this cuirassier lying on an ambulance waggon, escorted by his comrades. He had several knife and bayonet wounds in the abdomen, and a shot in the shoulder, and his eyes were cut out of their sockets. The body seems to have been found in this condition a day or two ago.

"Von Lüderitz,
"First Lieutenant in the 4th Westphalian
"Infantry Regiment, No. 17."

"I certify that at Villaria on January 1, I saw the corpse of a cuirassier, with both his eyes gouged out. I made no detailed examination of the body, but I believe more accurate information could be obtained. The body was escorted by dragoons of the 16th Regiment.

"D. Halle,
"Surgeon of the Second Battalion of
"Regiment No. 17.

"The Tuileries, *January* 9, 1871."

"The Division (20th Infantry Division) submits to the commander-in-chief, in the accompanying papers, the statement of First-Lieut. von Lüderitz, of the 4th Westphalian Infantry Regiment, No. 17, respecting the mutilation of a cuirassier of the No. 3 East Prussian Cuirassier Regiment, which may serve as material for the list which is to be drawn up of breaches of international law committed by the French. The Division further draws attention to the fact that in the battle of the 11th instant the enemy used explosive bullets in their rifles, which was remarked by the privates as well as by most of the officers, so that Major Blume is in a position to certify this on oath.

"Mantz.

"Chapelle, *January* 16, 1871."

*Monday, January* 23.—Weather dull and mild. I telegraph that the bombardment from our northern batteries is doing good work: the fort at Saint-Denis is silenced, while conflagrations are noticed in the town of Denis, as well as in Paris. I then wrote an article, with an appropriate moral upon the poisoning of four Prussians in Rouen, and completed the collection of French cruelties and breaches of international law, by the report of Dr. Rosenthal upon his imprisonment with the Red-breeches. The post is delayed again to-day, because the Francs-tireurs have blown up a bridge over the Moselle between Nancy and Toul. A vigorous fire is kept up by all our batteries, though we do not hear it. So says Von Uslar, lieutenant of hussars, who comes from the outposts to bring the Chief a letter from Favre. What does *he* want now?

General von Kameke, commander-in-chief of the engineers employed in the siege, and the light blue hussar and Johanniter, von Frankenberg, were present at dinner. There was no conversation worth noticing.

In the evening, soon after seven, Favre himself came in, and the Chancellor had an interview with him up in the little room next his own, where the widow Jessé's eldest son used to live. The conference lasted about two hours and a half. Meanwhile Hatzfeld and Bismarck-Bohlen entertained Favre's companion, his son-in-law, whose name was Del Rio, in the drawing-room below. He was, it appears, properly speaking a portrait-painter, but had come out as secretary with his father-in-law. Both of them got something to eat, whatever was to be had at a moment's notice, cutlets, buttered eggs, ham, &c., which will do them good, poor martyrs to obstinacy! Shortly before a quarter to eleven they both set off to return to their lodging here in a carriage standing at the door. Accommodation had been found for them on the Boulevard du Roi, where Stieber and the field police happen to be quartered. Hatzfeld escorted the gentlemen there. Favre seems depressed, and his dress somewhat neglected; his son-in-law, who is a little man of southern type, the same. Uslar had accompanied them here from the outposts.

After half-past ten the Chief goes to the King, and comes back in about three-quarters of an hour. When he came to us in the tea-room he seemed unusually pleased, sat down, let me pour him out some tea, and took a few bites of dry bread with it. After a while he said to his cousin, "Dost thou know this?" whistling a few bars—a hunter's signal, which signifies that the stag is killed. "Yes," said Bohlen; "a famous hunt." "No," said the chief, "that goes so," whistling a different air. "It was the signal to be in at the death. I think it is all over." Bohlen then remarked that Favre had looked "very shabby." The Chief answered: "I find him grown much greyer than in Ferrières—stouter, too, probably from the horseflesh. Otherwise, he looks like a man who has lately passed through much trouble and agitation, and to whom everything now has lost its taste. He was quite frank, and confessed that things were going on badly inside. I learnt from him, too, that Trochu is superseded, and Vinoy is now commander in the city." Bohlen then told us that Martinez del Rio had been extremely reserved. They had not, indeed, attempted to question him, but once they had asked how things were at Rothschild's villa at Boulogne, where Thiers said the staff of the Parisian army were quartered. He had replied quite curtly that he did not know. They had been talking to him all the rest of the time, somewhat ill-naturedly, about the first-class restaurants of Paris. Hatzfeld informed us, when he came back from accompanying the two Parisians, that Favre was glad that he had arrived in the dark, and would not leave to-morrow during daylight, lest he should attract attention, or be recognised by the people of Versailles. Before the Chancellor went up to his room, he asked whether anyone was left in the office who wrote legibly, if so, he must go up with him. Willisch was there, and accompanied him upstairs.

To go back a little. This afternoon I was in the Hall "du Jeu de Paume," the famous "tennis court" (German, *Ballhaus*) of 1789, which stands in a small street named after it near the Place d'Armes and the upper end of the Avenue de Sceaux. From reading of the Revolution in German books I had formed quite a different idea of the place; I imagined a stately house with a fine large hall for balls and concerts. I now saw that this was a mistake. It is a quite insignificant building, and the hall, which is not for dancing, but for playing ball, is neither elegant nor spacious. The door is approached from the outside by some small steps. The porter's wife led the way to the hall, which is very simple and without any adornment whatever. It is about 40 paces long by 20 broad, and about 30 feet high. The lower part of the wall is of stone, which is painted black, the upper part being boarded. The ceiling is of wood. In the woodwork are windows large and small, protected against the balls by wire gratings. Below, round the long side of the room, which is turned to the street, and the two short sides, runs a covered wooden corridor, with windows also protected by wire gratings. In the wall on the fourth side, about a man's height from the ground, a four-cornered brass slab is let in, containing the oath of June 20, 1789.[*] It was brought here in 1790 by a company of "patriots."

[*] This declared indirectly the sovereignty of the National Assembly, into which the third Estate of the States-General, shortly before led by

## The Tennis Court.

There is nothing else to remind one of what happened here. When I was examining this historical spot, clothes were hanging up in the corridor to dry, and cabbage leaves lay strewn about the floor. Probably the porter kept a rabbit-hutch where Mirabeau once thundered. A leather-covered ball and a bat reminded one of the proper use of the room.

*Tuesday, January* 24.—The day is cloudy and foggy. The Chief got up before nine o'clock, and worked with Abeken. Shortly before ten he went to the King, or as we now say, the Emperor. He did not come back till about one,

---

Bailly and Mirabeau, had been recently changed, after certain members of the other two Estates had been added to it. It ran thus: "The National Assembly, which is to give the kingdom a new constitution, must not be hindered in its deliberations; its members hereby pledge themselves by an oath not to break up, but to meet again continuously in one place, till the constitution is complete and firmly established." Three days after, on the 23rd of June, the Revolution began on the basis of this oath. The king caused a Constitution to be submitted to the Assembly of the three Estates, to which were prefixed fifteen articles, expressly forbidding a thorough reformation of the State, such as the Liberals desired and contemplated. The speech, drawn up for the king by his ministers, ended with these words: "I command you, gentlemen, to break up immediately, to meet to-morrow in the hall appointed for each individual Estate, and there to begin your sittings again." These were strong words, but they were spoken by a weak prince. The deputies of the Commons remained assembled in spite of the king's command, and when the Grand Master of the Ceremonies, the Marquis de Dreux-Brézé, required them to depart, Mirabeau answered him, "My lord, you cannot be the king's organ with the National Assembly, for you have neither seat nor voice here, nor even the right to remind us of what the king has said. Tell your master that we are assembled here by the will of the people, and that we can only be dispersed at the point of the bayonet." In answer to this opposition the king did nothing; when he was told of it, he replied: "Very well, if the gentlemen of the Third Estate will not leave the hall, we must let them stay there."

when we were sitting at breakfast. He ate a piece of fried ham, drank a glass of Tivoli beer, sighed, and said: "Till now I have always thought that the parliamentary method of conducting State matters was the most wearisome conceivable. I think so no longer. At any rate there is an escape with the last motion that is made. Here every one brings forward his individual opinion, and when one is deluded into hoping that the matter is settled, some one comes out with an opinion which he has already expressed, and which has been refuted, and we are back again where we started, and nothing gets done. No; I shall be pleased, nay thankful, if anything is yet decided, or will even be decided by to-morrow." He then observed that he expected Favre back, and had advised him to be off by three o'clock for he is going back to Paris, lest the soldiers should challenge him in the dark, and he not be able to answer them.

At half-past one, Favre again called on the Chancellor, talking with him for nearly two hours, after which he returned home, Bismarck-Bohlen accompanying him as far as the Bridge of Sèvres.

At dinner, where we had lobster mayonnaise, the talk did not turn upon this interview. But it seems to be understood as a matter of course that the preliminaries of the capitulation were discussed at it. The Chief first spoke of Bernstorff, and said: "I have not arrived at the point of writing with complacent diffuseness sides and sheets on the most unimportant things. A heap so high" (he showed it with his hand) "has come in to-day. And then come always back-references—'as I had the honour to inform you in my despatch of January 3, 1863, Number so-and-so;' or 'as I said, with the utmost respect, in my telegram, Number 1666.' Then I send it to the King, and he wants to know what he means, and pencils on the margin, 'I don't know this.'" Some one wanted to know whether Goltz had written as much. "Yes," said the Chief, "and sometimes, besides, private letters to myself, of six or eight closely-written sheets. He must have had a fearful amount of time on his hands. Luckily I quarrelled with him, and that blessing ceased." One of the company wondered: 'What he would have said if he had seen the Emperor in prison, the Empress in London, and Paris besieged and bombarded by us?' "Well," replied the Chief, "the Emperor was no such favourite of his, but—in spite of his being enamoured—he would not have been as pleased with all this as other people are."

The death of a Dutch or Belgian princess was mentioned, and Abeken, as in duty bound, expressed his sorrow. The Chief, however, said, "How can you take it to heart like that? There is no Belgian here at table, and no relation."

He then told us that Favre had complained to him that we fired upon the sick and blind in the Blind Institute. "I do not know what you find hard in that," said I. "You do far worse; you shoot at our men who are in sound and vigorous health. 'What a Barbarian!' he no doubt thought to himself."

Mention was made of Hohenlohe and his services in securing the success of the bombardment. "I have determined," said the Chief, "to confer on him the title of Poliorcetes (sacker of cities)." The conversation turned upon the statues and pictures of the *Renaissance*, and their want of naturalness and good taste. "That reminds me," said the Chief, "of the Minister Schuckmann, whom his wife painted—*en coquille*, I think it was called—in a rose-coloured cockle-shell, and dressed in a kind of antique costume, naked down to here—pointing to the bottom of his waistcoat—as I certainly never saw him." "He belongs to my earliest recollections. They often gave what were then called Assemblies, and are now called Routs—an Evening without supper. My parents usually attended them." He then again described the dress of his mother, and went on, "Some time after, there was an ambassador in Berlin, who also gave similar balls, where we danced till three o'clock, and there was nothing to eat. I know that, for I and a couple of good friends often went to them. At last we young people rebelled. When it grew late we produced bread-and-butter from our pockets and devoured it. Food was provided the very next time, but we were never invited again."

## CHAPTER XVIII.

#### NEGOTIATIONS FOR THE CAPITULATION OF PARIS.

WEDNESDAY, *January* 25.—In the morning I wrote letters, wrote out an article and a telegram, and read despatches and drafts. The latter contained nothing worthy of note. In the afternoon I looked up Dr. Good in the cloister in the Rue Saint-Honoré, where he had been taken on account of his illness. He pronounced himself past cure, and spoke of his death as imminent. Alas for a most amiable man!

Count Lehndorff dined with us. The conversation first turned upon the heavy losses sustained by the French in their sally of the 19th, and then upon our own during the whole campaign. After this the fish we are eating—mullet, as I understand, native to the Adriatic, and the gift of Bleichröder the banker—gave a topic for further conversation, in which the Chief took part with the animation of a connoisseur. As I have already said, he is extremely fond of fish, and of water animals generally.

From fish we pass to oysters, and after dwelling on their virtues, come to speak of bad oysters, which Lehndorff justly pronounces to be the most horrible things one can imagine.

Lehndorff told us then of the fine hunting grounds and numerous foresters of Prince Pless. The King had lately asked him: "Tell me now, has the calling out of your foresters inconvenienced you very greatly?" "Oh, no, your Majesty," replied the Prince. "How many of them then were called out?" "Oh! only forty, your Majesty." I fancy that I came across a similar story some years ago, only, if I recollect right, the Prince was an Esterhazy, and the foresters shepherds.

The Minister then spoke of his first journey to St. Petersburg. He set off in a carriage, because at first no snow had fallen. Later on, however, there was a heavy storm, the road was completely buried, so that his vehicle only got along, and very slowly. He passed five days and six nights in the narrow carriage, without sleep, and at thirty degrees of frost, before he reached the first railway station. But the moment he was in the railway carriage he fell so fast asleep that when he arrived at St. Petersburg, after a ten hours journey, he fancied he had only stepped into the train five minutes before.

"They had their good side, though, those days before railways," he went on; "one had not so much to do then. The post-day only came round twice a week, and then we worked with might and main. But the moment the post was off we got on horseback again, and had a good time till next post." Some one observed that the work in the Embassies as well as in the Foreign Office had been increased far more by the telegraph than by the railway. This led the Chief to speak of the reports of ambassadors and diplomatic agents generally, and he remarked that many of them, pleasant enough in form, contained nothing. "It is newspaper work, written just for writing's sake. Such, for example, were the reports of our Consul (name unimportant). I read them through, and am always thinking, 'Now it must be coming.' But nothing comes. It sounds ery nice, and one reads on and on. At the end, however, one finds that there really is nothing in it—it is all barren and meaningless." Another example is mentioned, a military commissioner, who had also come out as an author. On him the Chief passed judgment. "It was thought he would do something, and in quantity he has done a good deal, and the form is good. He writes pleasantly, as he would for a newspaper, but when I get to the end of his reports, closely written in a small neat hand, there is positively nothing in them for all their length."

Coming to speak once more of tiring journeys, and of long rides, he said, "That reminds me of the battle of Königgratz—I was the whole day in the saddle, on my big horse. I particularly wished not to ride it, because it was so high, and gave me so much trouble to mount. In the end, however, I did so, and had no reason to regret it. It was an excellent beast. The long ride across the valley had made me very tired, and my seat and legs were very sore. But I had not overridden myself. In my whole life I have never done that; but when I sat down afterwards on a wooden bench and began writing, I felt as if I was sitting on something else—some strange substance between me and the bench. It was only the swelling produced by the long ride.

"After Königgratz we arrived late in the evening at the market-place of Horsitz. Here the word was that gentlemen were to look out for their own quarters. It was easier said than done. The houses were shut up, and we ought to have had pioneers at hand to break open the doors. But they would not have come to their work till five o'clock in the morning." "Your Excellency got over that difficulty at Gravelotte," remarked Delbrück. "Well, I went then," proceeded the chief with his story, "to several houses in Horsitz—three or four, and at last I found a door open. When I had gone in a few steps I fell into a sort of wolf's-trap on the floor. Luckily it was not deep, and I was convinced there was horse-dung in it. At first I thought 'how would it do to stay here'? but I soon became aware by the smell that there was something else there; and, strangely enough this occurred to me among other things: 'If the hole had been twenty feet deep, and full, they would have had to look in the morning a long time for their Minister.' Well, I got out again, and found a place under the arcades of the market-place. There I laid down a couple of carriage cushions for myself, made a pillow out of a third, and settled myself to sleep. When I had lain down, my hand came in contact with something wet; and when I examined it I found it was a product of the country. Later on some one woke me. It was Perponcher, who told me the Grand Duke of Mecklenburg had a shelter for me, and a bed into the bargain. That was all right, only the bed was a child's bed. I stretched myself straight out, put the back of a chair at my feet, and fell asleep. But in the morning I could scarcely stand, from lying with my knees on the chair-back. If only one has a sack of straw, one can make oneself comfortable, even if there is very little in it, as often happens. You cut it open in the middle, shove the straw back, and lie in the trough thus formed. I have sometimes done that in Russia, when out hunting."

"That was when the despatch came from Napoleon," observed Bohlen, "and you promised you would pay the Gaul out for it when an opportunity came."

Finally the Chief said, "The day before yesterday Favre told me that the first shell which reached the Panthéon had knocked the head off the statue of Henri Quatre." "That must have affected him very much?" asked Bohlen. "Oh, dear, no!" replied the Chief. "I am inclined to think that he mentioned it as a democrat, glad that it should have happened to a king." "Well," said Bohlen, "this is the second bad time the king has had; the French stabbed him in Paris, and we have beheaded him there."

The dinner lasted this evening unusually long, from half-past five till after seven, and every moment Favre was expected back from Paris. After half-past six he came at last, again accompanied by his son-in-law with the Spanish name. Neither of them seems to have struggled against eating more than the first time. Like reasonable people they did justice to the good things set before them. One may conclude that in the main point which is being discussed they have either hearkened, or will hearken, to the voice of reason. That will appear when Favre again confers with the Chancellor in young Jessé's room.

After dinner I read drafts. Orders are sent out to Reims prescribing the course of procedure in the collection of taxes. Arrears are to be demanded of the communities at the rate of five per cent. increase for every day on the amount due. Flying columns with artillery are to present themselves at places which show themselves obstinate, to order them to pay at once. If they don't do so without delay, they are to proceed to bombard and burn the place. Three examples would make a fourth unnecessary. It is not our business to win the French by mildness, or to care for them. Judging by their character it is far more essential for us to infuse into them a greater terror of us than they have of their own government, which is also bringing stringent measures to bear upon them. On the night before last the Reds in Paris made a daring rush, set some of their ringleaders free from prison, and then got up a fight in front of the Hôtel de Ville. The National Guard fired upon the Garde Mobile, killed some, and wounded others, but quiet at last was restored. This information is to be relied on.

About ten o'clock, when Favre was still here, a brisk

fire of heavy artillery began, which lasted about an hour. After half-past ten I went down into the tea-room, where I found Hatzfeld and Bismarck-Bohlen talking to del Rio. He is a man of middle height, with a full dark beard, a bald patch on his crown, and an eye-glass on his nose. Soon after my entrance, he went home to his quarters at Stieber's, accompanied by Mantey, and a quarter of an hour later Favre followed him. Del Rio spoke of Paris as the centre of the world; so that in this bombardment the centre of the world is our bull's-eye. He said that Favre had a villa in Rueil, and a large cellar in Paris full of all kinds of wines, and that he himself had a property in Mexico, of a hundred and twenty square miles. After Favre left, the Chief came down to us, ate some cold partridge, ordered back a slice of the ham, and drank a bottle of beer. After a while he sighed, pulled himself straight, and said, "Ah, if I could only settle things myself and give my orders." He was silent a minute, then went on. "The wonder to me is that they do not send out a General. It is hard to make him understand military matters." He gave a couple of French words: "That means the mound in front of the trench on the outside," then another two: "and that is the inner side. He did not know that." "Well, I hope you found he had had a reasonable dinner to-day." The Chief said, Yes, and Bohlen remarked here that a rumour had spread below that this time he had not even despised champagne, but drunk it like any one else. "Yes," said the Chief, "the day before yesterday he refused it, but to-day he allowed some to be poured out for him. Even now, he had conscientious scruples about eating, but I talked him out of them, and hunger must have helped me; for he ate quite like a man who has long fasted."

Hatzfeld informed us that Rameau, the mayor, had been

here an hour ago to ask whether M. Favre was with us. He wished to speak to him, and to place himself at his disposal. Might he be allowed to visit him? Hatzfeld said that he, of course, did not know. Hereupon the Chief observed: "Any one who comes in the night to a man who is going back to Paris, deserves to be brought before a court-martial. Impudent fellow!" "Well," said Bohlen, "Mantey has no doubt already told Stieber. This M. Rameau probably has a longing to get back to his cell." (For writing in an impudent way about the arrangements for provisioning Versailles, he—with, I think, other magistrates—had been obliged to make acquaintance for some days with the inside of a room in the prison of Saint-Pierre.)

The Minister told us something of his interview with Favre. "I like him better than I did in Ferrières," said he. "He speaks fluently, and in long, well-balanced periods—often one is not obliged to attend to or answer him. He told some stories of old times, and he tells a story very well." "He did not take my last letter at all amiss. On the contrary, he said he was indebted to me for pointing out what he owed to himself." "He mentioned also that he owned a villa near Paris, which, however, had been plundered and ruined. I had it on my tongue to say, 'Not by us though;' but he at once added, of his own accord, that it might have been by the Garde Mobile." "He then complained that the town of Saint-Cloud had been burning for three days, and wanted to convince me that it was we who had set the castle there on fire." "Apropos of the Francs-tireurs and their misdeeds, he wished to refer me to our free companions in 1813, who had behaved far worse. I said to him, 'That I will not deny, but you must remember that the French shot them down whenever they could catch them. And they did not shoot them all at one time, but five at the place where the deed was done, then five more at the next halting-place, and so on, to spread terror.' He asserted that in the last action, on the 19th, the men of the National Guard who belonged to the better classes had fought best; the battalions taken from the lower classes of the population being of least worth."

The Chief was silent for a time, and wore a thoughtful expression. Then he went on, " If at first the Parisians get a supply of provisions, then are again put upon half rations, and have to starve a little, that will work, I think. It is just the same with flogging. If a man gets too many lashes one after the other, not much effect is produced. But when the flogging is stopped for a time, then begun again, it is very disagreeable. I know that from the criminal court in which I used to work. There flogging was still practised."

The conversation then passed to flogging, generally; and Bohlen, who regards it as useful,* observed that even the English had re-introduced it. " Yes," said Bucher; " first, for personal assaults upon the Queen—on some occasion when some one struck at her—then for garotters." The Chief then told how in 1863, when they infested London, he had often had to pass, after 12 o'clock at night, from Regent Street to his house in Park Street, through a lonely lane where there was nothing but stables and heaps of horse litter. To his horror, he read in the papers that several such attacks had taken place in that very lane.

After a while he said: "That is an unheard-of proceeding on the part of the English! They wanted (Odo Russell intimated as much, but the Chief refused it, as not

* Expressing thereby the feeling of nine-tenths of the German people —I mean the actual people, not the people of the liberal press and the public meetings.

permissible) to send a gunboat up the Seine, as they say, to fetch away such of the English families there as wished to come. They really want to see whether we have laid down torpedoes." "They are out of humour because we have fought great battles here, and won them by ourselves. They grudge the little, shabby Prussian his rise in the world. They look upon us as a people who are only here to make war for them, and for pay."

He was again silent for a while, then said: "I remember when I was in Paris in 1867, I thought, 'How would it have been had we let ourselves out about Luxemburg—should I be now in Paris, or the French in Berlin?' I believe that I was right in advising against it at that time. We were not then, by a long way, so strong as we are now. At that time the Hannoverians were not in the way of making such good soldiers as they do now. Of the Hessians I will say nothing of course. The Schleswig-Holsteiners, who have now fought like lions, at that time had no army at all. The Saxon army was broken up, and would have had to be reconstructed; and of the South Germans little was to be expected. What admirably practical fellows the Würtembergers are now! In 1866, every soldier would have laughed to see them march into Frankfort like a militia. The Baden men, too, were in a poor way, and the Grand Duke has done much since then." "Of course public opinion in Germany would have been with us, if we had wished to make war about Luxemburg. But it was not enough to make up for these shortcomings. And then the right was not on our side. I have never openly admitted it, but I may say so here: after the breaking-up of the German Confederation the Grand Duke became sovereign, and could do what he chose. His wishing to sell his dominions was mean, but he could have sold them. And our rights of occupation were not at all clear. We certainly were not entitled after the breaking-up of the confederation still to occupy Rastatt and Mainz. I said so in council, and I had then the idea of giving Luxemburg to Belgium. We should thus have connected it with a country on behalf of whose neutrality England, as was then thought, would step in. And we should, moreover, have strengthened the German element against the *Fransquillons*, and secured a good frontier to boot. But I found no support in this."

When the Minister left us, some one remarked that he had said nothing at all about the other side of the question. The French were not at that time so well-prepared for war as now. Their military stores had been exhausted by the war with Mexico, and the army was not yet provided with Chassepots. However, the reasons by which the Chief justified his moderation seem to me considerably to outweigh others.

About two o'clock in the morning, as I finished writing down this conversation, the heavy artillery in the north were still thundering, shot after shot, and Mont Valérien in particular hammering away like a Vulcan.

*Thursday, January* 26.—Bright weather, and again rather cold. Vigorous firing, while I was still in bed. To my jottings of last night I have to add an interesting speech of the Chancellor's. When at tea Bismarck-Bohlen said, "That is a happy idea, the picture in *Kladderadatsch;* Napoleon waiting for the train and saying, 'There is the whistle.' He has his ermine cloak round him for the journey back to Paris, and his travelling-bag in his hand." "Yes," replied the Chief; "so he really thinks, and he may be right. But I fear he will be too late in jumping in. At the end there may be no other way. It may be easier than

Favre can be got to believe. But he will need half the army, to establish his authority."

At this point I may also mention the patriotic fury displayed on the morning before last by the gardener's wife, who cleans out my room and makes the bed. Her name is Marie Lodier, a little person, of somewhat hectic appearance, with large dark eyes, rather lively and sprightly, though she can neither read nor write. When I told her that Paris would now be in our hands in a few days, she utterly refused to believe it. "Paris," she said, "was impregnable, invincible, not to be subdued by artillery, though possibly by hunger. But if she were commanding inside," she continued, with flashing eyes, and in the utmost excitement, "she would not give it up, even if she had to starve."

About half-past ten the Chief went to the King. We meanwhile had ourselves taken, a large group, by a Berlin photographer in front of the garden side of the house; the Minister is to be introduced later into the middle foreground of the picture. After breakfast B. told me a number of amusing stories of the English court, especially of the Prince of Wales—a pleasant personage, which is a hopeful fact for the future—and may he be found to agree with his disagreeable countrymen!

About two o'clock, not long after the Chief had returned from the King, Favre came again. When he went away in about an hour's time to go back to Paris, we heard that it was decided he should come again at eight o'clock in the morning, with a general, to settle the military questions—the military questions, that is, connected with the Capitulation! That then *is* the position! Paris is giving in. The bombardment has done good service in the South, and still more in the North, and the bread-basket is getting empty.

I go with L. to the town of d'Avray, where we see brisk firing proceeding in every direction. Short ruddy flashes dart from a French battery lying in the distant gloom. Our firing comes from the right hand, probably from Meudon. Again there seems to be burning in the town. We come back by Sèvres, where we notice marks of French shells on four houses.

When I told Hatzfeld of our excursion, he said, "I wish I had seen the Firing and the Burning! This is probably my last opportunity. At night one could make the fire out much better, if one only knew where to go for it." I promised, if the Chief would give me leave, to go out with him this very evening, and give him a good view of it. (He went out later—with Bohlen, I think—but they saw nothing.)

Mr. Hans von Rochow and Count Lehndorff were present at dinner. The Chief spoke of Favre, and among other things said, "He told me, that on Sundays the boulevards were still crowded with well and gaily dressed ladies with pretty children." I replied, 'I wonder they have not eaten *you* up before this.' It was then mentioned that to-day the bombarding had gone on with unusual vigour, and the Minister remarked, "I remember we once had an under-official in our Court—Stepki, I think his name was—who had to look after the flogging. He had a way of always applying the three last lashes with special force—as a wholesome reminder." The conversation passed to Stroussberg, and some one observed that he now was likely "to go to the dogs." On which the Chief said, "He once said to me, 'I know I shall never die in my house.' But the crash need not have come so quickly. Perhaps not at all, except for the war. He always covered his advances with fresh bonds, and that worked—although other Jews, who had got rich before him, tried with all their might to spoil his game. Then came the war, and down went his Roumanians, so low that they might be valued at so much the hundredweight. For all that, however, he is a clever fellow, and of restless activity."

The cleverness and restlessness of Stroussberg led some one to speak of Gambetta, who, he claimed to know, "had made his five millions out of the war," a statement which others of the guests, I think, reasonably doubted. After the Dictator of Bordeaux came Napoleon, of whom Bohlen said it was asserted that he had saved at least fifty millions during the nineteen years of his reign. "Others say eighty," added the Chief. "I look upon it as doubtful. Louis Philippe spoiled the game. He allowed *émeutes* to be got up, and then bought on the Amsterdam Bourse, till at last the commercial world saw what he was driving at." Hatzfeld or Keudell remarked that the industrious King had fallen ill from time to time with the same object in view.

It was then observed that under the Empire Morny in particular had known how to make money in every possible way, and the Chief told us "When he was appointed ambassador to St. Petersburg, he came with a whole long train of elegant carriages, and all his trunks, and chests, and boxes, full of laces, and silks, and woman's finery, for which as an ambassador he had not to pay duty. Every attendant had his own carriage; every attaché, or secretary, at least two, and he himself five or six. After he had been there a few days he sold all his things by auction—carriages, and lace, and fineries. He is said to have made 800,000 roubles by it. He was unscrupulous, but a good fellow—in fact, he could be a very good fellow." He illustrated this by examples, then went on: "In St. Petersburg, too, they had a very good notion of such things—the influential people, I mean. Not that they took money directly. But when any of them wanted anything, he went into a French shop and bought expensive lace, gloves, or jewellery, for thousands of roubles. But the shop was carried on in the interest of the official they wanted to get at, or his wife."

He then told us once more, but in rather a different form, the story of the Finn from whom he had wanted to buy wood. "He was at first quite willing to let me have it," said he. "Probably he took me for a merchant or something like it, from the Baltic. But when I told him it was" (a Russian word) "for the Prussian Embassy, he was startled; he was evidently very uneasy. He asked whether the" (Russian word) "was for the Crown? Perhaps Prussia was a province of the Russian empire? I told him, not quite that, but the Embassy had to do with the Crown. That was imprudent and undiplomatic; it clearly did not satisfy him, and it was no good my offering to pay him on the spot. He undoubtedly feared that I should extort the money from him again, and that he would be clapped in prison into the bargain and flogged." After giving an instance of that being done, he ended, "The next morning he did not come back."

Bohlen called across the table, "Pray tell the good story of the Jew with the worn-out boots, who got five-and-twenty." "Yes," said the Chief, "that was so. One day there came into our Chancery a Jew, who wished to be conveyed back to Prussia. But he was very ragged, and had particularly bad boots. He was told, yes, he should be taken back. But he wished first to have another pair of boots, claimed it as a right, and behaved so boldly and impudently, shrieking and using violent language, that the gentlemen of the office did not know what to do with him.

Even the servants did not feel safe with the raving fellow. At last, when the thing got too bad, I was summoned to give aid in person. I told him he must be quiet or I would have him locked up. He answered, defiantly, 'You cannot do it, for in Russia you have no such power.' 'We will see,' said I. 'I am bound to send you home; but I feel no call to give you boots, though I might have done so, had you not behaved so outrageously.' I then threw open the window and beckoned to a Gorodowoy, or Russian policeman, who was stationed a little way off. My Jew went on shrieking and scolding till the policeman, a big strong fellow, came in. To him I said" (some Russian words, not translated), "and the great policeman carried off the little Jew, and put him in prison. The morning after next he came back, quite a different man, and declared himself ready to go without new boots. I asked him how he had got on in the meanwhile. 'Badly—very badly!' 'What had they done to him?' 'Ah! they had—they had actually—ill-used him personally!' I expressed my regrets, and asked whether he would like to make any complaint. He preferred, however, to start off at once: and I have never heard of him since."

In the evening I studied drafts, while in the world without cannon were roaring, between nine and ten especially, louder than usual. The Chief was working alone in his room—probably upon the terms of the Capitulation and Armistice—and nothing was heard of him. Below it was rumoured that a negotiator from Napoleon at Wilhelmshöhe was on his way to us. The ever-accumulating business has caused the despatch to Versailles of a fourth secretary, who has arrived to-day. He is a Herr Zesulka, who will be useful as a copyist and decipherer, though he is still unemployed.

In the tea-room towards half-past ten I came upon the Chief in conversation with the deputies von Köller and von Forckenbeck. The former was saying that we should soon want money again. "We did not intend to ask any more from the Reichstag," said he, "for we never thought the war would last so long. I wrote to Camphausen, but he advises requisitions and contributions. These, however, are difficult to collect, for we have not enough troops in proportion to the large extent of ground which we cover, to exercise compulsion. To hold a country two hundred and forty thousand miles square completely in hand, one wants two millions of soldiers. War has raised the price of everything. When we make requisitions, we get nothing. When we pay cash, enough always comes upon the market, and cheaper than in Germany. A bushel of oats here costs four francs, but imported from Germany, six. At first I thought of having the matriculation fees paid in advance. But that only yields twenty millions, while Bavaria has seventy-two millions to her own account. I then thought of the plan of applying to our Diet, to advance us a sum. Only first we must find out what we can squeeze out of the Parisians, that is out of the city of Paris, for it is with her only we have now to deal." Forckenbeck was of opinion that the Chief's plan would meet with no insuperable difficulties in the Diet. Of course the Doctrinaires would oppose the claim, and others would say that Prussia must always be ready to help in return and make sacrifices for the rest, but we should in all probability have the majority, as Köller would confirm; which he did.

An officer of the dark blue hussars came in afterwards, an unusually handsome young fellow. He was a Count Arnim, who had just arrived from Le Mans, and had all sorts of interesting news from there. The inhabitants of the place, he said, seemed very sensible people, who condemned Gambetta's policy, and were always expressing their desire for peace. "Yes," replied the Chief, "that is very fine of the people, but how does it help us if, with all their good sense, they allow Gambetta to be constantly calling up from the earth fresh armies of 150,000 men with a stamp of his foot?" And when Arnim told us further that a great many prisoners had been again taken, he remarked, "That does not please me. What are we to come to at last with them all? Why do they make so many prisoners?"

*Friday, January* 27.—The bombardment ceased, they say, at twelve o'clock last night. It was, we are told, to have been resumed again, at six o'clock this morning, if the Parisian Government did not agree to our terms for the Armistice. As silence reigns, I presume the gentlemen have given in. But Gambetta?

In the morning I despatched a telegram upon the successful operations of our armies against Bourbaki. At half-past eight Moltke came, and was closeted with the Chief for about three-quarters of an hour. Shortly before eleven appeared the Frenchmen: Favre (who had cut short his grey demagogue's beard) with his pronounced underlip, his clear eyes and yellowish complexion; General Beaufort d'Hautpoule, with his adjutant Calvel, and a "chief of the engineers of the Eastern Railway," Dürrbach. Beaufort seems to have led the attack upon the fort at Montretout, on the 19th. The negotiations of these gentlemen with the Chief must have either been quickly brought to a point, or broken off; for soon after twelve, while we were seated at breakfast, they went out at the back of the house and got into the carriage which brought them here. Favre looks depressed.

The General had a remarkably red face, and seemed not quite firm on his legs. This was noticed also by the others. Soon after the Frenchmen had gone, the Chancellor came in to us, and said, "I only want a little fresh air; pray don't disturb yourselves, gentlemen." Then, turning to Delbrück with a shake of his head, he said, "There is no getting on with him! Really not a responsible person, I believe, a little tipsy. I told him he had better think it over till half-past one, and perhaps he may come to his senses. Hot-headed! ill-mannered! What does he call himself? Something like Bouffre or Bauffre?" "Beaufort," said Keudell. "Ah," said the Chief, "the name, but not the manners of a man of rank." The good general seems in fact—probably his ordinary capacities have been weakened by hunger—to have attempted more than he could stand, and eaten too good a *déjeuner.*

At breakfast it was mentioned that Fontenay, which was set on fire by our troops by way of punishment for the destruction of the railway bridge by the insurgent peasants, had been seen blazing by Forckenbeck, on his way here. Delbrück rejoiced with us "that at last once more a proper punishment had been inflicted."

When I remarked to our gardener's wife to-day that now surely she would no longer doubt that the fall of Paris was at hand; she must have seen the general who had come out to arrange matters, "This general" she answered, raging like an angry cat, "is a traitor" (she pronounced the word *traitre* like *trait*), "just like Bazaine and Napoleon, the swine, who began the war with the Prussians before we were ready for it. All our generals are traitors, and M. Favre is another. But wait till we have a firm Government, and make war on you again, then *tous les Prussiens, capot, capot, capot!*" ("All the Prussians are done for, done for, done for"). I remarked, "You will probably have your Emperor back in eight weeks." She answered, savagely, putting her arms a-kimbo, "*Mais non, Monsieur!* He must stop in Germany. If he comes to Paris, we shall send him to the scaffold, and Bazaine too." Lastly, she said that France was ruined, and she and her family also, for Madame Jessé was "near"; she had lost some of her property, and would no longer keep a gardener, but have her garden looked after by simple day labourers. Poor little woman! Let us hope things turned out better.

In the afternoon we heard that shortly before one o'clock the Chancellor had first gone to the King, and then called on Moltke, where besides Podbielski, he had again met the Frenchmen. The latter had gone back to Paris about four, and will come again to-morrow about twelve to conclude the Capitulation. I read a letter to the Chief with newspaper cuttings, which he handed over to me this morning to use at my discretion, and which contained much the same thing as English fools are always boring the Minister with in their sentimental epistles. It runs thus:

"I send you cuttings from the *Standard* and the *Times*, in which you will see something of the cruel and inhuman conduct of the Prussians during this war. Would to God you could deny it! In this country our heart bleeds at the thought, and we wonder how the soldiers of a civilised nation can commit such frightful acts, and how their officers can allow, or even encourage, them. You, my lord Count, will one day, and that before very long, have to regret the horrible and diabolical way in which this most cruel war has been conducted." This letter was signed, "A Soldier—but no murderer."

This "Soldier" was evidently not in the field in India against the Sepoys, and has not seen his countrymen in the

Crimean war burning down harmless Russian villages and towns on the Baltic. He has not even heard of these things. He has not even read his newspaper cuttings carefully, or he could scarcely have missed seeing, in one of them, a report upon the reprisals made for the slaughter of the men of the Landwehr by the Garibaldians (near Châtillon), and a remark by the writer, one of our artillerists, to the effect that "We are fighting no longer against the French army, but against assassins."

Later on I went with L. to Bougival, where we inspected more closely the famous barricade at the end of the place, and noticed the ravages which the war had made, in some of the houses near Barrot's. Here things looked worse in some ways than at Barrot's, and the library in particular, and a collection of old maps in one of the houses, had come off very badly. The soldiers told us that the German batteries planted above the place, not being informed of the commencement of the armistice, had fired a number of shots this morning. We, however, had heard nothing of it, and the story probably arises from a simple rumour, founded on some misunderstood speech.

At dinner the Chief said of Beaufort: "This officer behaved like a man of no education. Blustering, and shouting, with great oaths, and his '*Moi, général de l'armée française,*' he was hardly to be borne. He was always playing the 'plain soldier' and the 'good comrade.' Moltke was once or twice impatient, and as things went he might have burst out fifty times." "Favre, whose own manners are not 'first-rate,' said to me, '*J'en suis humilié!*' (I am ashamed of this.) However, it was drink, a common thing with him."

"On the general's staff it was believed that he had been chosen to settle matters, with the intention of letting it all come to nothing. 'On the contrary,' said I, 'they have chosen him because it makes no difference to him that he will sink in public opinion for signing the Capitulation.'"

He then told us: "At our last interview I said to Favre, in French, '*Vous avez été trahi—par la fortune*' ('You have been betrayed—by fortune'). He saw the point well enough, but he only said, 'To whom do you say that? Why, in three or four hours I also shall be numbered among the traitors.' He added that his position in Paris was a hazardous one. I proposed to him: 'Provoke an *émeute* then, while you still have an army to suppress it with.' He looked at me in horror, as much as to say, 'What a bloodthirsty fellow you are!' He has, moreover, no idea of how things are with us. More than once he pointed out to me that France was the land of Freedom, while Despotism reigned with us. I had told him, for instance, that we wanted money, and Paris must let us have some. He said that we might raise a loan. I told him that could not be done without the Reichstag or Diet. 'What!' said he, 'why, surely 500,000,000 francs could be raised without the Chamber.' 'No,' replied I, 'not five francs.' He could not believe it. But I told him I had had four years' experience of popular representation in time of war, and to raise a loan without the Diet had always been the point to which I had got, but it had never occurred to me to go beyond it. That seemed rather to shake him in his opinion. He only said that in France they would not stand upon ceremony (*on ne se gênerait pas*). Then he always came back to the assertion that France enjoyed infinite liberty. It is really very comical to hear a Frenchman talk like this— especially Favre, who has always belonged to the opposition. But they are constituted so. You may give a Frenchman five-and-twenty (lashes). If only you make a fine speech at the same time about Liberty, and the Dignity of man which it expresses, and make the appropriate attitudes, he imagines he is not being flogged."

"Oh, Keudell," he then said, suddenly, "that reminds me: I must have in the morning a commission from the King—in German, of course. The German Emperor must only write German. His Minister may be guided by circumstances. Official correspondence must be conducted in the language of the country, not in a foreign language. Bernstorff first decided to introduce this with us, but he carried it too far. He wrote in German to all the Diplomatists, and they all answered him—by arrangement of course—in their own languages—Russian, Spanish, Swedish, and I know not what; so that he had to establish a regular swarm of translators in the bureau. I found matters in this state when I came into office. Budberg (the Russian ambassador in Berlin in 1858) sent me a note in Russian. That would not do. If they had wanted to revenge themselves Gortschakoff would have been entitled to write in Russian to our ambassador in St. Petersburg. That would have been right enough. It is reasonable to wish that all the representatives of foreign Powers should understand and use the language of the country to which they are accredited. But for me in Berlin to answer a German letter in Russian was unreasonable. I made up my mind therefore—whatever comes in, that is not German, or French, or English, or Italian, remains as it is, and goes into the cupboards. Well, Budberg wrote reminder upon reminder, always in Russian. No answer; the things were always passed on to the cupboard. At last came the man himself, and asked why he had had no answer. 'Answer,' said I, in astonishment; 'to what? I have seen nothing from you.' Well, he had written four weeks ago, and sent several reminders since. 'Indeed! Ah, now I think of it, there is a heap of documents in Russian writing, lying below; they may perhaps be among those. But no one downstairs understands Russian, and whatever comes in, in an unintelligible language goes into the cupboard.'" It was then agreed, if I understand rightly, that Budberg was to write in French, and the Foreign Office might occasionally do so also.

The Chief then began talking of the French negotiators, and said: "Monsieur Dürrbach has represented himself as a member of the administration of the Eastern Railway, and as having a great interest in it. Yes; what would he say if he knew of our intentions?" (He meant probably that the Eastern Railway was to be conceded to us.) Hatzfeld observed: "He clasped his hands above his head when it was pointed out to him on the staff-map what destruction they themselves had done on bridges, tunnels, &c. 'I have always spoken against that,' said he, 'telling people that a bridge can be put up again in three hours, only they would not listen.'" "Yes," added the Chief; "a bridge for us certainly; but the railway bridges with the lines along them? They will find it hard to bring up provisions, especially if they have committed similar follies in the west. I suppose they count upon Brittany and Normandy, where sheep are in plenty, and upon the sea-ports. To my own knowledge there are many bridges and tunnels there, if they have only not destroyed them too. Otherwise they will be in a great scrape. I hope, too, that people in London will only send them presents of bacon, and not of corn."

In this wise the conversation turned for a while upon the satisfaction of the Stomach of Paris. At last the Chief told us a little story of his "good friend Daumer who would hear nothing of death. We were once out hunting in the Taunus, and had just breakfasted. I called attention to the beautiful view which the spot commanded. How prettily the village below lay among the trees, with its white church, and how lovely the churchyard looked beneath it! 'What?' asked he. 'I mean the graveyard there.' 'Ah! let me alone with your graveyards; you have quite ruined my appetite with them,' said he. 'How many sausages are there left?' said I. 'As many as you please; I can eat no more.' The recollection of death had quite upset him."

*Saturday, January* 28.—Like yesterday, it is rather cold, some four degrees of frost, and the sky is clouded. About eleven the French negotiators come in again: Favre, Dürrbach, two others who I suppose are also high railway officials, and two military men, another general with another adjutant, both stately persons of decorous bearing. They breakfasted with us. Then a long conference in Moltke's house. Afterwards the Chief dictates to his secretaries Willisch and Saint Blanquart two copies of the terms of the Capitulation and the Armistice, which are signed and sealed by Bismarck and Favre afterwards, at about twenty minutes past seven, in the green room next to the Minister's study.

Meanwhile my time had been free, and I employed it in a walk to the castle of Meudon and the batteries there, in which L. and another Saxon, Kohlschütter (belonging to the Government or the Civil Commissariat), joined me. The paved way through the wood had been very much broken up by our heavy artillery. At a little opening in the trees, where the paths cross one another, we passed a beautiful fir-tree. Farther on was a place arranged for an outpost. Barracks and walls pierced with loopholes were on the right, heaps of gabions and fascines on the left of the path. We pass through a door of open ironwork to the castle, on which the trees press closely, and which is surrounded at the back by a strong earthwork. Here we picked up some splinters of the shells which had been flying about, and which had torn many holes in the trees and knocked off branches. The castle, a stately but not very ornamental building of two stories, with no projecting buttresses, had suffered very little on the outside. Only the front turned towards Paris and Issy shewed some conspicuous traces of shells, and the ground immediately in front was strewn with petards great and small. The inside of the building, the steps, halls, and rooms were terribly wrecked, full of *débris* and shreds of furniture, splinters and crushed glass. On the walls soldiers and other visitors had made attempts at writing up their names and their mockery of the Gauls in German and outlandish tongues.

The terrace in front of the castle was upturned with pick and shovel, and converted into a sort of subterranean camp with deep ditches. In one of these had been set up a little block-house room with an oven, in which the field-telegraphist lived. In front, on the terrace, and immediately behind the stone breastwork, which runs round it towards the Parisian basin, was the battery with its high-mounted guns. We conversed for some time with the Prussian officer in command here, a very spruce and communicative young warrior. Below us lay, partly on the slope of the hill and partly at its foot, the houses and streets of Meudon, still deserted by their inhabitants. On our right we looked across to the pleasant wooded glen of Clamart. Far away on our left the bend of the Seine shimmered in the afternoon sun, and between the two, rather more towards the right on a bare piece of rising ground, rose in front of us, Fort Issy, the barracks of which had been reduced to ruins by our shells.

Returning to Versailles, I spent half an hour at the Hôtel de Chasse with H. and F., who have both been made lieutenants.

In the evening the Frenchmen dined with us. In consequence of the numerous company we sat farther apart than usual, and as the Parisian guests generally did not talk loud the conversation yielded little matter for jotting. The general (whose name was Valden) ate little, and hardly spoke at all. Favre, too, was dejected and sparing of his words. The adjutant, a M. d'Hérisson, seemed not to take the matter so much to heart, and the railway officials devoted themselves with praiseworthy zeal to the long-withheld eatables. As far as I could make out from their talk, dreadful scarcity has actually existed for some time in Paris, and in the past week the mortality, if I understood right, reached the total of about five thousand deaths. A great many children, especially between one and two years old, had died, and everywhere one met people with coffins for such little Frenchmen. "Favre and the general," said Delbrück afterwards, "looked like poor culprits, who are to-morrow to go to the scaffold. They made me sorry for them."

Keudell is very hopeful about the conclusion of peace; he thinks we may probably be back in Berlin in four weeks. Short'y before ten, a gentleman with a full beard and apparently between forty and forty-five, came in, who called himself Duparc, and was at once conducted to the Chief, with whom he remained for about two hours. He came, it is said, with proposals of peace from Wilhelmshöhe. Capitulation and Armistice do not, then, mean quite the end of the war with France.

*Sunday, January* 29.—A cloudy sky. Our troops march to occupy the forts. In the morning I read despatches upon the London conference, and other business, as well as the

Armistice and Capitulation convention signed yesterday. The latter fills, in our copy, ten folio pages, and is sewn together with threads in the French colours, to the ends of which Favre has affixed his seal. The contents are briefly as follows: An armistice of twenty-one days is agreed upon, which is to hold good over the whole of France. The contending armies maintain their positions, which are signified by a line of demarcation, defined in the memorandum of agreement. The object of the armistice is to enable the Government of National Defence to summon a freely-elected assembly of representatives of the French people, to decide the question whether the war is to be continued, or peace concluded, and on what conditions. The elections are to be perfectly free and undisturbed. The Assembly meets at Bordeaux.

The forts of Paris are to be handed over to the German army, which is to occupy other parts of the outer line of defence of Paris up to an appointed boundary. During the armistice German troops are not to enter the city. The *enceinte* loses its guns, the carriages of which will be taken into the forts. The whole garrison of Paris and the forts, with the exception of 12,000 men, who are left to the authorities for service inside, become prisoners of war, and must, officers excepted, give up their arms and remain in the city. After the armistice has run out, in case peace is not then concluded, they are to give themselves up to the German army as prisoners of war. The Francs-tireurs will be disbanded by the French Government. The National Guard of Paris retain their arms, so as to preserve order in the city, and the same applies to the gendarmes, the republican guard, the excise officers, and the firemen. After the surrender of the forts and the disarming of the *enceinte*, the revictualling of Paris will be allowed by the Germans. Only the provisions destined for this object must not be taken from regions occupied by our troops. Whoever wants to leave Paris must have a pass from the French military authorities, with a *visé* by the German advanced posts. This pass and *visé* is to be given to those who wish to canvass the provinces, as well as to the deputies elected to the National Assembly at Bordeaux. The town of Paris pays within fourteen days a war-contribution of two hundred million francs (£8,000,000). During the armistice none of the public property which might contribute to this payment, is to be removed. During this time also the introduction of arms or ammunition into Paris is forbidden.

Count Henckel, who has been appointed prefect in Metz, was present at breakfast. He maintained that in his province the elections, after some five years or so, would turn out in favour of the government! He would even pledge himself to bring that about. In Elsass, on the other hand, things did not promise so well, for the Germans were not so compliant to all authority as the French were. He told us also that his province had certainly suffered greatly. At the beginning of the war it had probably from 32,000 to 33,000 horses, but now he believed it had not more than 5000. At breakfast the rumour was spoken of that Bourbaki had shot himself, in despair because he had had no success with his army against Werder, and was now forced to retreat before him and Manteuffel.

In the afternoon I made an excursion to Petit Chesnay, where I wished once more to look up my friends of the Forty-sixth, who had marched in and halted there. I found an officer whom I did not know, who told me that the regiment had been ordered this morning to occupy Mont Valérien, which it had probably done by this time. Before dinner I again read drafts, and among them a letter in which the Chief explains to the King the impossibility of demanding from Favre, in addition to what he has granted, the flags of the French regiments interned in Paris.

Count Henckel and the French adjutant of yesterday dined with us. The latter, whose full name is d'Hérisson de Saulnier, wore a black hussar's uniform, with yellow epaulettes, and embroidery on the fore arm. He is said to understand German, and to speak it, though the conversation, in which the Chief took an active part, was carried on mostly in French. To-day, when Favre and the General were not present—the former was in the house, but he was so busy he had his dinner taken to him in the little drawing-room—the Frenchman was even more lively, sprightly, and amusing than yesterday. For a long time he bore the whole burden of the conversation, telling us good stories and anecdotes one after the other. He stated also, that the starvation in the city had latterly been very much felt, though he appeared to know the cheerful, better than the serious aspect of it. He said that the period in the fast which he had found most interesting was when they "ate up the Jardin des Plantes." Elephant's flesh, he told us, cost 9 francs the pound, and tasted like coarse beef. Then there had been actually *filet de chameau* and *côtelettes de tigre*—on which, as on other points in his narrative, we made no remarks. The dog's flesh market was set up in the Rue Saint-Honoré, and a pound cost about a shilling. There were hardly any dogs now to be seen in Paris, and when one came round the corner three or four people at once started off in chase. The same with the cats. Whenever a pigeon was seen on a roof the street was in a moment full of men anxious to catch it. Only the carrier-pigeons were spared. These carried the despatches in the middle of their tail-feathers, of which they ought to have nine. If one had only eight, it was at once said, "He's only a civilian, and he must go the way of all flesh." A lady is supposed to have said, "I shall never eat pigeon again; I should always be feeling that I had swallowed the letter carrier."

In return for these and other stories the Chief told him various things that could not have been known of in the Paris clubs and *salons*, and which he might like to hear, as, for instance, the ordinary behaviour of Rothschild in Ferrières, and the metamorphosis by which the Elector of Hesse had converted grandfather Amschel from a small Jew into a big one. He called him repeatedly " Juif de la cour," and thereby hit off a characteristic of the household Jews of the Polish nobility.

After dinner I read drafts and reports; among the latter a very interesting one, recommending that we should leave Metz and German Lothringen to the French, and appropriate Luxemburg. The suggestion was declined, because we regarded Metz as indispensable for securing Germany against the French, and because the German nation would not tolerate any departure from the programme drawn up five months ago.

Favre, with the other Frenchmen, stays till late. He does not go till about a quarter to eleven, and then not back to Paris, but to his lodgings in the Boulevard du Roi. He will come again to-morrow at noon.

Later on the Chief came in to tea. The talk was of the capitulation and armistice. "But how," asked Bohlen, " if the others refuse—Gambetta and the Prefects in the South?" " Well, in that case," replied the Chief, "we have the forts, and with them control of the town. If the people in Bordeaux do not accept the convention, we remain in the forts, and keep the Parisians shut up, and in that case may possibly not prolong the armistice to the 19th of February

Meanwhile they have given up their arms and gun-carriages, and must pay the contribution. It is always the worse for a man who has given a pledge like what Faust gave for his agreement, and then cannot keep it."

Bohlen then turned the conversation upon d'Hérisson, and the bright and amusing way in which he had told us of the dog-hunts in Paris. He had been with them in China, and it was supposed that he had carried away a memorial or two from the Emperor's summer palace. He mentioned that on his way home from that country, Montauban, who was in great favour with the Emperor, and thought it probable he might be raised to a peerage, sent him, d'Hérisson, on in advance, in order to prevent his being made Count or Duke of Pekin, which, from the word *pequin*, might have given an opening for bad jokes.* He had accordingly been named Palikao, which meant "the bridge with nine arches," and was a place near which the troops of the French expedition had routed the soldiers of the Celestial Empire in battle. It was then mentioned that Bourbaki had really intended to shoot himself, but had not injured himself mortally. The Chief afterwards remarked that Favre had admitted to him to-day that he had acted a little rashly in the matter of revictualling. He really did not know whether it would be possible to provide the many hundred thousands of people in the town with food in time. Somebody said, "Storch can hand over some oxen and flour in case of need." "Yes," replied the Chief, "that he must do, but he must see that we come to no harm by it." Bismarck-Bohlen thought we need not give them anything; they might see for themselves where they could get it, and so on. "What?" said the Chief, "Do you want, then, to let them starve?"

* *Pequin* in French military slang means "the civilian," with a touch of "the stay-at-home."

"Certainly," said Bohlen. "Then," said the Chief, "how should we manage to raise our war contribution?"

In the course of further conversation he said: "Important State business and negotiations with the enemy do not worry me. If they make objections to my ideas and demands, even when I am unreasonable, I take it calmly. But the small wrangling of mere land-lubbers in political affairs, and their ignorance of what is or is not possible! First comes one and wishes this, then another who considers that indispensable. When you have got rid of them, up comes a third, an adjutant or adjutant-general, who says, 'But, your Excellency, that is impossible,' or 'We must have that, else—' Why, yesterday they actually wanted a clause which had never been discussed to be inserted in a document already signed!"

Bohlen or Hatzfeld then recurred to another of d'Hérisson's anecdotes. After the 4th of September the police-sergeants of Paris appeared in altered guise. Moustaches and imperials were cut off, and only a small peaceable-looking whisker left. The curl on the left ear was also gone, and the side arms, and the whole military uniform—all but the policeman's helmet. So it had been ordained by the democratic wisdom of Kératry. All Paris laughed. The guardians of public order were instructed moreover always to parade the streets in threes. This went on for some weeks, when the order fell into oblivion, and they were always to be seen in pairs. When provisions had become scarce, the street wits said, "Look, there are two sergeants; they must have eaten the third!"

Hatzfeld told us that a Spanish secretary of legation had been here, who had come from Bordeaux, and wanted to get into Paris. He wished to fetch out his countrymen, had with him a letter from Chambord to Favre, and seemed in a great hurry. What is to be said to him? The Chief bent forward a little, then sat upright again, and said, "The attempt to carry despatches through our headquarters from one member of the hostile government to another is matter for a court-martial. When he comes again treat the matter very seriously, be cool, look astonished, and tell him what I have said, and that we shall bring against the new King of Spain the charge of violating neutrality, and shall demand satisfaction. I wonder, too, how the military came to let him through. They always are absurdly over-respectful in dealing with foreign diplomatists. Even if he had been an ambassador, they ought to have turned him back, though he might have died of hunger and cold in consequence. Such letter-carrying borders very closely upon spying."

We then talked of the general rush into and out of Paris that would likely follow. He replied, however, "Oh, the French will not let many out, and we only let those through who have a passport from the authorities inside—perhaps not even all of them."

Some one then said that Rothschild had been supplied with a passport, and wanted to be let out. Thereupon the Chief remarked, "It would be a good thing to detain him as a Franc-tireur—to be reckoned among the prisoners of war." (To Keudell): "Just find out about that." "Then Bleichröder will appear," cried Bohlen, "and beg on his knees in the name of the entire Rothschild family." Reference was then made to the surprising fact that an accurate *résumé* of the convention signed yesterday was already to be seen in the *Daily Telegraph*. Then we talked of Stieber.

"How often one is deceived about people," the Chief struck in. "I hardly recognise people till I hear them speak. When I went within the last few days to call upon Favre, I saw a man standing before the door in the dusk, who made me uncomfortable. I thought it must be his son-in-law's servant who was lounging about there, for he looked like a Spaniard. When he came up to me I half drew my sword so as to have it ready. Then he greeted me: 'Good evening, your Excellency,' and when I examined him more closely, it was Stieber."

*Monday, January* 30. — A foggy morning, moderately cold, somewhere about freezing-point. Favre seems not to have stopped in Versailles, but, late as it was, to have gone back to Paris. I despatch various telegrams to Berlin, Cologne, and London, concerning our completed occupation, without hindrance, of the forts of Paris, the possibility of a famine there, the difficulty of bringing provisions quickly from a distance, and our readiness to avert the momentary danger by the use of our own stores. Warning, too, is to be given in the press against a rush to the headquarters.

I went out in the afternoon with L. to the bridge at Sèvres, and thence as far as Bellevue on the way to Meudon. On the road there, which at the end rises very steeply from the river, we saw hardly anybody but soldiers. A barrier, guarded by riflemen, prevents our further progress. We learn from the soldiers, to our astonishment, that the castle at Meudon is in flames. A French shell seems to have hit the wall of one of the rooms during the last few days of the bombardment, remained sticking there, and later on been exploded by accident. Probably the accident was due to some carelessness. It will, however, make a lovely ruin, something like the castle at Heidelberg.

Favre, and other Frenchmen, such as the President or Prefect of the Paris police, were again working busily with the Chief in the afternoon, and dined at half-past five with him and the Councillors. The secretaries and I were to dine this time in the Hôtel des Réservoirs, there being no room for us at table. I, however, stayed at home, translated Granville's latest peace proposals for the Emperor, and then dined in my room.

Abeken came up to me in the evening, to fetch away the translation. He expressed regret that he had not known I was in, or they would have made room for me below. It was a pity I had not been there, as the conversation had been particularly interesting. The Chief had said, among other things, to the Frenchmen, that consistency in politics often became simply blundering, obstinacy, and self-will. One must be ruled by facts, by the position of things, and by probabilities, taking into account the conditions, and serving one's country according to circumstances, and not following one's own opinions, which are often mere prejudices. When he first entered upon political life, as a green young man, he had had very different ideas and aims. But he had changed his mind after thinking the matter over, and then had not shrunk from sacrificing his own wishes, if anything was to be gained thereby, to the necessities of the day. One must not force one's own inclinations and wishes upon one's country, he said further, and then concluded, "La patrie veut être servie et pas dominée." This saying made a great impression upon the Parisian gentlemen (particularly, of course, its form), and Favre said, " C'est bien juste, Monsieur le Comte, c'est profond!" Another Frenchman exclaimed with equal enthusiasm, " Oui, messieurs, c'est un mot profond!" Bucher, while confirming this report, told me further that Favre had been foolish enough to follow up the Chief's speech—which had, of course, been intended to convey a hint to the French, as many earlier sayings had been aimed at other guests—and his own praise of its truth and profundity, by saying, "Nevertheless it is a fine thing to see a man who has never changed his principles." The railway director, too, whom Bucher, however, thought a far shrewder person than Favre, had added, *à propos* of the expression "servie et pas dominée," that this of course would imply the subordination of individual genius to the will and opinion of the majority, and majorities had always shown but little understanding, experience, or character. To this, however, the Chief answered finely, in a sense which showed conclusively his consciousness of responsibility before God as one of his guiding stars. In opposition to the claims of genius, exalted by the former speaker, he said that duty— by which he meant what is defined by Kant as the Categorical Imperative—is the weightier and more excellent of the two.

Late in the evening—it was past eleven—the Chief came down to take tea with us. There were assembled on this occasion, besides Wagner and myself, Barons Holnstein and Keudell, and a regular shoal of counts: Hatzfeld, Henckel, Maltzahn, and Bismarck-Bohlen. The Chief remarked, "I am still curious to know how Gambetta will take it. Gambetta —the Italian partner!—*the smallbone à l'Italienne.*\* He still seems to intend thinking over it; for he has not yet answered. I fancy that he, too, will give in in time. However if he does not, there is no harm done. A little of the line of the Maine business in France would be by no means unacceptable." Then he continued, "These Frenchmen are really the oddest fellows. Favre comes to me with the face of an injured saint, and an air of having the most important communication to make. When I notice it I say, 'Shall we go upstairs?' 'Yes,' says he, 'by all means.' Once up there he sits down and writes letter after letter, and I wait in

---

\* *Gambetta* is the name of a little long-legged stork, or marsh-bird of the heron tribe.

vain for any important utterance or information. He had nothing at all to say to me." "Two small pages of notepaper would contain all that he has done here." "And this Prefect of Police! I never in my life saw a more impracticable fellow. We have to advise and assist him in everything. In a single half-hour he made me requests of every possible kind, till at last I almost lost patience, and said to him: 'But, my dear sir, had you not better give it me in writing? It is impossible for me to carry everything in my head, and it is only in this way that the matter can profitably be settled. Thousands of things pass through my brain, and when I begin thinking carefully about one of them, I lose sight of the others.'"

We then spoke of the difficulties which we should in all probability afterwards encounter in providing the Parisians with food. Several of the railways, for the time at least, are not available. To draw provisions from the parts of France lying behind those which we occupy, might bring ourselves into want and embarrassment, and the harbour of Dieppe, which was counted upon for supplies from foreign countries, was only fit for small ships. The Chief calculated roughly how many portions a day would be needed, and about how many could be brought in, supposing that the conditions were not too abnormal, and found that the supply could only be a scanty one, and that many people may yet have to succumb to hunger. He added, "Favre himself told me they had held out too long. But he admitted it was only because they knew there were stores in our hands ready for them in Lagny. They were quite correctly informed about this. We had there for them at one time about 1400 loaded waggons."

The talk then turned upon the difficulties we encountered in collecting the taxes and contributions, and the Chief explained to Maltzahn what arrangements he had made accordingly. "We must, as far as possible," he added, "avoid scattering our troops, keep them together as a rule at the chief places in the Departments or Arrondissements, and from these centres operate with flying columns against the refusers of taxes, the free companions, the people who hide away their property, and all their accomplices."

Some one spoke of the ten million francs which had been imposed upon the district of Fontenay on account of the destruction of the railway bridges, and Henckel declared, with an air of authority, that it was a demand that could not be met; they would not be able to wring two millions out of the people. "Probably not one," said the Chief. "But it is our way. We have always been threatening all kinds of horrible things, and then been unable to carry them out. The people notice this at last, and get used to our threats."

Count Maltzahn told us he had been to Fort Issy. It looked very horrible there, holes, coals, splinters, and rubbish, and above all heaps of filth, and an abominable smell. "Had they no latrines?" asked some one. "Apparently not," answered Maltzahn. "*Ove? dove volete*, as the Italians say," remarked another. "Yes, they are an uncleanly people, the French," said the Chief, reminding us of the horrible arrangements in the town school-house at Clermont, and the similar state of things at Donchery.

Then followed a very interesting and detailed account of the various phases of the scheme for uniting the South German States with the Northern Confederation. "At last, after many difficulties," he went on to say, "we came to deal with the Bavarians, and people said, 'Now there is only one wanting'—but that was the most important of all. I saw a way out of it, and wrote a letter; then a high Bavarian official did good service. In fact, he almost accomplished an impossibility. He made the journey, there and back, in six days, eighty miles without a railway, and up the mountain to the Castle where the King was living. All the while his wife was ill. Yes, it was a great thing for him to do."

In the course of conversation the imprisonment of Jacoby was mentioned, and the Chief observed, " Falkenstein behaved very reasonably, but that measure of his was the reason why we were unable to summon the Diet four weeks earlier, as he would not consent to let Jacoby go when I asked him. If he had eaten him in rhinoceros cutlets, well and good; but to put him in prison—he could get nothing out of that but an old dried-up Jew. Other people, too, would at first listen to none of my remonstrances, so we had to wait ; for the Diet would have had a right to insist on his liberation."

The conversation drifted from Jacoby to Waldeck, whom the Chief described as of "a similar disposition to Favre, always logical, and true to principle, with his opinion and conclusion ready made beforehand; a handsome figure ; a white venerable beard ; phrases in the chest tones of conviction, even about trifles. That impressed people. In a voice which quite shook with the earnestness of his feeling, he would declare that this spoon here was in this glass, and proclaim that every one who would not admit it was a scoundrel. Every one admitted it and praised him in all possible keys for the energy of his nature."

*Tuesday, January* 31.— In the morning I telegraphed various small successes in the South-Eastern departments, where, by agreement, the armistice does not at present hold good. The King of Sweden has delivered a warlike sounding speech from the throne. Wherefore, ye gods ? I prepare two articles by command of the Chief, and then a third, describing the sufferings endured through the siege by a number of unoffending German families, who for one cause or another had remained in Paris during the siege; and mentioning with praise the services in alleviating the lot of these unfortunates rendered by Washburne, the United States ambassador. His conduct in this respect is really most worthy of our gratitude, and his subordinates faithfully seconded his efforts.

The Parisian gentlemen are here again, with Favre, who is urgently entreating Gambetta, by telegram, to give in. It is to be feared that he will not do so. The Prefect of Marseilles at least has mounted the high horse, and snorted down upon poor Favre the patriotic speech: "*Je n'obéis le capitulé de Bismarck. Je ne le connais plus.*" ("I owe no obedience to the man who has capitulated to Bismarck; I know him no longer.") Proud and valiant; but it is well to be far away from the firing. It is not yet certain whether Bourbaki has shot or only wounded himself: his army, however, is clearly in a bad way. It will turn out to have been made up like the other creations of the Dictator of Tours.

Our Frenchmen again dine with the Chief, and I with Wollmann at the Hôtel des Réservoirs, where we see at table, among others, the Marquise ——— with some young lieutenants. She is the fair-haired, spare, and rather free-living lady I have already met with her dogs several times in the streets and in the Park. She came from London, and is serving under the Geneva Cross.

We have again several degrees of frost. Bucher told me at tea that the Chief spoke strongly again at dinner about that old visionary, Garibaldi, whom Favre declared to be a hero. In the evening Duparc is with the Minister. After ten o'clock the latter came down and sat with us. He began talking directly about the unpractical character of the Frenchmen who had been working with him lately. Two Ministers—Favre, and the Finance-Minister, Magnin, who had come out with him this time—had actually spent half an hour toiling over a telegram. He then took occasion to speak of the French generally, and the whole Latin race, and to compare them with the German nations. "The Teutonic, or Germanic race," said he, "is, so to speak, the masculine element, which goes all over Europe and fructifies it. The Celtic and Slav peoples represent the female sex. The former element extends up to the North Sea, and across it to England." I ventured to say: "Even to America; to the Western States of the Union, where men of our race are the best part of the population, and influence the *morale* of the rest." "Yes; these are its children, its fruits," replied he. "We have already seen in France what the Franks are worth. The Revolution of 1789 meant the overthrow of the German element by the Celtic; and what is the result?

"In Spain, too, the Gothic blood long preponderated; and the same in Italy, where the Germans had also taken the lead in the northern provinces. When that died away, farewell to order. It was much the same in Russia, where the German Waräger, the Ruriks, first gathered. If the national party were to overcome the Germans who have settled there, or those who cross over from the Baltic provinces, the people would not remain capable of an orderly constitution." "Certainly things don't as a matter of course, go straight, even with full-blooded Germans. In our South and West, for example, when they were left to themselves there was nothing but Knights of the Empire, Towns of the Empire, and Villages of the Empire, each for itself, so that the whole thing went to pieces. The Germans are all right when they are united by compulsion or by anger—then they are excellent, irresistible, invincible—otherwise every man 'gangs his ain gate.'" "After all, a kindly, upright, and sensibly-conducted absolutism is the best form of government. Unless there is something of that kind everything goes wrong; one man wishes one thing, another another, and there is perpetual hesitation, perpetual delay." "But we have no longer any thorough-going Absolutists. They have gone—the species has died out." I took the liberty to tell him that when I was a small child I had imagined the king to be like the king on German cards, with crown and ermine, sceptre and ball, stiff, gaily-dressed, and always the same, and I had been bitterly disappointed when my nurse took me one day to the walk between the castle at Dresden and the Catholic Church, and pointed out a little, crooked, feeble old man as King Antony. "Yes," said the Chief, "the peasants also about us had the most extraordinary ideas. There is a story that some of us—young people—were assembled in a public place, and had said something against the King, who was present *incognito*. Suddenly he stood up, threw open his cloak, and showed the star on his breast. The others were frightened, but I was believed not to have cared, and to have treated him rudely. For this I would have got ten years' imprisonment, and not been allowed to shave. Well, I grew a long beard at that time, to which I had been used in France in 1842, when the fashion came in, and the story went that every year on St. Sylvester's Eve the executioner came and cut it off. This story was told by well-to-do and in other respects not stupid country people, who repeated it, not out of spite to me, but quite in good faith, and full of pity for the poor young man."

*A propos* of this myth it was said that even to this day sayings spring up, with little or no foundation in fact. In this connection I said, "Might I ask, your Excellency, whether there is any truth at all in the story of the beer-jug, which you are supposed to have broken in two over some one's head in a Berlin public-house, because he had insulted the Queen, or had refused to drink to her?"

"Yes," replied he, "but the circumstances were different, and there were no politics in the matter. I was going home late one evening—it must have been in the year 1847—when I met a man who had had too much, and wanted to pick a quarrel with me. When I upbraided him for his offensive language I found he was an old acquaintance. I think it was in the Jägerstrasse. We had not met for a long time, and when he proposed to me to go to such-and-such a place I went with him, though he had clearly had enough. After we had our beer, however, he fell asleep. Well, near us was a party of people, one of whom had also had more than was good for him, as was evident from his boisterous behaviour. I was quietly drinking my beer. My being so quiet vexed him, so he began to taunt me. I sat still, and that made him only the more angry and spiteful. He went on taunting me louder and louder. I did not wish for 'a row,' but I would not go lest they should think I was afraid. At last his patience seemed exhausted, he came to my table and threatened to throw the jug of beer into my face, and that was too much for me. I told him he must go, and when he then made a gesture as if to throw it, I gave him one under the chin, so that he measured his length on the floor, smashed the stool and the glass, and went clean to the wall. The hostess came in, and I told her she might make herself quite easy, as I would pay for the stool and glass. To the company I said, 'You see, gentlemen, that I sought no quarrel, and you are witnesses that I restrained myself as long as I could, but I was not going to let him pour a glass of beer over my head, because I had been quietly drinking mine. If the gentleman has lost a tooth by it, I am sorry. But I acted in self-defence. Should any one want more, here is my card.' They turned out to be quite sensible people, who took much the same view of the matter as I did. They were indignant with their comrade, and said I was right. I afterwards met two of them at the Brandenburg Gate. 'You were present, gentlemen, I think,' said I, 'when I had the adventure in the beerhouse in the Jägerstrasse? What became of your friend? I should be sorry if he sustained any injury.' They had been obliged to carry him out. 'Oh,' said they, 'he is quite well and lively, and his teeth, too, are all right again. He kept very quiet, and was very sorry. He had just entered upon his year's service as a doctor, and it would have been very unpleasant for him had the affair come to the ears of people, especially of his superiors.'"

The Chief then told us that, when a student in Göttingen, he had twenty-eight duels in three terms, and had always come well out of them. "But once," said I, "your Excellency got hit. What was the name of the little Hannoverian—Biedenfeld?" "Biedenweg," he replied; "and he was not little either, but nearly as big as I was. But that only happened because his sword-blade, which was probably screwed in badly, came off. It flew into my face and stuck there. Otherwise I was never once hit. Once, however, in Greifswald, I came near it. They had introduced there a marvellous sort of head-dress—like a felt coffee-bag. They had broadswords too, to which I was not accustomed. Now I had taken it into my head that I would cut off the peak of my opponent's coffee-bag, and in so doing I exposed myself, and his stroke whistled quite close to my face; but I sprang back just in time."

*Wednesday, February* 1.—In the morning the sky was moderately clear, with a slight rain and sleet. At breakfast we are told that Gambetta has consented to the armistice, but expressed surprise that the French are still being attacked by us in the South. Of course, Favre, in his unbusinesslike way, has omitted to telegraph to him that the war is kept up there by his own wish. We have company at breakfast. Besides Privy Councillor Scheidtmann, of the Exchequer, a rather peculiar gentleman, Count Dönhoff (the blue and handsome, not the red and corpulent one), and "my nephew, Count York," honour us with their presence. It is said that none of the Frenchmen are coming out to-day.

This was a mistake. About one, Favre appeared, and set to work for two hours upstairs with the Chief. Meanwhile I went with L. through the Ville d'Avray, and the park of Saint-Cloud, to the town of that name, or, more properly speaking, to the heap of ruins to which the raging conflagration of the last few days has reduced it. On the way there I learn the welcome news that Belfort has capitulated, and that the remnant of Bourbaki's army, 80,000 strong, and commanded by Clinchant, has retired before our troops into Swiss territory. So the war here also is ended, as Bismarck-Bohlen informed me on the stairs.

In the Park of Saint-Cloud we saw, immediately behind the open ironwork gate at the entrance, under some trees on the left hand, a little neglected graveyard, with ten or twelve graves of German soldiers who had fallen there. Farther on we passed some more graves of the same kind, and a redoubt and a barricade stretched across the street. Under a bridge, crossing the road, tunnelwise, the troops had found quarters for themselves, as in a casemate. On the right and left as one enters the town, and at the edge of the wood, blockhouses had been built against a wall, and behind them, in a long street, stands for cannon were put up. The town here consists first of broad streets of detached villas, surrounded by gardens; farther on, of narrower streets, with rather tumble-down houses closely packed, and running finally down the hill-slope to the bank of the Seine. Without exception the villas were either wholly or partly burnt down. Of the more slightly-built ones only a level heap of bricks, slates, plaster, and coal remained. In the more confined streets of the inner town hardly anything was left standing but outside walls, and even these had fallen in here and there, bringing down with them the flooring of the different stories. On what remained of these were still to be seen standing book-shelves, plate-racks, writing-desks, washhand-stands, &c., while pictures and mirrors hung on the papered walls. Whole house fronts, three stories high, were lying in the side and main streets, and others bending forwards or backwards, apparently ready to fall. Everywhere smoking ruins and the smell of burning. In three or four buildings flames still flickered about the chimneys, the framework of the walls, and the wooden dressings. The church, a newly-built edifice in a pleasing Gothic style, was uninjured, save for a few holes in the roof. All around was ruin—a frightful picture of the seriousness of war! From the heights of the demolished town we had a lovely view of the valley of the Seine, of the bridge with one of its arches broken, and of the South side of Paris, with the Bois de Boulogne. We did not stop here, but hurried on to the castle, which before the war was Napoleon's summer retreat, now also a silent heap of ruins. French shells had done it. Only the *enceinte* and a few of the partition walls were still standing. We scrambled through its heaps of rubble, climbed over the fallen remnants of ceiling and roof from room to room, wherever no further downfall seemed imminent, and carried away with us *souvenirs* from the prostrate marble capitals and mutilated statues.

As we went home to Saint-Cloud we met several small parties of people returning from Paris to their native villages with beds and household gear, and at Ville d'Avray a company of Prussian artillery passed us on its march to Mont Valérien.

When I got back to the Rue de Provence, at half-past five, I found the Chief and the rest of the party already at dinner. There were no guests present. As I entered, the Minister was just speaking of Favre: "I believe he came only because of yesterday's discussion, when I would not admit that Garibaldi was a hero. He was clearly uneasy about him, because I refused to include him in the Armistice. Like a true advocate he drew attention to the first article. I, however, told him, 'Yes, that was the rule, but next came the exceptions, and he was one of them.' If a Frenchman bore arms against us, I maintained, he was fighting for his country, as he had a right to do. But as for this foreign adventurer, with his Cosmopolitan Republic and his band of revolutionaries from all quarters of the globe, I could not recognise his rights. He then asked what we should do with him if we caught him. 'Oh,' said I, 'we will show him about for money, with a placard round his neck, labelled "Ingratitude."'"

He then asked, "Where is Scheidtmann?" Some one said what he knew about him. "I had thought of him as a legal assistant in the matter (referring to the contribution of two hundred million francs to be paid by Paris)—he is a lawyer?" Bucher replied, No, he had not studied at all, he had originally been a merchant, or something of the kind. "Well," said the Chief, "Bleichröder must go to the front. He must go into Paris at once, to ferret among his colleagues, and consult with the bankers how it is to be done. He is coming, is he not?" "Yes," said Keudell, "in a few days." The Chief, "Please telegraph to him that we want him immediately. Then comes Scheidtmann—he speaks French?" No one knew. "As a third man I think of Henckel. He is at home in Paris, and known among the financial people. 'We on the Bourse,' one of the leading financiers once said to me, 'are in the habit of spotting lucky speculators, and if we want to spot one here, it is Count Henckel.'"

The conversation afterwards turned upon the story of the fortunes and development of the German question. The Chief observed, "I remember, thirty or more years ago, in Göttingen, I made a bet with an American as to whether Germany would be united in twenty years. We wagered five-and-twenty bottles of champagne, which the man who won was to stand, while the loser was to cross the sea for it. He was against and I for the Unity. I thought of it in 1853, and intended to go across. But upon inquiry I found he was dead. He had just the sort of name which promised no length of life—Coffin! The most remarkable thing is that I must at that time, in 1833, already have had the ideas and hopes, which now by God's help have been realised, although then my relations with the party that wished for Unity had only been antagonistic."

The Chief lastly expressed his belief in the influence of the Moon upon the growth of hair and of plants, and then proceeded to joke Abeken upon the excellence of his barber. "You look quite young again, Mr. Privy Councillor," said he; "would I were your wife! You have had it cut just at the right time, when the moon was waxing. It is just so with trees. If they are wanted to grow again, they are felled during the first quarter; if you wish to cut them clean away, you do it when the moon is on the wane, and then the root decays more quickly. There are people, scholars, who do not believe this; but the State itself acts on the belief, though it will not openly confess it. No forester is allowed to fell a birch-tree, which is to throw off suckers again, when the moon is waning."

In the evening I read a number of documents, bearing upon the armistice and the revictualling, and among them several autograph letters of Favre, who writes a neat legible hand. In one of them it is stated that Paris only has meal up to the 4th of February, afterwards nothing but horse-flesh. In another letter Moltke is entreated not to put Garibaldi on the same footing with the French, and in any case to grant the complete laying down of their arms by him and his people. The Minister asks for this on political grounds. Instructions are sent to Elsass not to hinder the elections to the Assembly at Bordeaux, which is to decide the question of war or peace, and eventually the conditions of the latter. They are to be ignored. In the regions occupied by us, not the Prefects but the Mayors will guide the elections. The instructions issued by the Parisians on this subject are to this effect. "The Mayors of the chief places in the Department will put themselves in communication with those of the chief places in each Arrondissement, and these again with the mayors of the chief places in the Cantons and Communes. They will appoint a day on which the deputies to the National Assembly are to be nominated. The Mayor of each commune will furnish every enrolled elector with the list from which he has to choose. In default of a list the electors will be allowed to vote notwithstanding, after their identity has been established. The Mayor of the chief place in the department will determine the number and limits of the electoral circles. The election will be decided by casting up the votes according to the relative majority. In consequence of difficulties arising from the war, the election is to be valid whatever the number of voters." The Parisian members of the French Government further issued the following directions on January 29th:

"Considering the importance, in present circumstances, of allowing the electors perfect liberty of choice, so far as is consistent with a true expression of the will of the people, the Government of National Defence enacts: that articles 81 to 90 of the law of March 15, 1849—with the exception of the provisions made in paragraph 4 of article 82, and paragraph 5 of article 85—are not to apply to this election to the National Assembly. Accordingly, prefects and sub-prefects are not eligible in the departments where they exercise their functions."

*Thursday, February* 2.—The weather is bright and mild, as if spring were close at hand. Betimes in the morning I was summoned to the Chief. I am to telegraph that 80,000 Frenchmen of Bourbaki's army have been driven across the Swiss frontier at Pontarlier, while only 8000 have escaped to the south. Soon after, I am called up once more, to draw attention in the press here, as well as in Germany, to a circular from Laurier (inspired by Gambetta) which has just reached us by telegraph, and to state our views thereupon. I write the following article on the subject at once:

"A circular was issued to the Prefects, signed by C. Laurier, from Bordeaux, on January 31, after the conclusion of the Convention of January 28 had become known there. It contained this passage: 'The policy maintained and carried out by the Ministers of the Interior and of War remains the same as before: War to the last, Resistance till every resource is exhausted. Lend, therefore, every aid in your power to maintain a good spirit among the population. The interval of the armistice must be devoted to strengthening our three armies with men, ammunition, and provisions.

Our aim must be to turn the armistice to account at any price, and we are in a position to do so. In short, before the elections the whole advantage rests with us. What France needs is a representative body which wishes for war, and is determined to carry it on at all costs.'

"So runs the circular signed by Laurier. In the eyes of sensible people it passes judgment upon itself; we might therefore refrain from commenting upon it. It is, however, important to remark that the German authorities have been very mild and liberal both in their interpretation and administration of the Convention of January 28th. They have given effect to the proposals of the Parisian government in a far greater degree than was implied in that Convention. They have granted full liberty of election to the assembly which is to meet in Bordeaux, to decide the question of peace or war. In spite of this, the public authorities in Bordeaux proceed to preach war to the last, and are working openly for the election of such people as they hope will vote for carrying on the war till the resources of France are exhausted. Is this conduct not such as to suggest to the German authorities the question, whether their magnanimous reading of the obligations entered into by France is not a case of misplaced confidence, and whether they ought not, in the interests of France herself, to substitute a stricter interpretation of the Convention of January 28th?

"As to the three armies mentioned by M. Laurier, we may remark that since Bourbaki's troops have partly been made prisoners, partly escaped into Swiss territory, France has only the remnants of two armies. In conclusion, compare with M. Laurier's manifesto the following extracts from the *Daily Telegraph*, upon M. Gambetta's views of the position of things and the course which France ought to take. The correspondent of the English paper says:

" ' The conversation turned upon the war in general, and on my asking whether it was at an end with the surrender of Paris, Gambetta answered, that the surrender of Paris had no bearing on the question of the continuance of the war, if the Prussians persisted in their present schemes. " I am speaking now," he continued, " not only in my own name or in that of the Government Delegation here. On the contrary, I am repeating, the final decision of my Colleagues both in and out of Paris, that the war must be continued whatever the cost and whatever may be the consequences. If Paris falls to-morrow, it will have nobly fulfilled its duty to France, but I cannot believe that Paris will ever surrender. I believe that the inhabitants would themselves burn it to the ground, and turn it into a second Moscow, rather than allow it to fall into the hands of the enemy." " But just suppose," replied I, " that in spite of this the capitulation should take place."

' " In that case," answered Gambetta, " the struggle must be continued in the provinces. Without counting the army of Paris, we have actually at the present time half a million of troops, and 250,000 men more behind, ready to join the army, or to leave their depots. We have never called out the Contingent of 1871, and we have not yet pressed married men into the regiments. The former will yield us 300,000 recruits, the latter will furnish two millions of strong men. Arms are coming in to us from all sides, and there is no lack of money. The nation, including all shades of political opinion, is on our side, and the only question will be, which is the stronger and more persevering race, ours or the German." " No," he continued, bringing his fist down heavily on his writing-table, " I look upon it as a mathematical impossibility for us, if we persevere and continue the war, not to succeed in the end in driving the invader out of France. Every four-and-twenty hours is for us only one day, but for our enemies each hour's delay brings fresh difficulties. England has made a great mistake in not having stepped in before now, to tell Prussia that her passing a certain limit would be in the eyes of England a *casus belli.*"'"

Soon after one, the Frenchmen came again, but the Chief had ridden out with the War Minister, as was supposed, to one of the forts, or to some more commanding point of view, for they had taken field-glasses with them. Gerstäcker and Duboc called on me, and with the latter, who is living as correspondent in the Saxon camp, I went for an hour into the castle park. On the way home I learnt that the Chief had been to Saint-Cloud, and the Frenchmen were waiting for him meanwhile in our park.

At dinner Odo Russell, and a tall, strong young man in dark blue uniform, were our guests. The latter, I was told, was Count Bray, son of the Minister, and formerly in the Bavarian Embassy at Berlin. The Chief said to Russell, "The English papers, and some German ones too, have found fault with my letter to Favre, and called it too harsh. He himself does not seem to be of that opinion. He said to me of his own accord, 'You have done right to remind me of my duty. I ought not to go away before the end.'" After praising this self-renunciation, the Minister repeated that our Parisians were unpractical people, and that we were continually obliged to advise and assist them. He added, that they now showed signs of wishing amendments in the Convention of January 28. Outside the city of Paris very little willingness to help in its re-provisioning was displayed. The directors of the Rouen and Dieppe Railway, for instance, whose assistance had been counted upon, said they were short of working stock, as their locomotives had been taken to pieces, and carried over to England. Gambetta's action was still doubtful, though he seemed to be thinking of continuing the war. It was necessary that France should soon have a regular Government. "If they do not soon establish one," he went on, "we will give them a king. Everything is ready for it. Amadeo, with a travelling-bag in his hand, entered Madrid as King of Spain. Our King is coming immediately with a train, with ministers, cooks, chamberlains, and an army."

The conversation then turned upon the property of Napoleon, which was very differently estimated, now as great, and again as inconsiderable. Russell seemed to doubt whether he had much. The Empress, at least, he thought, could not have much, for she never had more than six thousand pounds deposited in the Bank of England.

It was then said that Count Maltzahn had already gone into Paris, and when some one added that he had not yet appeared again, the Chief said, "I only hope nothing has happened to that stout person." He then told us that on his way to Saint-Cloud to-day he had met many people with beds and household gear, probably inhabitants of the villages hereabouts, who had not been able to get out of Paris. "The women looked quite friendly," he said, "but, as soon as they caught sight of our uniform, the men assumed a hostile expression and a heroic attitude. It reminds me of the old Neapolitan army, which had a word of command, answering to our 'Arms to the charge! right!' —'*Faccia feroce!*' With the French, everything lies in a magnificent attitude, a pompous speech, and an impressive theatrical mien. If it only sounds right and looks like something, the meaning is all one. They are like the Potsdam burgher and householder, who once told me that a speech of Radowitz had touched and affected him deeply. I asked him whether he could point out any passage which had specially gone to his heart, or seemed particularly fine. He could not name one. Thereupon I read the whole speech out to him, and asked him what was the affecting passage. It turned out that there was nothing of the sort there, nothing either striking or affecting. It was nothing but the manner and attitude of the orator which looked as if he were saying the deepest, most important, and most striking things—the thoughtful glance, the devout eyes, the voice full of tone and weight. It was the same with Waldeck, though he was not so able a man or of such distinguished appearance. In this case it was rather the white beard, and his intellectual force.

"The gift of oratory has ruined much in parliamentary life. Time is wasted because every one who feels ability in that line, must have his word, even if he has no new point to bring forward. Speaking is too much in the air, and too little to the point. Everything is already settled in committees: a man speaks at length therefore only for the public, to whom he wishes to show off as much as possible, and still more for the newspapers, who are to praise him. Oratory will one day come to be looked upon as a generally harmful quality, and a man will be punished who allows himself to be guilty of a long speech. We have one body," he continued, "which admits no oratory, and has yet done more for the German cause than almost any other—the Council of the Confederation. I remember that at first some attempts were made in that direction. But I put a stop to them.

"I said to them something like this: 'Gentlemen, we have nothing to do here with eloquence and speeches intended to produce conviction, because everyone brings his conviction with him in his pocket—I mean, his instructions. It is so much time lost. I propose that we confine ourselves here to the statement of facts.' And so it was; no one again made a long speech. We get on so much the faster with our business; and the Council of the Confederation has really done a great deal."

In the evening I read despatches, as well as some drafts; then drew up and sent off three telegrams, one upon Belfort and the three South-Eastern departments, one upon the hindrances in the way of revictualling Paris, and one upon the difficulties raised by Faidherbe and d'Argent.

*Friday, February* 3.—Weather damp and cold. In the forenoon, while the Chief was busy, I went again with Wollmann to Saint-Cloud, the ruins of which still smoke continually, and smell of burning, and then beyond to the first houses of Suresnes, at the foot of Mont Valérien. Our sentries are still posted along the banks of the Seine, but everything has the most peaceable look, and one is struck only by the deep stillness which reigns on the further side of the stream, though a great town lies close to it. No people are to be seen on that side, and the only sign of life is on the water, where two boats, apparently fishing-smacks, are gliding along.

At breakfast Bucher told us all kinds of characteristic stories from the life of Gladstone. About one, I have a call from Wachenhusen, who wishes to smuggle himself into Paris.

About a quarter to four I was sent for by the Chief. Gambetta has followed Laurier's example, and himself made a declaration which is thoroughly warlike and despotic. A proclamation to the French, signed by him, was issued on January 31, and contained these words:—

"The enemy has inflicted on France the most grievous injuries which our people have been fated to endure in this unfortunate war. Impregnable Paris, sorely pressed by hunger, has been unable to keep the German hordes any longer at a distance. On January 28th it fell." "It seems as if a gloomy fate had in store for us still greater calamity, and even bitterer pain. Without our being taken into counsel, an Armistice has been signed, the reprehensible wantonness of which we have only learned too late; an armistice which hands over to the Prussians the Departments still occupied by our troops, and obliges us to remain quiet for three weeks, while, in the present unfortunate condition of the country, a National Assembly is being called together. We have demanded explanations as to the state of Paris, and remain silent till they are vouchsafed. We wish to wait for the expected arrival of some member of the Government from Paris, into whose hands we may resign our authority."

"No one has yet come from Paris. We must therefore, at any price, take steps to frustrate the shameful plans of the enemies of France. Prussia counts on the armistice unnerving and breaking up our armies. It lives in hope that an assembly, meeting after a long train of disasters, and under the terrible shock of the fall of Paris, will be disheartened and ready to agree to an ignominious peace. It lies with us to disappoint this calculation, and to use every endeavour, that the means intended for stifling the spirit of resistance may, in fact, add to it fresh life and strength. Let us employ the Armistice in drilling our young soldiers, and in bringing the organisation of Defence and of the War to a state of greater efficiency than ever. Let us do our utmost that, instead of the reactionary and fainthearted body of representatives expected by our enemies, a truly national and republican assembly may meet, ready for peace if the honour and inviolability of the country is secured, but equally able and ready to vote for war, to prevent France becoming the victim of assassination.

Frenchmen, let us think of our fathers, who handed France down to us as a United and Indivisible State. Let us guard against treason to our history, let us see that our inheritance does not pass into the hands of barbarians!" This fanatic document ends with the appeal "To arms! *Vive la France!* Long live the Republic One and Indivisible!"

Gambetta issued at the same time a document in which a number of persons were declared ineligible. In it he observed:—

" Justice demands that all the accomplices of the Government which began with the *Coup d'état* of December 2, and ended with the capitulation of Sedan, should be struck for the future with the political impotence of the dynasty, whose tools and abettors they were. This is the necessary consequence of the responsibility which they undertook in assisting the Emperor to carry out a certain policy. To this category belong all persons who, between the 2nd of December, 1851, and the 4th of September, 1870, have held the rank of minister, senator, privy councillor, or prefect. Furthermore, all individuals who were in any way concerned as Government candidates in the elections to the legislative body during the same period, and the members of those families who have ruled in France since 1789, are debarred from election to the National Assembly."

In reference to this last manifesto, I telegraphed by the Chief's orders to London and Cologne, that the Government in Bordeaux has, by an election circular, declared whole classes of the population ineligible—ministers, senators, councillors, and all who were formerly official candidates. The fear expressed by Count Bismarck during the negotiations for the Convention of January 28, that free elections would not be allowed, has thus been justified. On this account the Chancellor proposed at the time to summon the

Legislative Body, but Favre would not consent. He has now protested in a note against the exclusion of those men, and it is only an Assembly constituted by free election, in the sense of the Convention, that will be recognised by the Germans as representative of France.

The Chief went with Gambetta's election circular to the King, while the Parisian prefect of police was waiting to speak to him in the drawing-room. He did not come to dinner, but stayed to dine at the Prefecture. Abeken therefore took the head of our table, Scheidtmann and Count Henckel being present as guests.

Summoned to the Chief at eight o'clock, I received instructions to send for insertion in the *Moniteur* a copy of a Reuter's telegram dated Bordeaux, February 2. It ran thus:—

"The journals *La Liberté*, *La Patrie*, *Le Français*, *Le Constitutionnel*, *L'Universel*, *Le Courrier de la Gironde et Provence*, publish a protest against the Manifesto issued by the Delegation of Bordeaux on January 31st, restricting the freedom of election. They say, that before publishing this protest they considered it their duty to send three deputies to M. Jules Simon, to ask whether there was not existing a proclamation bearing upon the elections, which had been issued by the Parisian Government and published in the *Journal Officiel*. M. Jules Simon answered, that this manifesto did exist, that it bore date January 31st, and had been unanimously accepted by the members of the Government; and that in it there were no restrictions on the liberty of election. The only point insisted upon had been that prefects were not eligible in the provinces where they exercised their functions.* The elections in Paris have

---

* The main heads of this manifesto have been given above.

been fixed for February 5th; in the provinces for February 8th. The Deputies are to meet on the 12th. The *Journal Officiel*, containing this proclamation, has been sent out, by order of the Parisian Government, into all the Departments. Jules Simon obtained a passport on January 31, and started off on the same morning. On his arrival at Bordeaux he summoned a meeting of the members of the Delegation, in order to explain fully to them the state of matters. At four o'clock in the afternoon a long discussion took place. Jules Simon declared to the representatives of the press that he was prepared to stand by the proclamation of the Parisian Government, and authorised them to publish this declaration. The undersigned representatives of the press have therefore only to await the execution of the Parisian proclamation." Then follow the signatures. Gambetta's dictatorship, then, has probably at last come to an end. His stubbornness has cut the ground from beneath his feet.

I was once more summoned to the Chief. I telegraphed the news of the successful battles of Manteuffel's southern army at Pontarlier. We have taken there 15,000 French prisoners, including two generals, nineteen guns and two eagles.

Count Herbert has returned to-day to his father's house from Germany. He was with him at nine o'clock.

*Saturday, February* 4.—The weather is warmer than yesterday. In the morning I read the news and some drafts. I see that the Chief has protested against Gambetta's Election Circular in a double way—in a telegram addressed to himself, and in a note to Favre. The former runs:—" In the name of the freedom of election guaranteed by the Armistice-Convention, I protest against the instructions issued in your name, depriving numerous classes of the French people of the right of election to the Assembly. The rights, which are given in the armistice-convention to freely-elected deputies, cannot be acquired through elections carried on under the influence of oppression and despotism." After briefly summarising the contents of Gambetta's election-decree, the despatch to Favre proceeds:—" I take the liberty of putting to your Excellency the question whether you consider this in accordance with the provision of the convention, that the Assembly is to be constituted by free election. Will your Excellency allow me to recall to your recollection the negotiations which preceded the convention. Even then I expressed my fear that it would be found difficult under existing conditions to secure full liberty of election, and to prevent any attempt that might be made against it. Having this fear, which has now been justified by M. Gambetta's circular, I raised the question whether it would not be better to summon the Legislative Body, which was a lawful authority, elected by universal suffrage. Your Excellency declined this, and gave me your express promise that no pressure should be put upon the electors, and the fullest freedom of election should be assured to them. I appeal to your Excellency's sense of fairness in asking you whether you think the exclusion of whole categories of candidates, declared fundamentally in the decree now in question, is compatible with the liberty of election guaranteed in the convention of January 28th. I consider myself entitled to express a confident hope that that decree, the application of which would appear to contradict the provisions of the Convention, will be immediately withdrawn, and that the Government of National Defence will take such measures as will effectually guarantee the carrying out of the second article of the convention, regarding the liberty of election. We could not allow to persons elected according to the stipulations of the Bordeaux Circular, the rights guaranteed to the deputies of the National Assembly by the Armistice-Convention."

As early as nine o'clock two officers of the National Guard of Paris, an old man and a young one, appeared, bringing a letter for the Chief—probably Favre's answer.

After ten the Chief sent for me, to say, "Here is a complaint from Berlin that the English papers are far better informed than ours, and that we communicated to our papers so little of the negotiations for the armistice. How is this?" "Well, your Excellency," replied I, "it is because the English have more money, to go everywhere and pick up information. And then they are so well recommended to eminent personages, who tell them about everything—and, besides, the military are not always quite close about things which ought to be kept secret. I could only allow such of the negotiations for the Convention to be published as it was proper should appear." "Well, then," said he, "write, pray, on this subject, and say that circumstances, and not we, are to blame."

I ventured then to congratulate him upon the announcement of honorary citizenship, which he is said to have received lately, and to remark that Leipzig was a good town, the best in Saxony, and one that I had always held dear "Yes," replied he, "an honorary citizen—I am a Saxon, now, and a Hamburger, too, for I have one from there also. That could not have been hoped for in 1866."

I was going, when he said, "That reminds me—it is one of the marvels of this time—write, please, something in detail upon the singular fact that Gambetta, who has so long had the character of representing liberty, and of fighting against the influence of Government in the elections, now, when he is himself in power, authorises the most flagrant encroachments upon freedom of election, and is de barring from the privilege of being elected all whom he believes not to hold his own views—that is, the whole of official France, with the exception of thirteen republicans. That I should have to restore to the French their liberty of election, in opposition to this Gambetta and his accomplice and confederate, Garibaldi, is another wonderful thing." I said, "I do not know whether it was intentional, but in your protest to Gambetta it had a very strange effect: the contrast between the sentence where 'in the name of the freedom of election' you guarded yourself against 'the directions issued in your (Gambetta's) name for depriving numerous classes of the right of election.' Might that be pointed out?" "Yes," said he; "pray do so."— "You may also," he added, smiling, "remind people that Thiers, after his negotiations with me, called me *an amiable barbarian*. They now call me in Paris *a shrewd barbarian* ('*un barbare astuticux*'), next time I shall probably be the *constitutional barbarian*."

I here insert, by way of comparison, other remarks upon the Prince from French papers and books of 1870-1874. The record is given in a German paper, the name of which I cannot give, as the label stuck upon the cutting which contains it came off. It runs somewhat as follows :—

\* \* \* \* \* \*

The Chancellor remarked of himself in the Reichstag this spring (1874) that he was the best hated man in Europe, from the banks of the Garonne to the Neva. The following may help to show the feelings entertained towards Bismarck by his chief enemies the French, and to illustrate that soon celebrated utterance. The German Chancellor occupies the same place in the thoughts of the French, as Hannibal did in those of the Romans. If the great Carthaginian was to the minds of the Quirites, the incarnation of all that went against the grain with them or could thwart their plans, the expression of every perfidy and intrigue, these are also the relations between Bismarck and the French to-day.  His name has become a bugbear to France, just as the *Hannibal ante portas* (Hannibal at the gates) was a terror to Rome.  Wherever anything happens in the world which goes against the grain with the French, Bismarck is the cause of it.  In this way this utterly hated man has qualities attributed to him which no mortal is conscious of possessing : omnipresence, omniscience, omnipotence.  With the outbursts of hatred, however, there is always mingled a good deal of involuntary admiration.  Like Balaam, the French must now and then bless when they mean to curse.

This phenomenon may be traced in the French press with tolerable accuracy.  The French papers usually speak of the Chancellor, if they have no quarrel with him, without ceremony as *M. de Bismarck*.  They do not, however, always ignore the elevation of rank which he has acquired; at times, though not very frequently, they have to do with *le Prince de Bismarck*.  The title of Prince reminds them at once of the services by which it was won, connected as they are with the repulse of French insolence, and the weakening of the French power of offence.  Officially speaking he is, according to his friends west of the Vosges, Chancellor, to which is usually added some epithet, such as Prince Chancellor, Illustrious Chancellor, Arch-Chancellor, or Grand Chancellor.  In regard to his political bias, the French are not all of one opinion, but maintain in that respect very various views.  At one time the papers call him "the defender of aristocratical ideas," at another "the champion of modern Liberalism and of human reason," or again, "the apostle of Liberalism."  In the French papers, which hold liberal views, these designations, which presuppose Bismarck to have two souls, appear harmoniously side by side. The Legitimist and clerical prints express themselves more logically; with them he is always "this revolutionary." The Chancellor's high statesmanlike qualifications are fully recognised by the French.

From a diplomatic point of view he is "the illustrious diplomatist," "*l'homme de Biarritz*," which seems to signify a magnificent success, just as "*l'homme de Sedan*" implies a frightful defeat. He is "an able man, always on the spot, with his finger in everything. He sees in the most trifling opportunities the way to attain his end." *A propos* of the policy by which the Chancellor triumphed over France, they say, "He profits by our perplexities with admirable skill; and always turns them adroitly to account." As opposed to poor innocent France, who has troubled no man's water, who loves peace, who has no other ambition than to live and prosper quietly, he is "the implacable German Chancellor." A phrase is used to express Bismarck's home and foreign policy, borrowed from the party of progress, "the man of might above right." Like the German democratic papers, the French papers also speak of him as a politician of blood and iron. He is "the celebrated author of the policy of blood and iron." Again, he is "the Machiavellian Chancellor," while he is at the same time described (ironically, no doubt), as "the high-minded and God-fearing man." As is known, this expression is properly used only of the country of Prussia, but from the French point of view the country has become incarnate in Bismarck; the Chancellor is the collective embodiment of Prussian qualities, their type and quintessence : "*le Grand homme Prussien*," "*le Grand-Prussien*." The last expression was invented by the "Union," and is clearly modelled upon the Grand Turk.

To the French Ultramontanes Bismarck is neither more nor less than the Turk, the incarnation of the Evil Principle itself, the Antichrist, Beelzebub, as the clerical *Revue de la Presse* may boast to have dubbed him. With extremely abortive envy and jealousy the *Constitutionnel* calls him further "the pivot of society," the pole round which the whole of existing society revolves. If the French wish to sum up in a word the magnificent successes of Bismarck they call him in characteristic fashion not "the conqueror of Sedan" or the like, but "the conqueror of Sadowa." His victories over the French are ignored, they have no existence as such, they are regarded rather as the treasons of the Emperor Napoleon and his generals. The poor Austrians must suffer accordingly for not being invincible like the French.

To express his greatness the proud title is given him of "*Le Richelieu de la Prusse*," which in a Frenchman's mouth sums up all statesmanlike and diplomatic ability. Others again cannot put him so high; but bring him down one place and call him only "*Polignac en politique*," but certainly "Polignac successful, the bold and powerful minister." Finally Bismarck's Creation, the new German Empire, is called by the clerical press in France, "the Godless Empire of M. de Bismarck"—of course, why what else could be expected of Beelzebub? Their doubts as to the permanence of this creation are expressed by the French in these words, "He is a terrible gambler." That there is nothing so very extraordinary in their eyes in the establishment of the Empire they signify by saying, "Bismarck is only a plagiarist."

\* \* \* \* \* \*

I return to what the journal has to tell of events in Versailles on *February* 4, 1871.

This morning the Chief had more time and interest than

usual recently for the papers. I was sent for six times before noon. At one of them he gave me a lying French *brochure:* "War as made by the Prussians," and remarked thereupon, "I should like you, please, to write to Berlin. They must draw up something similar on our side, with reference to the cruelties, barbarities, and breaches of the Convention (of Geneva) committed by the French. But not too long, or no one will read it, and it must appear quickly." The next time the question was of several newspaper cuttings "for my collection." Then again, he showed me a small paper, published by a certain Armand le Chevalier, 6, Rue Richelieu, with a woodcut portrait of the Chancellor on the frontispiece, and said, "Look here, here is a recommendation with reference to Blind's attempt to assassinate me, and my portrait is given too—like the photographs of the Francs-tireurs. You know that in the forests of the Ardennes, photographs of such of our skirmishers as were to be shot were found in the pockets of the Francs-tireurs. Luckily no one can say that my likeness is specially well hit off in this—nor for the matter of that my biography either. This passage" (he read it aloud and then handed me the paper) "should be sent to the papers with a moral to it, and then appear as a pamphlet."

Finally he gave me some more French newspapers, saying, "Just look whether there is anything there for me or the King. I shall be off, or the gentlemen from Paris will catch me again."

In M. Chevalier's paper it is in fact stated in rather plain terms by a certain "Ferragus," that France would welcome with approval the Chief's assassination, although he is, properly speaking, a benefactor to the French. The author, whose style savours of Victor Hugo's school, says:

"Bismarck has probably done better service to France

than to Germany. He has worked for a false unity in his own country, but very effectually for a regeneration of ours. He has freed us from the Empire. He has restored to us our energy, our hatred of the foreigner, our love for our country, our contempt for life, our readiness for self-sacrifice, in short, all the virtues which Buonaparte had killed in us.

"Honour therefore to this grim foe who saves us, when seeking to destroy us. Meaning to kill us he summons us to immortality, at the same time adding impetus to our earthly life. The blood which he spills fructifies our country; the twigs which he lops off allow the tree to absorb more sap. You will see how much greater we shall be when we escape from these fearful but wholesome toils. We have to expiate twenty years of forgetfulness of duty, of luxury, and of servility. The visitation is severe, but the result will be glorious. I call to witness the manly attitude of Paris, and the hunger after justice and honour with which our bosoms swell. To-day when one passes the door of the opera-house, one is smitten with shame. Those nudities, which were so brightly illumined by the sun of the Empire, shock the modesty of the Republic; we turn away from this typical memorial of another age, another grade of civilisation. It is Bismarck who has imbued us with this Puritan pride. Let us not thank him for it, but pay back with manly hatred this involuntary benefit from a man who, mightier to destroy than to construct, is more easily cursed than hailed with applause. Prussia has made him its great man, but on the 8th of May, 1866, the whole country mourned the fate of a young fanatic, a student, who seeing in Bismarck an enemy of freedom, fired five pistol-shots at him.

"Bind [as the author further on calls Blind's stepson] belonged to that class of inspired people, represented by Karl Sand, the murderer of Kotzebue, Stapss, who tried to stab

Napoleon at Schönbrunn, and Oscar Becker, the author of the attempt upon the King of Prussia. Bind was not deceived when he gave himself credit for a Roman soul, for he behaved like a Stoic after his capture, and himself opened the artery in his neck, to rob the executioner of his victim.

"If we were to hear to-day that a more successful attempt had been made upon Bismarck, would France have the generosity not to applaud it? So much is certain that this frightful question of political assassination will always remain one of relative morality, until it is eradicated from the minds of nations together with capital punishment and war. At this time, in October, 1870, one would hail as saviour a man, who, three months before, would have been branded as a common 'murderer,'"—a fine sign truly of the regeneration, which, according to the opening words of the article, is supposed to have taken place in France, and of the hunger after justice and honour, with which the writer sees his countrymen's bosoms swelling.

The Chief rode out about one o'clock, but was "caught" after all by Favre, who came in in the meantime, and worked with him up in the little drawing-room.

Prince Putbus and Count Lehndorff were present at dinner. The Chief told us first that he had called Favre's attention also to the remarkable fact that he, who was decried as the despotic and tyrannical Count von Bismarck, had been obliged to protest, in the name of freedom, against the proclamation of Gambetta, the advocate of freedom, who wished to deprive many hundreds of his countrymen of eligibility, and all of freedom of election. He added that Favre had acknowledged this with a "*oui, c'est bien drôle.*" However, the restrictions upon free election, authorised by Gambetta, had been by this time withdrawn and repealed by the Parisian part of the French Government. "He told me so," said he, "this morning by letter (that which was brought by the officers of the National Guard), and has now confirmed it by word of mouth."

It was then mentioned that several German papers had been discontented with the Capitulation, having expected our troops to march at once into Paris. Thereupon the Chief remarked: "That arises from total ignorance of the situation here and in Paris. I might have arranged it with Favre, but the population— They had strong barricades, and 300,000 men, of whom certainly 100,000 would have fought. Enough blood—German blood—has been shed in this war. If we had tried to use force, far more would have been spilt in the irritation of the inhabitants. Merely to inflict another humiliation upon them,—it would have been bought too dear." After a little meditation he went on, "And who told them we should not still march in and occupy a part of Paris? Or at least march through, when they have cooled down and listened to reason. The Armistice will probably have to be prolonged, and in return for this concession we can demand to occupy Paris on the right bank. I think we shall be there in some three weeks." "The 24th"—he thought a little— "yes, it was a 24th when the Constitution of the North German Confederation was proclaimed. It was on the 24th of February, 1859, that we lived to see a shameful event in Frankfort. I told them at the time that they would be paid out for it. You will soon see. *Exoriare aliquis*— I am only sorry that the Würtemberger (the ambassador of the Diet), old Reinhart, has not lived to see it. But Prokesch has, I am glad to say, who was the worst. He is now quite at one with us, praises the energetic and spirited policy of Prussia, and *always*" (here the Minister laughed ironically) "or long ago, at least, recommended Union with us."

The Chief then mentioned that he had been to-day at Mont Valérien. "I was never there before," said he, "and when one sees the strong earthworks and numerous provisions for defence—we should have left many men lying there if we had attempted to storm it; I cannot think of it."

He next informed us that Favre had to-day come over to ask us to let out of Paris the crowds of country people who took refuge in the town in September. They were mostly people from the suburbs, and must number about 300,000. "I refused him," he went on; "giving him for answer, 'Our soldiers are occupying their houses, and if the possessors come out and see how their property has been carried off and ravaged, they will be furious (and I cannot blame them), and tax our people with it; and that might lead to awkward scuffles, and perhaps something worse.'" He then recurred to his excursion to Saint-Cloud and Suresnes, and said incidentally: "When I was looking at the place in the castle where the fire was, and thinking of the room where I had dined with the Emperor, a well-dressed gentleman, who had probably come from Paris, was there, being taken about by a man in a blouse. I could easily make out what they were saying, for they spoke loudly, and I have good ears. '*C'est l'œuvre de Bismarck,*' said the man in the blouse. But the other only answered: '*C'est la guerre.*' If they had known that I heard them!"

Count Bismarck-Bohlen then told us that the Landwehr somewhere hereabouts had punished a Frenchman who resisted an officer and struck at him with a penknife, by giving him seventy-five blows with the flat of a sword. "Seventy-five!" said the Chief; "H'm, that is too much." Some one told of a similar case that had happened near

Meaux, where, when Count Herbert lately passed through, the soldiers had laid hold of a miller, who had abused Count Bismarck and expressed a wish to have him between two mill-stones, and had flogged him with such terrible severity, that he was not able to move for several hours after.

The Election Programmes, which the candidates for the National Assembly had posted at the street corners to recommend themselves to their dear fellow-citizens, were then spoken of. Some passages were quoted from them, and it was remarked generally, that they still rode very much the high horse in Bordeaux, and promised to do mighty things. "Yes," said the Chief, "that I can imagine. Favre even tried once or twice to assume the high-heeled buskin. But it did not last long. I always brought him down at once with a light jest."

Some one spoke of Klaczko's speech in the Senate on January 30, against a combination between Austria and Prussia, and of Giskra's disclosure which appears in the morning edition of the *National Zeitung* for February 2. The latter had said that Bismarck sent him from Brünn to Vienna with peace proposals to the following effect: a *status quo ante bellum* except in Venetia; the Prussian Hegemony to be bounded by the Maine; no war expenses, but the mediation of France to be declined at the conclusion of peace. Giskra sent Baron Herring to Vienna with the proposals, but he had been coldly received by Moritz Esterhazy, and sent away with an evasive answer after waiting sixteen hours. He then went to Nicolsburg, where he met Benedetti, and received the answer, "You come too late." The French mediation, therefore, as Giskra maintained, cost Austria a war indemnity of thirty millions.

It was remarked that Prussia might at that time have

easily taken more from Austria, even in land, as for instance Austrian Silesia, and perhaps Bohemia. The Chief answered, "That is possible. But money—what more could they give! Bohemia might have been of some use, and there were people who thought of it. But it would have involved us in difficulties, and Austrian Silesia would have been of little value to us. It is just there that the sympathy for the Imperial house, and the attachment to Austria are strongest. The question in such cases is not what one can get, but what one wants."

*A propos* of this, he continued, that once in Nicolsburg he had gone out in plain dress, and had met two gendarmes, who had arrested a man. "I asked them what he had done, but of course as a civilian I got no answer," said he. "I then enquired of the man himself, and he told me it was because he had spoken disrespectfully of Count Bismarck. They were nearly carrying me off, too, because I said that many people had done that. That reminds me that I was once obliged to give a cheer for myself. It was in 1866, after the entry of the troops, in the evening. I happened to be unwell, and my wife would not let me go out. I slipped out, however, and when I wanted to cross the street back again by Prince Karl's palace, there was a great crowd of people collected, with the intention of giving me an Ovation. I was in plain clothes, and in my broad hat, which for some reason I had pressed down over my brow, must have looked suspicious, for some of them looked askance at me. I thought it best, therefore, to join in with their hurrahs."

From eight o'clock I read drafts and letters, including Favre's answer to the Chief's inquiry about Gambetta's election manœuvre. It runs thus :—

"You are right to appeal to my sense of justice, in which

you will never find me wanting. It is quite true that your Excellency urged me strongly to adopt as the only possible expedient—the summoning of the former Legislative Body. I declined this on several grounds, which I need not recall, but which you have certainly not forgotten. In answer to the remonstrances of your Excellency, I said that I believed myself sufficiently sure of my country to be able to assert that its only wish is for free election, and that the principle of the Sovereignty of the People is its only resource. That will be enough to show you that I cannot agree to the restriction which has been laid on the elector's right of voting.

"I have not fought against the system of official candidatures, to re-introduce it for the benefit of the present Government. Your Excellency may therefore rest assured that if the decree, of which you speak, has been issued by the delegation at Bordeaux, it will be recalled by the Government of National Defence. I only ask to be allowed to procure for myself an official assurance of the existence of this decree, which I can do by a telegram to be despatched to-day. Accordingly there is no difference of opinion between us, and we must work each with the other for the execution of the convention we have signed."

At nine o'clock I am called to the Chief, who wishes an article. written to the effect that the entry of our troops is impracticable just now, but possible later on. It was a criticism of the armistice in the *National Zeitung*, which suggested this. It began:—"As a war is at any time fertile in inscrutable surprises, we find that great event, the fall of Paris, accompanied in its last phases by unexpected circumstances. Most people, not in Germany alone, had assumed that our armies would one day make a brilliant entry through the open gates of the enemy's capital, and these brave armies themselves had counted upon this well-earned satisfaction of war. Instead of this, they are content with the occupation of the outworks, from which they look down upon the vanquished city, in which all the soldiers of the line and the Garde Mobile, except 12,000 men, lay down their arms and remain prisoners." "This Convention of Versailles not only appears on the face of it wanting in brilliancy, but it gives the impression of our acquisition being less complete than if we had at once marched into the city and seized upon all their materials of war." Further on it is asserted,

"In November Favre thought of war; in January, of peace." I am to say, on the other hand, that the "brilliant entry" might have been an entry over barricades. To wish for it is completely to mistake the position of things, and to show total ignorance of what is possible, or likely, under existing circumstances. The French Government might probably have agreed to an occupation of Paris by our troops, had we insisted upon it; but a very large mass of the population would, in their present state of excitement, have taken up arms to resist it, and the entry would have cost us further bloodshed, when surely enough blood has been shed in this war already. Let us wait awhile, till circumstances have changed, till people in Paris have cooled down. The brilliant entry, the occupation of some part of Paris, is by no means excluded by the convention of January 28; it is even suggested in it. Article 4 only says: "*During the armistice* the German army will not enter Paris." The armistice will, in all probability, have to be extended, and then, as a compensation for our consent to this, we can impose the condition that we march into Paris, and so, in about three weeks' time, this may be done without a struggle and with no loss to us. The National Guard will also be disbanded and reorganised, but gradually, by the French Government. We can do nothing towards that; we have not to help in the government. Favre declined to negotiate about peace, with the remark that the representatives of the people were alone competent to the task.

Later, I am once more called to the Chief. An article in the *Volks-Zeitung*, from Cologne, points out that the Ultramontanes have offered money support to the leaders of the Universal German Workmen's Union, if they will work for the election of clerical candidates. We shall remark upon this, and at the same time speak in the press of a Savigny-Bebel party, or of the Liebknecht-Savigny fraction.

*Sunday, February* 5.—A milder day; the spring seems already drawing near. In the morning I worked diligently. The Chief's guests at dinner are Favre, d'Hérisson, and the Director of the Western Railway, a man apparently about thirty-six years old, with a broad, jolly-looking, laughing countenance. Favre, who sits at the upper end of the table, looks anxious, harassed, and depressed, hangs his head on one side or by way of a change upon his breast, drops his under-lip. When he is not eating he folds his hands upon the table-cloth, in token of his submission to the will of fate, or crosses his arms like the first Napoleon, to show that on a closer consideration of matters he still feels like himself. During dinner the Chief speaks only French, and mostly in a subdued voice. I was too far off to be able to follow him distinctly.

In the evening I am several times sent for by the Chief, and various matters are prepared for the press. The four members of the Bordeaux Delegation have, we learn by telegraph, issued a proclamation confirming Gambetta's decree about the elections. It is stated therein that Jules Simon, member of the Parisian Government, has brought news to Bordeaux of an election decree, which does not tally with that issued by the government in Bordeaux. The Government in Paris had been shut up for four months, and cut off from all connection with public opinion; nay more, they are at the present time in the position of prisoners of war. There is nothing against the supposition that, had they been better informed, they would have acted in accord with the government in Bordeaux; and as little to prove that, when they gave Jules Simon orders to see after the elections, they would have expressed themselves in unqualified and offensive terms against the ineligibility of certain persons. The Bordeaux government therefore considers itself bound to abide by its election decree; and, in spite of the interference of Count Bismarck in the internal affairs of the country, maintains its position in the name of the honour and the interests of France.

An open quarrel has thus been introduced in the enemy's camp, and Gambetta's retirement may be looked for at any moment. The Parisian Government, in a proclamation to the French on the 4th, which appears in the *Journal Officiel*, and will be printed in the *Moniteur*, has branded Gambetta as "unjust and foolhardy" (*si injuste et si téméraire*), and then declared: "We have summoned France to the free election of an Assembly, which shall make known her wishes at this extreme crisis. We recognise no man's right to force a decision upon the country, whether it be for peace or for war. A nation which is assailed by a powerful foe, fights to the uttermost, but retains the right of judging at what moment resistance ceases to be possible. This, then, is what the country will decide when questioned as to its destiny. In order that its will may be imposed on all as recognised law, we need the sovereign expression of the free votes of all. We do not admit that arbitrary restrictions can be put upon the voting. We have overcome the Empire and its practices, and we do not intend to begin them over again by introducing the expedient of an official exclusion of candidates. Nothing is more true than that great mistakes have been made, entailing severe responsibilities, but all this is hidden by the misfortunes of the country. Should we condescend to the *rôle* of partisans, by pointing the finger at our former opponents, we should bring upon ourselves the pain and the disgrace of punishing men who are fighting and shedding their blood in our cause. To remember past dissensions at the moment when masses of the enemy are in occupation of our blood-drenched soil, is so far to injure the great work of delivering our country. We place our principles above these expedients. We do not wish the first proclamation summoning the Republican Assembly in the year 1871, to be an act of disrespect to the electors. To them belongs the ultimate decision; let them give it without weakness, and our country may be saved. The Government of National Defence rejects, therefore, the illegally-issued decree of the Bordeaux Delegation, and declares it, as far as is necessary, null and void; and it calls upon all Frenchmen without distinction to give their votes for such representatives as seem to them best fitted to defend France."

At the same time to-day's *Journal Officiel* publishes the following proclamation:—"The Government of National Defence, in regard to a decree dated January 31st, issued by the Delegation in Bordeaux, in which various classes of citizens, who are eligible according to the Government decree of January 29, 1871, are declared ineligible, gives notice as follows: 'The before-mentioned decree issued by the Bordeaux Delegation is annulled. The decrees of January 29, 1871, remain in full force throughout.'"

The *Kölnische Zeitung* has become, with some reservations certainly, an organ of complaint against the asserted destruction of the French forests by our officials. It might, one would think, do better than trouble itself as to whether we are taking toll from the state forests of France on a right system. We act upon scientific principles, if not according to French ideas about tree-felling. Moreover, the most reckless exhaustion of this source of help to the enemy would be justifiable, on the ground that it might induce him to make peace with us sooner.

The conduct of the Duke of Meiningen deserves warm recognition. Instead of sitting still in Versailles, consulting his comfort, and enjoying the sight of an action from a safe distance, he has followed his regiment in the army corps commanded by Prince Albert; has taken his share in all its hardships, privations, and dangers, and many times over has helped his subjects, who are fighting for their fatherland in the ranks of the German army.

*Monday, February 6.*—Mild weather. In the morning the Chief wishes an article written against Gambetta. I drew up the following:—

"The Convention of January 28, concluded between Count von Bismarck and M. Jules Favre, raised to new life the hopes of all true friends of peace. Since the events of September 4, enough satisfaction had been given to the military honour of Germany, so that there was room for the wish to enter into negotiations with a Government really representing the French nation, for a peace which should guarantee the fruits of victory, and place our future upon a safe footing. When the Governments represented in Versailles and Paris were able to come to terms about a convention, in accordance with the urgent pressure of circumstances, and which would restore France to herself, they were justified in the expectation that this first step in a new era of mutual relations between the two countries would be generally approved. The decree of M. Gambetta, which declared the former high officials and dignitaries, senators and official candidates, ineligible, was probably necessary to show France the whole depth of the abyss which lay open before her, when the Dictatorship, lavish of the most precious blood of France, refused to call regularly together the representatives of the nation.

"Article 2 of the Convention of January 28 is thus worded: 'The Armistice thus agreed upon has for its object, to allow the Government of National Defence to call together a freely-elected Assembly, which shall decide whether the war is to be continued, or whether, and under what conditions, peace is to be concluded. The Assembly will meet in the town of Bordeaux. The commanders of the German army will afford every facility for the election and the assembling of the Deputies, of whom it will consist.'

"In this sentence it is clearly and unmistakeably implied that liberty of election is one of the conditions of the Convention itself, and it would be wholly out of the question for any one to seek to avail himself of its other advantages, and to limit the area of the conditions, which in their entirety alone contain the elements of reconciliation. When Germany lent its aid to the elections, it had in view only the laws actually existing in France, not the whim and pleasure of this or that popular tribunal. On this principle it would be quite as easy to summon a Rump Parliament in Bordeaux, and create an instrument with which to strike the other half of France. At the outset we are convinced of this: that all true and honourable patriots in France will protest against the act of the Delegation in Bordeaux, which every man in his senses would call sheer despotism. If this act had as its object to rally all those anarchical parties, which endure a Dictatorship, when it promotes their pet ideas, complications of the worst kind would infallibly have resulted from it.

"Germany has no intention of in any way interfering in the internal affairs of France. But by the Convention of January 28th she acquired the right to see a public power appointed, with the necessary qualifications for carrying on peace negotiations in the name of France. If Germany's right to treat for peace with the assembled nation is questioned; if the representation of one party is to be put in place of the representation of the nation, the Armistice-Convention itself will become null and void. We freely admit that the Government of National Defence has lost no time in acknowledging the justice of the complaints made by Count Bismarck in his despatch of February 3rd. In noble and honourable language this government has given its account to the French people of the difficulties of the situation, and the exertions it has made to avoid the last consequences of an unfortunate campaign. It has at the same time declared the decree of the Delegation in Bordeaux null and void. Let us then hope that M. Gambetta's attempt will meet with no response in the country, but that the elections will take place in complete accordance with the letter and spirit of the Convention of January 28th."

I wrote another article to the following effect. Hunger in Paris cannot yet be very extreme, or at least cannot be so dangerous as one might suppose from Favre's expressions. Though our stores have been at the disposal of the Parisians for the last eight days, no use has yet been made of them. General von Stosch reports that not a pound of meal or of meat has yet been carried away by them. They left moreover considerable stores of biscuits and salt meat behind them in the forts which they evacuated, and our people, who have been in Paris, have seen a great quantity of meal—even considering the number of the inhabitants—in one of the magazines there. "The reason, it must be remembered," remarked the Chief, "for the re-provisioning going on so slowly is, that the necessary orders have a long way to go from the general to the sentry."

About eleven o'clock I am once more summoned to him. I am to defend Favre against certain attacks of a severe character, which have been published in some French papers. "The Paris journals reproach Favre for having dined with me," said the Chief. "I had great trouble in bringing him to it. But it is quite absurd to expect that after working eight or ten hours with me he was either to starve, like a staunch Republican, or go to a hotel, where people would run after him as a notable personage, and the street boys would stare at him."

From two to four o'clock the Frenchmen are here again, six or seven strong, including Favre, and, if I heard aright, General Leflô. The Chief's elder son and Count Dönhoff were our guests at dinner.

In the evening I drew up a paragraph upon the *Times* telegram from Berlin, to the effect that at the conclusion of peace we shall demand from the French twenty ironclads, the colony of Pondicherry, and ten Milliards of francs as war indemnity. I described it as a downright invention, which one could hardly imagine would have been believed or would have given anxiety in England; and I indicated the source from which it was probably derived—the brain of some clumsy person in the diplomatic world, who wishes us ill and is spinning intrigues against us.

*Tuesday, February* 7.—The weather is mild; in the morning there was a fog, which did not lift till noon. The government of Prince Charles seems really likely to come to an end soon in Bucharest. In Darmstadt, owing to Dalwigk's staying in office, the old party opposed to the Empire remains firm, and the well-known Cabal goes on weaving its intrigues. From Bordeaux the expected news is telegraphed, that Gambetta has informed the prefects by circular, that in consequence of the annulment of his election decree by his Parisian colleagues, he has sent them his resignation—a good sign. He must know that he has no strong party at his back, or he would not have gone so easily. In Paris the mobilised National Guard, the regiments of Paris, have been disbanded by the Government.

General von Alvensleben, Count Herbert, and Bleichröder, the banker, dine with us. There is nothing remarkable in the conversation, the Chief speaking mostly in a low voice to Alvensleben. I feel exhausted, probably on account of my sitting up every night over my journal. I must stop it, or cut it shorter. There is to-day a fine additional trait to be noted in Gambetta's activity. The *Soir* states, that some days after the last sortie of the Parisians the following despatches were publicly posted up by the Dictator's orders in all the country communes not occupied by us:

"Three days' battle! On the 17th, 18th, and 19th, Wednesday, Thursday, and Friday. On the last day, Friday, a magnificent sortie; 200,000 men, the troops commanded by Trochu, broke through Saint-Cloud and over the heights of Garches. The Prussians were driven out of the park of Saint-Cloud, where terrible slaughter took place. The French forced their way up to the toll-gate of Versailles. Result: 20,000 Prussians *hors de combat*, all their works destroyed, their guns taken, spiked, or thrown into the Seine. The National Guard fought in the van." If Gambetta talks like this of Paris, where his statements can easily be checked, what fictions may he not have imposed upon the provincials!

*Wednesday, February* 8.—The air mild, as yesterday, the sky bright and sunny. I am still more worn out, and I am so giddy that I am like to fall. It may only be the ordinary spring languor; I will keep it under as well as I can. The Chief is up in unusually good time, and goes to the King as early as a quarter past nine. Shortly before one comes Favre with a whole swarm of Frenchmen, as many as ten or twelve. He has an interview with the Minister, who had previously breakfasted with us. There were also present Dönhoff and Hatzfeld's brother-in-law, a Mr. Moulton, a somewhat confident, but amusing young gentleman.

In the evening the Chief dines with his son at the Crown Prince's, but first he was with us for a while. He again observes that Favre had not taken his "malicious letter" amiss, but thanked him for it, and adds that he (the Chief) had repeated to him by word of mouth that it was his duty to help to eat up the broth he had had a hand in brewing. He then mentioned that to-day the bringing in of the contribution from Paris had been spoken of, that they wanted to pay part of it in bank-notes, by which we should have been losers. "How much what they offer comes to I know not," said he. "In any case they would gain by it. But they must pay all that has been agreed upon; not a franc will I abate." As he rose to go, he gave Abeken a telegram on pink paper, and said, "This is mere bosh. I can get on without Orleans, and if need be without Louis too."

*Thursday, February* 9.—To-day, for once in a way, the Parisians did not come. In the morning I read the text of the address, with which Gambetta, at 6 P.M., took his leave of the French people. It runs—

" My conscience obliges me to resign my office as member of a government whose views or hopes I am no longer able to share. I have the honour to inform you that I have to-day sent in my resignation. I thank you for the patriotic and indulgent support I have always received from you when it was a question of carrying to a satisfactory conclusion the task I had undertaken, and I beg to be allowed to tell you that my deeply-formed conviction is, that considering the short notice and the grave interests which are at stake, you will do a great service to the Republic, if you take in hand the elections on the 8th of February, and reserve to yourselves the right of coming after this period to such conclusions as become you. I pray you to accept the expression of my fraternal sentiments."

The Chief rode out to-day before two o'clock with Count Herbert, and a young lieutenant of the body-guard, the son of his cousin Bismarck-Bohlen (who is Governor-General in Elsass). He did not come back till after five. Of the conversation at dinner, where both these gentlemen were present, the following is noteworthy. The Chancellor, speaking again of the Paris contribution, said, " Stosch told me he could use fifty millions in bank-notes to make payments inside France for provisions and the like. But the other hundred and fifty must be funded in due course." Speaking afterwards of the fable of our thinking of taking possession of Pondicherry, after giving other explanations of this clumsy invention, he said, " I want no colonies. They are good for nothing but supply stations. For us in Germany, this colonial business would be just like the silken sables in the noble families of Poland, who have no shirts to their backs." He added further remarks in the same sense.

In the evening the Chief sent me for consideration a very confused and wrong-headed letter from Jacoby, teeming with slanders and misrepresentations, in *La France*. I afterwards prepared three articles, including the following for our *Moniteur*.

"The line of demarcation defined in the Convention of January 28 divides the town of Saint-Denis in such a way that the greater part of it falls into the neutral zone. Now as the inhabitants of this part being without certificate have no claim on provisions in the German zone, and can no longer enter Paris, the consequence is that considerable scarcity has arisen, during which this hard-pressed population has unceasingly besieged the stations of the German officers charged with the scrutiny of certificates. Being informed of this state of things, Count Bismarck wrote to Jules Favre a letter which we here publish in full. At the same time the Chancellor applied to the German military authorities, and induced them to let the inhabitants of Saint-Denis have food provisionally and as a present. His Majesty the Emperor issued orders accordingly, and 15,000 portions have been distributed from the magazines of the German army.

Count Bismarck's letter runs ' The commune of Saint-Denis has been so cut in two by the line of demarcation, that the greater part of it falls within the neutral zone. Up to the time of the Convention provisions were procured from the city of Paris and distributed through the mayoralty of Saint-Denis. The inhabitants who are in the neutral zone now see themselves cut off from Paris, which no longer gives them anything, and they are forbidden to look for food outside the line of demarcation. This unfortunate population, therefore, which has already suffered severely by the war, has now fallen into a condition which calls for aid in the interests of humanity. I have the honour to direct your Excellency's attention to this point, and to ask you to take the necessary measures to secure means of sustenance to that portion of the inhabitants of Saint-Denis which is in the neutral zone. Pending these measures I have requested the German military authorities to assist in providing for this population by handing over to them as a present some food from our own stores.'"

## CHAPTER XIX.

FROM GAMBETTA'S RETIREMENT TO THE CONCLUSION OF THE PEACE PRELIMINARIES.

FRIDAY, *February* 10.—Fresh complaints about the intrigues of Dalwigk, and especially about measures which threaten the national constituencies of Hesse with the loss of their representatives and the victory of the combined Ultramontanes and Democrats. It will be necessary at once to set on foot an active campaign in the press against these and other mischievous proceedings of our good friend Beust.

The Chief wishes printed in the *Moniteur* the long list of French officers, who have broken parole and escaped from Germany. I send it on. There are altogether (not counting the three well-known generals) 142 names, including Colonel Thibaudin, of the 67th regiment of the line, two lieutenant-colonels, three majors, and thirty captains. The *Mot d'Ordre* gives the following strange story: "M. Thiers is carrying on his intrigues in the provinces. He is attempting to represent to Herr von Bismarck the possibility of a combination worthy of his advanced age, by which the crown of France is to be offered to the King of the Belgians, who, in order to obtain this extension of territory, would gladly sign with both hands the cession of Elsass and Lothringen, and in the end even that of Champagne itself. This wonderful idea is moreover not new. M. Thiers proposed it four or five months ago in Vienna and Petersburg, when the Government of National Defence, in spite of the energetic protests of Rochefort and Gambetta, despatched him to plead in the name of the Republic for the intervention of the Emperors of Austria and Russia. So that at the very time when France arose to repulse the invader, Thiers, with 'bold front, was ready to betray the Republic, and cover his own white hairs with dishonour.'" It can do no harm and may possibly do good for the *Moniteur* to bring this information to-morrow, without comment, before the notice of the public. The paper is not writing history, but it will help in the making of it.

At dinner the Duke of Ratibor and a Herr von Kotze, the husband of the Chief's sister's daughter, were present as guests, two men to outward appearance strikingly different from one another. The Minister remarked, *inter alia*, when Strousberg had been spoken of, that all or many of the members of the Provisional Government were Jews : Simon, Crémieux, Magnin, as well as Picard, which he would not have believed, "very probably Gambetta, too, to judge from his face." " I suspect even Favre of it," he added.

*Saturday, February* 11.—Fine bright weather. In the morning I read newspapers, and especially certain proceedings of the English Parliament down to the end of last month. It would seem as if our good friends across the Channel were seriously leaning to the French side, and were not indisposed to interfere once more, so that an Anglo-French alliance might possibly come to pass. Let those who have this in their eye take care that they do not fall between two stools. There is another result more probable.

From what one hears and reads in the papers, the feeling here towards England is almost as unfavourable as towards us, in some circles even more so, and it might quite easily happen in case of our seeing ourselves threatened by the attitude of England, that all at once the very contrary of an Anglo-French alliance against Germany might astonish our cousins in London. We might see ourselves obliged to take into serious consideration the bringing back of Napoleon, which hitherto we have been far from entertaining.

About mid-day a number of shots were heard from heavy artillery, as if the bombardment were breaking out again. It turns out, however, to be only the bursting up of the guns which have been handed over to us with the fortresses, and which are not worth their carriage into Germany.

Count Henckel and Bleichröder were the strangers present at dinner. It was mentioned that Scheidtmann, in his dealings with the French financiers, had used expressions about them that were more forcible than complimentary, not knowing that some of the gentlemen understood German. The Chief, speaking of the insolence of the Parisian papers, who behaved just as if the town were not in our hands, said, "If this goes on, they must be told plainly that we will put up with it no longer; it must cease, or we will throw in a few shells from the forts in answer to their articles." When Henckel spoke of the bad feeling in Elsass, he remarked further that the elections ought never to have been allowed there at all, indeed his wish had been against it. But by an oversight the same instructions had been given to the German authorities there as everywhere else. Mention was then made of the sorrowful situation in which the Prince of Roumania found himself, and from Roumanian Radicals the conversation turned to Roumanian bonds. Bleichröder said that the speculation of financiers in stocks was always based upon the ignorance of the masses, and their blind desire to get money. This was confirmed by Henckel, who said, "I had many Roumanians, but after I had made about 8 per cent. on the rise, I took care to get rid of them, for I knew they could never bring in 15 per cent., and this alone could keep them lively." It was mentioned that the French were carrying on all kinds of smuggling in the provisioning of Paris. It was not from pride that they had not availed themselves of our contributions, but simply because nothing was to be made out of them. This extends even to Government circles, as —— during these few days has made 700,000 francs by the purchase of sheep. "We must let them see that we are aware of this," said the Chief, glancing at me; "it will do us a turn in the peace negotiations." It was attended to at once.

In the evening I prepared several articles by the Chief's instructions. We ought no longer to allow the shamelessness of the Paris journalists. It passes the bounds of endurance, and the limits of reasonable toleration, when the French press presumes to mock and insult us to our faces, their conquerors, before the walls of their capital, which is wholly in our power. Besides, their lies and insults are hindrances to the conclusion of peace, by embittering both sides and delaying the approach of a calmer state of feeling. This behaviour could not have been foreseen at the conclusion of the Armistice-Convention; and in the case of a prolongation of the armistice, which may be necessitated by this delay, we shall be obliged to consider what means there are of effectually preventing further insults. The best means would undoubtedly be the occupation of the city itself by our troops. We should thus relieve the French Government of a grave anxiety; and in regard to the prevention of worse consequences from irritating press manifestations we may perhaps do on our side what probably it might be impossible to do on theirs.

The *Progrès de Lyon* has asserted that the Chancellor duped Favre in the matter of Belfort and the three South-Eastern departments. This is a falsification and mis-statement of the circumstances, which were as follows: In the negotiations for the armistice the Chief wanted the siege of Belfort not to be included in it, but things there to be allowed to take their course. Thereupon Favre, misled probably by the fictitious successes of the French arms reported in the provincial papers, and with the idea that Bourbaki might still do great things against us and relieve Belfort, made the proposal that the latter also should retain his full liberty of action. We had not certainly calculated upon this request, but still we saw no reason to oppose it. On the contrary, had we shown ourselves unfavourable to it, the French would have considered it a great hardship. It is therefore mere impudence for the Lyons paper to charge us with foul play in this affair. The lying reports of the French, and the proposal they induced Favre to make, were alone to blame for what happened.

A leader for the *Moniteur* discussed the two subjects jointly, and was as follows :

" The *Progrès de Lyon* of February 4 writes : ' It will be noticed that Herr Bismarck has not forgotten to introduce a characteristic trick of the trade of which he is such a master, into the conditions of the armistice, which bears a great resemblance to a surrender. According to Jules Favre's despatch the military operations in the East were only to last till the moment when an understanding was arrived at in respect of the line of demarcation, the drawing of which across the three Departments in question was reserved for a final settlement. Bismarck, like a crafty trickster (*roué compère*), says in few words, but very plainly, that hostilities continue before Belfort, in Doubs, in Jura, and the Côte d'Or. Favre was apparently bamboozled here, and it is possible that he deserves the charge of levity which Gambetta has brought against him on the score of the armistice. This *slight* misunderstanding has brought on terrible consequences. In Jules Favre's sense but little time was needed to mark off the neutral territory between the combatants; it should have been accomplished without delay, and our army in the East would have remained unimpaired till the peace. Bismarck, on the other hand, construes the matter like a disciple of Escobar: instead of giving orders to have the limits of the armistice immediately traced out, he instructs his armies to press on the pursuit with the utmost zeal, so as speedily to complete the ruin of the French army in the East. We all know the rest: Bismarck's dishonest interpretation of the armistice costs us the complete annihilation of a fresh army of some 100,000 men, in the event of the National Assembly deciding to continue the War.'

"This is a statement which must be decidedly refuted, and shown to be what it is, a dishonest misrepresentation. In reality the case was as follows:

"In the negotiations for the armistice-convention of January 28 a request was made on the German side that the siege of Belfort should be continued, even after the conclusion of the convention, unless Belfort should at once surrender, on the garrison being allowed to retire. This request was refused on the French side, and a fresh one put forward; that, if the siege were to continue, full liberty of action should also be reserved to the army of Bourbaki. This was conceded by the Germans, and that was the reason why hostilities went on before Belfort and in the three departments mentioned above."

The preceding article, however, is only an example of the heaps of misrepresentations and inventions, silly fables groundless accusations, mean aspersions, and barefaced insults, which the French press, headed by the papers of Paris, fabricate and circulate day by day, no less since than before the armistice. It is, however, asking too much that the Parisians should have the right to insult and defy the conqueror at their gates, during an armistice which is to pave the way for peace. This attitude of the Parisian press, which after all was one of the chief causes of the whole war, is one of the main hindrances to peace. It prevents the French from seeing the necessity for it, and makes the Germans less willing to conclude it, and to trust to it for the future. When the expected negotiations for some extension of the armistice come on, the Germans will have to consider that the occupation of the city of Paris is the most effective means of putting a stop to these excitations against peace.

*Sunday, February* 12.—We learn by telegraph that Napoleon has issued a proclamation to the French. The telegram is to be printed in our paper to-day. The Chief seems to be unwell. He does not come to dinner. Abeken therefore takes the chair, in virtue of the position he delights to feel that he occupies in the office, of Vice-Secretary of State. The entry into Paris is spoken of as inevitable, and the old gentleman wishes to ride in the train of the Emperor. He intends, therefore, to send for his three-cornered hat from Berlin: " It would never do to put on a helmet for the occasion," said he; "although, when one comes to think of it, Wilmowski has one." Hatzfeld thought that a Greek helmet with big white feathers would look fine. "Or one with a visor, that could be dropped at the moment of the entry," put in another guest. Bohlen finally proposed a velvet cloth, trimmed with gold lace, for the Privy-Councillor's gray horse. He took all these quizzing suggestions as put forward quite seriously for discussion.

I wish I were rid of this limpness and giddiness, which constantly recur.

*Monday, February* 13.—Yesterday and the day before I worked, though I was not well. To-day the same. I again called attention to the incivility of the Paris press, hinting that the irritation it created must be regarded as delaying peace, and could most surely be removeb py the Occupation of Paris. The article is intended for the *Moniteur*, which is to append extracts from the insulting and threatening papers. The main substance is as follows :—

"History will point to the Convention of January 28 as a conclusive proof of the moderation shown by Germany to France on that day. The Government of National Defence itself recognised this when, in its proclamation of the 10th inst. it says, 'Never has a besieged town surrendered under such honourable conditions, and these conditions were accepted, because outside help is impracticable, and our bread is eaten up.' At the very moment, however, when Germany is giving to conquered France the means of freeing herself from the burden of a Dictatorship, and becoming once more mistress of her own destinies, the Parisian and provincial press spits at the German army, the German princes, and the political and military leaders of Germany, so as to call an angry blush to the cheek of even the mildest man, and embitter thoes who have directed their efforts to saving thousands of innocent persons from the punishment which has been brought on by the blunders of the Demagogues, and of a press drivelling in madness. If the French armies remained uninjured; if 'the elected of eight millions' were not a prisoner of war in Germany; if more than half a million Frenchmen, in consequence of numberless defeats, were not sharing qis fate, interned partly in Germany, partly in Belgium, and partly in Switzerland; if, in a word, the fortune of war had not already clearly been decided—these incessantly repeated swaggerings and affronts would in any case have seemed most unseasonable. But what are we to say of the ideas and behaviour of this section of the French nation, in its own opinion so particularly prudent and high-toned, if while the public welfare depends on the conqueror's clemency, it takes pleasure in insulting him aimlessly and without cause? Germany might treat these manifestations with the contempt that they deserve, had she not to keep in view the object which she has proposed to herself to attain.

"This object is Peace, and Peace of a nature to last as long as possible. The excitement which the Parisian press is stirring up works against this in two ways: it infatuates the French, and it embitters the Germans. In Paris the true state of affairs—namely, that the city is in our hands—is not clearly understood. People do not see that these manifestations cannot further a reasonable decision of the question of war or peace, to which the National Assembly is now addressing itself. The entry of the German army, and the occupation of the city appear, therefore, to be the only means of hastening the work of peace, and removing the opposition, which has long been a matter of offence to Europe."

*Wednesday, February* 22.—I wrote last week articles of all kinds, large and small, and sent off about a dozen telegrams. I have been in the meantime at Fort Issy, at Mont Valérien, and at the Castle of Meudon, reduced to ruins by fire. We came to Mont Valérien just at the time when our people were carrying away the biggest of the cannon there, festooned with leaves. The remaining guns, both here and in Fort Issy have either been blown to bits, or pointed at the city. To enable them to do this, the walls and breastworks have been rebuilt.

The Assembly in Bordeaux shows an intelligent regard

for the situation which the last four weeks have produced. They have turned out Gambetta and elected Thiers as chief of the Executive Power, and spokesman for France in the peace negotiations, which began here yesterday. *A propos* of this, the Chief said yesterday at dinner, where Henckel was present, "If they gave a Milliard more, we might perhaps let them have Metz. We would then take eight hundred million francs, and build ourselves a fortress a few miles further back, somewhere about Falkenberg, or towards Saarbrücken—there must be some suitable spot thereabouts. We should thus make a clear profit of two hundred millions. I do not like so many Frenchmen being in our house against their will. It is just the same with Belfort. It is all French there too. The military, however, will not be willing to let Metz slip, and perhaps they are right."

Generals von Kamecke and von Treskow were our guests to-day. The Chief told us of his second interview to-day with Thiers. "When I demanded that of him" (I missed hearing what) "though he is usually well able to control himself, he rose to his full height and said, '*Mais c'est une indignité!*' (That is an indignity!) I would not allow myself to make a blunder, but I spoke to him in German after this. He listened for a time, and probably did not know what to make of it. Then he began in a querulous tone, 'But, M. le Comte, you are aware that I know no German.' I replied to him—this time in French, 'When you spoke just now of "indignity," I found that I did not understand French sufficiently, so I proceeded to speak German, where I know both what I say and what I hear.' He at once caught my meaning, and as a concession wrote out what I had proposed, and what he had formerly considered an indignity.

"'And yesterday,' he went on, 'he spoke of Europe as likely to step in if we did not abate our demands.' I answered him, 'If you speak to me of Europe, I speak to you of Napoleon.' He would not believe in this: 'From him there was nothing to fear.' But I proved to him that he must think of the plebiscite, the peasantry, and the officers and soldiers. The Guard could regain their old position only under the Emperor, and, with a little address, it would not be hard for him to get for himself a hundred thousand of the soldiers who were prisoners in Germany. Then all we had to do was to let them go armed across the frontier, and France would be his again. If they would grant no good terms of peace, we would, in the end, put up even with an Orleans prince, though we knew that with them the war would break out again in two or three years. If not, we would interfere, which we have hitherto avoided doing, and they would get Napoleon again.' That must have made an impression upon him; for to-day, when he was going once more to speak about Europe, he pulled himself up suddenly and said, 'I beg your pardon.' He pleases me, however, very much; he has a fine intellect, good manners, and can tell a story very agreeably. I was often sorry for him, too, for he is in a bad position. But all that cannot help him."

The Chancellor came afterwards to speak of the conversation he had had with Thiers about the cost of the war, and said, "His idea throughout was to agree to a war indemnity of only 1500 millions, for it could not be believed what the war had cost them; and besides, everything that had been supplied to them had been bad. If a soldier only tripped and fell down, his breeches were at once torn, so wretched had been the cloth. The same with the shoes with the pasteboard soles, as well as the arms, especially those from

America. I replied, Yes, but just suppose that a man were to attack and try to flog you, and after having beaten him off, you came to settle with him and demand reparation, what would you answer were he to appeal to you with ' You must take into consideration that the rods with which I tried to beat you cost me a lot of money and were so badly made?' Besides, there is a very considerable difference between 1500 and 6000 millions."

The conversation hereupon, I do not remember how, lost itself in the gloom of the Polish forests and their swamps, and turned for a while upon the great solitary farms, and upon the colonisation of these "Backwoods of the East," and the Chief remarked, "In former days when so many things were not and did not seem likely to be as they should be, I often thought, if things did not get better, I would take my last thousand thalers, put up a farm for myself in the woods, and keep house there. But matters turned out differently."

The talk turned at last upon ambassadors' reports, of which for the most part, the Chief seems to have a low opinion. "Great part of them is mere paper and ink," said he. "The worst is when they make them long. With B. one is used to his sending every time such a ream of paper, with antiquated newspaper cuttings. But if any one else writes much, one gets disgusted, because as a rule there is nothing in it." "If people write history out of them, there is no proper information to be got there. I believe the archives will be opened to them after thirty years; they might be allowed to see them much earlier. Despatches and reports, even if they contain anything, are not intelligible but to those who know the persons and circumstances. Who knows after thirty years what sort of a man the writer was, what view he took of the case, and how far his representation of it was biassed by his individuality? And who has any intimate acquaintance with the persons of whom he writes? It ought to be known what Gortschakoff, or Gladstone, or Granville thought of their ambassador's report. Better information may be gleaned from the newspapers, of which even governments avail themselves, and where one often says more plainly what one thinks. But in this case, too, knowledge of the conditions is necessary. The main points always lie in private letters and confidential communications, even by word of mouth, nothing of which finds its way into the records." He added a number of examples, and concluded, "This is only to be learned confidentially, not officially."

*Thursday, February* 23.—We are to keep Metz. The Chief announced this distinctly to-day at dinner. Belfort, on the other hand, there seems no desire to keep. The entry of a part of our army into Paris is now quite decided. I wrote this evening in the *Moniteur* to the following effect:

"We have repeatedly characterised as it deserved the unmeasured abuse which the Parisian press is heaping upon the victorious German army, while it stands at the gates of their capital. We have also remarked that the Occupation of Paris by our troops would be the most effective means of putting a stop to this insolence. Their swaggerings, lies, and slanders have to-day quite passed bounds. Read for instance the Figaro *feuilleton* for February 21, entitled '*Les Prussiens en France*,' and signed Alfred d'Aunay, in which the most shameful outrages, thefts, and plunderings are laid to the charge of the German officers and the Germans generally. We understand that this behaviour, which escapes the notice it deserves, has rendered perfectly fruitless the strenuous efforts made by the Parisian negotiators to prevent the entry of the German army into

Paris, and that all hope of avoiding this entry has gone by. We are assured on good authority that this will take place immediately after the expiry of the armistice."

*Friday, February* 24.—In the morning we had the brightest and loveliest spring weather, and the garden behind the house was filled with the twitter of birds. Thiers and Favre were here from one till half-past five. When they were gone the Duc de Mouchy and Comte de Gobineau called to complain, they said, of oppression on the part of the German prefects, like the one in Beauvais, who is apparently governing harshly, or at least not with winning mildness. The Chief appeared at dinner in plain clothes —for the first time during the war. Can this mean that peace has been concluded?

*Saturday, February* 25.—Again unpleasant news from Bavaria. Odo Russell is supposed to have called in the course of the day, but not to have presented himself to the Chief. This has led to people saying that England intends to interfere in the peace negotiations.* In the evening there is a rumour that the war indemnity to be paid by the French has been reduced from 6000 to 5000 million francs, and that the preliminaries of peace will probably be signed tomorrow, the consent of the National Assembly in Bordeaux being alone wanting. Metz is handed over. Our soldiers are to enter Paris next Wednesday, in order to occupy, to the number of 30,000 men, that part of the inner town which lies between the Seine, the Rue du Faubourg Saint-Honoré, and the Avenue des Ternes, until the National Assembly has declared its concurrence in the preliminaries of peace. This will undoubtedly come soon, and so we may turn our faces homewards in the first week of March.

* The Chancellor told me later, that on March 4**th,** they had only attempted it in regard to the money question, when it was too late.

*March 1, Wednesday.*—In the morning I went out to the bridge of boats at Suresnes, and across to the grassy plain of Longchamps, as far as the Bois de Boulogne, and looked on from the roof of the half-ruined View-house of the racecourse at the review which the Emperor is holding of the troops which are to enter Paris. There were Bavarian regiments among them. They say that the Guard is to go home to-morrow. At dinner, where the Würtemberg Minister von Wächter and Mittnacht joined us, the Chief told us he had ridden into Paris, and been recognised by the populace. No demonstration, however, had taken place against him. One person, who threw at him a very sinister glance, and up to whom he accordingly rode to ask for a light, readily complied with his request. Mittnacht told another story about the high personage whose curiosity had already formed the topic of conversation. "I don't know whether you have heard before," said he, "how he remarked to some one who was presented to him, 'Ah, I am delighted; I have heard so very much to your credit—what was it, pray?'" General laughter. Only Abeken seems as usual to hear such frivolous talk with pity and surprise.

*Thursday, March 2.*—Favre comes as early as half-past seven in the morning, and wishes to be announced to the Chief. Wollmann, however, refuses to wake him, and his Parisian Excellency is much put out. Favre has to communicate the news received during the night that the National Assembly in Bordeaux has assented to the Peace Preliminaries, and he wishes therefore to claim the evacuation of Paris, and of the forts on the left bank of the Seine, a request which he left in the form of a letter.

*Monday, March 6.*—A beautifully fine morning. Thrushes and finches warble the signal for our departure. We must breakfast at the Sabot d'Or, for all our plate is already packed up. About one o'clock the carriages are put into motion, and we pass with a light heart out of the gate through which we entered five months ago, by way of the Villa Coublay, Villeneuve Saint-Georges, Charenton, and the pheasantry, to Lagny, which we reached after seven o'clock, taking up our quarters in two summer-houses on the right bank of the Marne, about three hundred paces beyond the fallen bridge.

From Lagny we went next day by express train to Metz, which we entered late in the evening, putting up at an hotel, while the Chief lodged with Count Henckel at the Prefecture. The next morning we walked through the town in various directions, went to see the Cathedral, and had a view from one of the forts over the country to the north-west. Shortly before eleven we again took train to go by way of Saarbrücken and Kreuznach to Mainz, and thence to Frankfort. The Chief was enthusiastically received everywhere, especially in Saarbrücken and Mainz. It was only in Frankfort that there was no demonstration. From this city, though we reached it late in the evening, we went on still further in the night, and by the next morning at half-past seven we were in Berlin, from which I had been absent exactly seven months. It was clear, on consideration, that as much as was possible had been done in the interval.

THE END.

*A FASCINATING BOOK.*

# Prince Bismarck's Letters

TO

## HIS SISTER, WIFE, AND OTHERS,

### From 1844 to 1870.

TRANSLATED FROM THE GERMAN,

### By FITZH. MAXSE.

One Vol. 16mo, cloth, . . . . . . . . . $1.00

---

These select letters of Prince Bismarck, which have been collected, translated, and published with his express consent, illustrate, and perhaps as forcibly as ever before, the wide separation there may be between the public and private life of a great statesman. No matter how familiar the reader may be with Bismarck's political career, this volume will contain for him a revelation as remarkable as it is intensely interesting. For in them we see not the diplomatist but the man.

*From the "New-York Evening Post."*

"The careful reader will see on nearly every page some sentence which reveals the character of this remarkable man as it has never been revealed in his public acts or words."

*From the "Boston Transcript."*

"Even the most confirmed Bismarck-hater cannot help feeling his prejudices softened, and his respect for this wonderful man increased in reading these revelations of his inner life. The work which contains them will have the effect of changing in no small degree the popular estimate of his character in this country, and will form an important volume in autobiographic literature."

*From the "Nation."*

"The impression conveyed throughout these letters is that Bismarck, in respect to his political life, is a Diogenes, who, in an hour of weakness, has been persuaded out of his tub, and who regrets the emergence as an error. But in its humor, its melancholy, its self-consciousness, Bismarck's is a thoroughly modern mind; in his lack of intellectual subtilty, and in his downright religious convictions, he is less evidently of our time, orthodoxy being now in Germany, for the most part—at least among the *Hofwelt*—an anachronism. * * * Complete vigor and genuineness of nature, combined with rare patience and good humor, rather than a profound insight, have given Prince von Bismarck his position in European affairs. These letters alone are enough to show that their writer was never destined to an inferior place."

\*\*\* *The above book for sale by all booksellers, or will be sent, prepaid, upon receipt of price, by*

### CHARLES SCRIBNER'S SONS, PUBLISHERS,

743 AND 745 BROADWAY, NEW YORK.

AUTHORIZED AMERICAN EDITIONS.

# Froude's Historical Works.

## THE HISTORY OF ENGLAND,
### From the Fall of Woolsey to the Death of Elizabeth

*THE COMPLETE WORK IN TWELVE VOLUMES.*

#### By JAMES ANTHONY FROUDE, M.A.

"MR. FROUDE is a pictorial historian, and his skill in description and fulness of knowledge make his work abound in scenes and passages that are almost new to the general reader. We close his pages with unfeigned regret and we bid him good speed in his noble mission of exploring the sources of English history in one of its most remarkable periods."—*British Quarterly Review.*

#### THE POPULAR EDITION.
In cloth, at the rate of $1.25 per vol. The set (12 vols.), in a neat box..$15.00
The same, in half calf extra................................................ 36.00

This edition is printed from the same plates as the other editions, and on firm, white paper. It is, without exception, the cheapest set of books of its class ever issued in this country.

#### THE CHELSEA EDITION.
In half roan, gilt top, per set of 12 vols.; 12mo........ ...............$21.00

Elegance and cheapness are combined in a remarkable degree in this edition. It takes its name from the place of Mr. Froude's residence in London, also famous as the home of Thomas Carlyle.

#### THE LIBRARY EDITION.
In twelve vols., crown 8vo, cloth............... ......................$36.00
The same, in half calf extra.................................. .................. 50.00

The edition is printed on laid paper, at the Riverside press, and is in every respect worthy a place in the most carefully selected library.

## SHORT STUDIES ON GREAT SUBJECTS.
**POPULAR EDITION.** Three vols. 12mo, cloth, per vol................$1.50
**CHELSEA EDITION.** Three vols. 12mo, half roan, gilt top, per vol.. 2.00
**LIBRARY EDITION.** Three vols. crown, 8vo, cloth, per vol.......... 2.50

### HISTORY OF ENGLAND AND SHORT STUDIES.
#### Fifteen volumes in a neat box.
**POPULAR EDITION** .....................................................$19.50
**CHELSEA EDITION**............. ...................................... 27.00

## THE ENGLISH IN IRELAND
### During the Eighteenth Century.

Three vols. crown 8vo, uniform with the Library Edition of the "History of England," price per volume........ ................... ..........$2.50

※* The above books for sale by all booksellers, or will be sent, post or express charges paid, upon receipt of the price by the publishers,

### CHARLES SCRIBNER'S SONS,
#### 743 AND 745 BROADWAY, NEW YORK.

"These volumes contain the ripe results of the studies of men who are authorities in their respective fields."—THE NATION.

# Epochs of Modern History.

Each 1 vol. 16mo., with Outline Maps. Price per volume, In cloth, $1.00.

EACH VOLUME COMPLETE IN ITSELF AND SOLD SEPARATELY.

EDITED BY EDWARD E. MORRIS, M.A.

The ERA of the PROTESTANT REVOLUTION. By F. SEEBOHM, Author of "The Oxford Reformers—Colet, Erasmus, More." *(Now ready.)*

The CRUSADES. By the Rev. G. W. Cox, M.A., Author of the "History of Greece." *(Now ready.)*

The THIRTY YEARS' WAR, 1618—1648. By SAMUEL RAWSON GARDINER. *(Now ready.)*

The HOUSES of LANCASTER and YORK; with the CONQUEST and LOSS of FRANCE. By JAMES GAIRDNER, of the Public Record Office. *(Now ready.)*

The FRENCH REVOLUTION and FIRST EMPIRE; an Historical Sketch. By WM. O'CONNOR MORRIS, with an Appendix by Hon. ANDREW D. WHITE, Prest. of Cornell University. *(Now ready.)*

The AGE OF ELIZABETH. By the Rev. M. CREIGHTON, M.A. *(Now ready.)*

The PURITAN REVOLUTION. By J. LANGTON SANFORD. *(Now ready.)*

The FALL of the STUARTS; and WESTERN EUROPE from 1678 to 1697. By the Rev. EDWARD HALE, M.A., Assist. Master at Eton. *(Now ready.)*

The EARLY PLANTAGENETS and their relation to the HISTORY of EUROPE; the foundation and growth of CONSTIUTIONAL GOVERNMENT. By the Rev. WM. STUBBS, M.A., etc., Regius Professor of Modern History in the University of Oxford. *(Now ready.)*

The BEGINNING of the MIDDLE AGES; CHARLES the GREAT and ALFRED; the HISTORY of ENGLAND in its connection with that of EUROPE in the NINTH CENTURY. By the Very Rev R. W. CHURCH, M.A., Dean of St Paul's. *(Now ready.)*

The above Ten Volumes in Roxburg Style. Leather Labels and Gilt Top. Put up in a handsome Box. Sold only in Sets. Price per Set, $10.00.

The AGE of ANNE. By EDWARD E. MORRIS, M.A., Editor of the Series. *(Now ready.)*

The NORMAN KINGS and the FEUDAL SYSTEM. By the Rev. A. H. JOHNSON, M.A. EDWARD III. By the Rev. W. WARBURTON, M.A., late Her Majesty's Senior Inspector of Schools.

FREDERICK the GREAT and the SEVEN YEARS' WAR. By F. W. LONGMAN, of Balliol College, Oxford.

*\*\** *The above book for sale by all booksellers, or will be sent, post or express charges paid, upon receipt of the price by the publishers,*

CHARLES SCRIBNER'S SONS,

743 AND 745 BROADWAY, NEW YORK.

*Now in process of publication, uniform with* Epochs of Modern History, *each volume in 12mo. size, and complete in itself,*

# Epochs of Ancient History.

A Series of Books narrating the HISTORY OF GREECE AND ROME, and of their relations to other Countries at Successive Epochs. Edited by the Rev. G. W. COX, M.A., Author of the "Aryan Mythology," "A History of Greece," etc., and jointly by CHARLES SANKEY, M.A., late Scholar of Queen's College, Oxford.

---

Volumes already issued in the "Epochs of Ancient History." Each One Volume 12mo, cloth, $1.00.

---

The GREEKS and the PERSIANS. By the Rev. G. W. Cox, M.A., late Scholar of Trinity College, Oxford: Joint Editor of the Series. With four colored Maps.

The EARLY ROMAN EMPIRE. From the Assassination of Julius Cæsar to the Assassination of Domitian. By the Rev. W. Wolfe Capes, M.A., Reader of Ancient History in the University of Oxford. With two colored maps.

The ATHENIAN EMPIRE from the FLIGHT of XERXES to the FALL of ATHENS. By the Rev. G. W. Cox, M.A., late Scholar of Trinity College, Oxford: Joint Editor of the Series. With five maps.

The ROMAN TRIUMVIRATES. By the Very Rev. Charles Merivale, D.D., Dean of Ely.

EARLY ROME, to its Capture by the Gauls. By Wilhelm Ihne, Author of "History of Rome." With Map.

---

## OPINIONS OF THE PRESS.

"Brief but comprehensive in its narrative, it is written in a plain and simple style which will attract the attention of the general reader as well as the philosophical student."—*The Providence Journal.*

"It would be hard to find a more creditable book *(Greeks and Persians)*. The author's prefatory remarks upon the origin and growth of Greek civilization are alone worth the price of the volume."—*The Christian Union.*

"The volume is compact, convenient, clearly written, and well illustrated by maps. This is a very valuable series for general readers."—*The Watchman.*

---

*\*\** *The above books for sale by all booksellers, or will be sent, post or express charges paid, upon receipt of the price by the publishers,*

CHARLES SCRIBNER'S SONS,
743 AND 745 Broadway, New York

# Prof. F. Max Muller's Works.

## LECTURES ON THE SCIENCE OF LANGUAGE.

By F. MAX MULLER, M.A., Fellow of All Souls College, Oxford.

FIRST SERIES:—Comprising those delivered in April, May, and June, 1861. One vol., crown 8vo, half calf, $4.50; cloth, . $2.50

SECOND SERIES:—Comprising those delivered in February, March, April, and May, 1863 *With thirty-one illustrations.* One vol., crown 8vo, half calf, $5.50; cloth, . . . . . . $3.50

*From the Atlantic Monthly.*

"Easily comprehensible, and yet always pointing out the sources of fuller investigation, it is ample, both to satisfy the desire of those who wish to get the latest results of philosophy, and to stimulate the curiosity of whoever wishes to go further and deeper. It is by far the best and clearest summing up of the present condition of the science of language that we have ever seen, while the liveliness of style and the variety and freshness of illustration make it exceedingly interesting."

## CHIPS FROM A GERMAN WORKSHOP.

By F. MAX MULLER, M.A., Fellow of All Souls College, Oxford. Reprinted from the Second Revised London Edition, with copious Index. Vol. I. ESSAYS ON THE SCIENCE OF RELIGION. Vol. II. ESSAYS ON MYTHOLOGY, TRADITIONS, AND CUSTOMS. Vol. III. LITERATURE, BIOGRAPHY, AND ANTIQUITIES. Three vols., crown 8vo, cloth, per vol., $2.50; the set in half calf, . . $13.50

*From the New York Evening Post.*

"This book of Prof. Müller would afford no end of interesting extracts; 'Chips' by the cord, that are full both to the intellect and the imagination; but we must refer the curious reader to the volumes themselves. He will find in them a body of combined entertainment and instruction such as has hardly ever been brought together in so compact a form."

## LECTURES ON THE SCIENCE OF RELIGION.

WITH PAPERS ON BUDDHISM, AND A TRANSLATION OF THE DHAMMAPADA, OR PATH OF VIRTUE. By F. MAX MULLER, M.A. One vol., crown 8vo, half calf, $4.50; cloth, $2.00

*From the Chicago Evening Journal.*

"The thoroughness of its method, the vigor and clearness of its discussions, and the extensive learning wrought into the text of the work, give it the high character which commands for such a production the rank and authority of a standard."

## THE ORIGIN AND GROWTH OF RELIGION,

As illustrated by the Religions of India. By F. MAX MULLER. One vol., crown 8vo, $2.50.

There can be no doubt that this volume will be welcomed by all earnest and thoughtful minds.

\*\*\* *The above books for sale by all booksellers, or will be sent, prepaid, upon receipt of price, by*

### CHARLES SCRIBNER'S SONS, PUBLISHERS,
743 AND 745 BROADWAY, NEW YORK.

New Edition in handsome Binding. Each 1 vol. 12mo. uniform.
Extra cloth, $1.25 per vol.

# The Erckmann-Chatrian Novels.

**FRIEND FRITZ: A Tale of the Banks of the Lauter.** Including a Story of College Life—"MAITRE NABLOT."

"'Friend Fritz' is a charmingly sunny and refreshing story."—*N. Y. Tribune.*

**THE CONSCRIPT: A Tale of the French War of 1813.** With four full-page illustrations.

*From the Cincinnati Daily Commercial.*

"It is hardly fiction—it is history in the guise of fiction, and that part of history which historians hardly write, concerning the disaster, the ruin, the sickness, the poverty, and the utter misery and suffering which war brings upon the people."

**WATERLOO: A Story of the Hundred Days.** *Being a Sequel to "The Conscript."* With four full-page illustrations.

*From the New York Daily Herald.*

"Written in that charming style of simplicity which has made the ERCKMANN-CHATRIAN works popular in every language in which they have been published."

**THE PLEBISCITE: The Miller's Story of the War.** A vivid Narrative of Events in connection with the great Franco-Prussian War of 1872.

**THE BLOCKADE OF PHALSBURG: An Episode of the Fall of the First French Empire.** With four full-page Illustrations and a Portrait of the Authors.

*From the Philadelphia Daily Inquirer.*

"Not only are they interesting historically, but intrinsically a pleasant, well-constructed plot, serving in each case to connect the great events which they so graphically treat, and the style being as vigorous and charming as it is pure and refreshing."

**INVASION OF FRANCE IN 1814.** With the Night March past Phalsburg. With a Memoir of the Authors. With four full-page Illustrations.

*From the New York Evening Mail.*

"All their novels are noted for the same admirable qualities—simple and effective realism of plot, incident and language, and a disclosure of the horrid individual aspects of war. They are absolutely perfect of their kind."

**MADAME THERESE; or, the Volunteers of '92.** With four full-page Illustrations.

*From the Boston Commonwealth.*

"It is a boy's story—that is, supposed to be written by a boy—and has all the freshness, the unconscious simplicity and *naïveté* which the imagined authorship should imply; while nothing more graphic, more clearly and vividly pictorial, has been brought before the public for many a day."

\*\*\* *The above books for sale by all booksellers, or will be sent, post or express charges paid, upon receipt of the price by the publishers,*

## CHARLES SCRIBNER'S SONS,

743 AND 745 BROADWAY, NEW YORK.

*A NEW WORK BY PRESIDENT WOOLSEY.*

# Political Science;
## OR, THE STATE THEORETICALLY AND PRACTICALLY CONSIDERED.

*IN THREE PARTS:*

I. The Doctrine of Rights as the Foundation of a Just State.
II. The Theory of the State.
III. Practical Politics.

By THEODORE D. WOOLSEY, *Lately President of Yale College.*

In two volumes royal octavo, of nearly 600 pages each. Handsome cloth, extra. Price per vol., $3.50.

---

## IMPORTANT WORKS
### By THEODORE D. WOOLSEY, D.D., LL.D.,
EX-PRESIDENT OF YALE COLLEGE.

### INTERNATIONAL LAW.

INTRODUCTION TO THE STUDY OF INTERNATIONAL LAW. Designed as an Aid in Teaching and in Historical Studies. The edition revised and enlarged. Cloth, $2.50.

"Though elementary in its character, it is still thorough and comprehensive, and presents a complete outline of that grand system of ethical jurisprudence which holds, as it were, in one community the nations of Christendom."—*New York Examiner.*

"He has admirably succeeded. The want was that of a compendium treatise, intended, not for lawyers nor for those having the profession of law in view, but for young men who are cultivating themselves by the study of historical and political science."—*St. Louis Republican.*

"The editor and politician will find it a convenient companion. Its appendix contains a most useful list of the principal treaties since the Reformation."—*New York Evening Post.*

### THE RELIGION OF THE PRESENT AND FUTURE.
One volume, crown 8vo, cloth, $2.00.

The thousands of graduates of Yale College, as well as the very large number who are only in a general way familiar with the deserved reputation of President Woolsey, will welcome this volume, which is a selection from the discourses which President Woolsey has delivered in Yale College Chapel during the last twenty-five years. For the direct application of truth, severe logical simplicity, that eloquence which springs from unaffected earnestness and single-hearted sincerity of desire to convince the understanding, and persuade the hearts of those to whom they were addressed, these sermons are preëminent.

### ESSAYS ON DIVORCE AND DIVORCE LEGISLATION.
WITH SPECIAL REFERENCE TO THE UNITED STATES.
One volume, 12mo. Price, $1.75.

The Essays here brought together originally appeared in the *New Englander*, where they attracted wide attention from the exactness and thoroughness with which they discuss the legal aspect of this great question, as well as from the sound discrimination displayed in the examination of its social aspects.

---

*⁎⁎⁎ The above books for sale by all booksellers, or will be sent, post or express charges paid, upon receipt of the price by the publishers,*

### CHARLES SCRIBNER'S SONS,
743 AND 745 BROADWAY, NEW YORK.

# Gleanings of Past Years.

BY THE
### Right Hon. W. E. GLADSTONE, M.P.

*Six Volumes, 16mo, Cloth, per volume, $1.00.*

The extraordinary scope of Mr. Gladstone's learning—the wonder of his friends and enemies alike—and his firm grasp of every subject he discusses, make his essays much more than transient literature. Their collection and publication in permanent shape were of course certain to be undertaken sooner or later; and now that they are about to be so published with the benefit of his own revision, they will need little heralding in England or America. What Mr. Gladstone has written in the last thirty-six years—the period covered by this collection—has probably had the attention of as large an English-speaking public as any writer on political and social topics ever reached in his own life-time. The papers which he has chosen as of lasting value, and included here under the title of *Gleanings of Past Years*, will form the standard edition of his miscellanies, both for his present multitude of readers and for those who will study his writings later.

## NOW READY:

### VOL. I.

## THE THRONE, AND THE PRINCE CONSORT.
## THE CABINET, AND CONSTITUTION
(Containing "*Kin beyond the Sea*").

### VOL. II.

## PERSONAL AND LITERARY.

*⁎⁎⁎ The above books for sale by all booksellers, or will be sent, prepaid, upon receipt of price, by*

**CHARLES SCRIBNER'S SONS,** Publishers,
743 AND 745 BROADWAY, NEW YORK.

www.ingramcontent.com/pod-product-compliance
Lightning Source LLC
Chambersburg PA
CBHW020238240426

43672CB00006B/572